Glycemic Index
Cooking
made easy

Glycemic Index Cooking
made easy

Lose Weight, Eat Well, and Boost Your Energy Levels Using Low-GI Foods

Dr. Jennie Brand-Miller, Kaye Foster-Powell, Johanna McMillan-Price,
Johanna Burani, Dr. Nadir R. Farid, and Kate Marsh

RODALE

The GI logo (page 12) is a trademark of the University of Sydney in Australia and other countries. A food product carrying this logo is nutritious and has been tested for its GI by an accredited laboratory.

Book design by Susan Eugster

Front cover recipe: Roasted Vegetable and Mushroom Lasagna (page 200)
Back cover recipes (from left to right): Buckwheat Pancakes with Berries (page 72); Mixed Grain Cereal with Dried Fruit Compote and Yogurt (page 66); Pan-Fried Lamb and Greens Salad with Tzatziki (page 316); and Chocolate Mousse with Berries (page 339)

Portions of this book have been previously published as *The New Glucose Revolution Pocket Guide to Diabetes* 2nd revised and expanded edition (Marlowe and Company, 2003); *The New Glucose Revolution Guide to Living Well with PCOS* (Marlowe and Company, 2004); *Good Carbs, Bad Carbs* 2nd revised and updated edition (Marlowe and Company, 2002, 2005); *The New Glucose Revolution Life Plan* (Marlowe and Company, 2004); and *The Low GI Diet Cookbook* (Marlowe and Company, 2005). The Rodale Inc. direct mail edition is published in 2007 under license from Avalon Publishing Group Incorporated, New York.

Library of Congress Cataloging-in-Publication Data

Brand-Miller, Jennie, date
    Glycemic index cooking made easy : lose weight, eat well, and boost your energy levels using low-GI foods / Dr. Jennie Brand-Miller, Kaye Foster-Powell, Johanna McMillan-Price, Johanna Burani, Dr. Nadir R. Farid, and Kate Marsh.
       p.   cm.
    ISBN-13 978–1–59486–609–8 hardcover
    ISBN-10 1–59486–609–0 hardcover
    1. Low-carbohydrate diet—Recipes.   2. Glycemic index.   I. Foster-Powell, Kaye.
II. McMillan-Price, Joanna.   III. Title.
RM237.73.B73 2007
641.5'6383—dc22   2007007580

    6   8   10   9   7   5   hardcover

RODALE
LIVE YOUR WHOLE LIFE™

We inspire and enable people to improve their lives and the world around them
For more of our products visit rodalestore.com or call 1-800-848-4735

CONTENTS

INTRODUCTION

The Glycemic Index (GI), a ranking of foods by their ability to raise blood sugar levels, has become one of the most enduring and inspiring dietary concepts to arise at the turn of the 21st century. Low GI is *the* new way of eating that everyone's talking about—and one of the few programs around with years of scientific research to support it.

Eating low-GI foods can benefit everyone by positively affecting a wide range of diseases and conditions, including diabetes, heart disease, and obesity. Below, we offer some frightening disease statistics and describe how using the Glycemic Index can help steer you clear of illness and tilt the good-health odds in your favor.

DIABETES

Did you know that every day in the United States, more than 3,500 people are diagnosed with diabetes? And even more striking is the number of people who have the disease and don't even know it: In addition to the 13 million who have already been diagnosed with diabetes, another 5.2 million people remain undiagnosed—unaware that they're even sick! And in 2000, diabetes killed 69,301 Americans, and nearly 1.3 million new cases of diabetes are diagnosed every year.

In fact, many people don't even know they are suffering from the seventh leading cause of death in the United States until they develop one of its life-threatening complications such as blindness, kidney disease, heart disease, stroke, or nerve damage.

Glycemic Index Cooking Made Easy can help because:

- We provide an easy and effective way to eat a healthy diet and control fluctuations in blood sugar

- We offer a lifestyle plan that includes many traditionally taboo foods (because they don't cause the unfavorable effects on blood sugar they were believed to have)

- Diets containing low-GI foods may improve blood sugar control in people with both type 1 (insulin-dependent) and type 2 (non-insulin-dependent) diabetes

OBESITY

You can't go anywhere these days without people talking about what they're eating—and not eating. It seems everyone's uttering those five golden words: "I'm on a new diet." But would you believe that even with all those diets, the number of overweight and obese people in our society is actually climbing? In fact, one study found that 400,000 deaths in the U.S. each year can be attributed to obesity. That makes obesity the second leading cause of preventable death—surpassed only by smoking.

The problem is so pervasive that an estimated 64 percent of American adults are overweight or obese. Childhood obesity statistics have reached an unprecedented 30 percent. Worse yet, if this trend continues, experts say that within just a few generations, every adult American will be overweight. And excess weight brings with it a host of other health problems, such as heart disease, diabetes, some types of cancer, and high blood pressure.

WHY DIETS DON'T WORK

If you're overweight (or consider yourself to be) chances are that you have looked at countless books, brochures, and magazines offering a solution to losing weight. At best, a weight-reducing "diet" will reduce your calorie intake. At worst, it will change your body composition for the fatter. The reason? Many diets teach you to reduce your carbohydrate intake to bring about quick weight loss. The weight you lose, however, is mostly water (that was trapped or held with stored carbohydrate) and eventually muscle (as it is broken down to produce glucose). Once you return to your former way of eating, you regain a little bit more fat. With each desperate repetition of a diet, you lose more muscle. Over a course of years, the resulting change in body composition to less muscle and more fat makes it increasingly difficult to lose weight.

Glycemic Index Cooking Made Easy can help because low-GI foods:

- Fill you up, keep you satisfied for longer, and help you burn more of your body fat and less of your body muscle

- Enable you to increase your food intake without increasing your waistline

- Control your appetite

HEART DISEASE

Heart disease is the single biggest killer of Americans. So big, in fact, that every 26 seconds an American will either suffer a heart attack or go into cardiac arrest. According to 2001 estimates, more than 64 million Americans have one or more forms of cardiovascular disease. What's more, in 2001, cardiovascular disease accounted for 38.5 percent of all deaths.

So what causes this deadly disease? It's often caused by atherosclerosis or "hardening of the arteries." Generally, people develop atherosclerosis gradually, and live much of their lives blissfully unaware of it. If the disease develops fairly slowly it may not cause any problems—even into great old age. But if its development is accelerated by one or more of many processes, the condition may cause trouble much earlier in life.

Glycemic Index Cooking Made Easy can help fight heart disease by:

- Reducing blood cholesterol levels

- Increasing "good" high-density lipoprotein (HDL) cholesterol

- Helping you lose weight

- Reducing "bad" low-density lipoprotein (LDL) cholesterol

- Increasing your body's sensitivity to insulin

HOW THE GLYCEMIC INDEX CAME TO BE

The Glycemic Index concept was first developed in 1981 by a team of scientists led by Dr. David Jenkins, a professor of nutrition at the University of Toronto, Canada, to help determine which foods were best for people with diabetes. At that time, the diet for people with diabetes was based on a system of carbohydrate exchanges or portions, which was complicated and not very logical. The carbohydrate exchange system assumed that all starchy foods produce the same effect on blood sugar levels even though some earlier studies had already proven this was not correct. Jenkins was one of the first researchers to question this assumption and to investigate how real foods behave in the bodies of real people.

Jenkins' approach attracted a great deal of attention because it was so logical and systematic. When scientists, using Jenkins' technique, began to study the actual blood sugar responses to different foods in hundreds of people, they found that many starchy foods (such as some types of bread and potatoes) were digested into sugar and entered the bloodstream very quickly and that many sugar-containing foods, such as fruit and

What Is the GI?

The GI (Glycemic Index), a proven measure of how fast carbohydrates hit the bloodstream, helps you choose the right amount and type of carbohydrates for your health and well-being. Foods with a high-GI value contain carbohydrates that will cause a dramatic rise in your blood glucose levels, while foods with a low-GI value contain carbohydrates that will have a lesser impact.

Low GI 55

Medium GI 56–69

High GI > 70

even some cookies, were not responsible for high blood sugars. That was quite a surprise!

Over the next twenty-five years medical researchers and scientists around the world, including the authors of this book, tested the effect of many foods on blood sugar levels and developed a new concept of classifying carbohydrates based on their Glycemic Index.

Now, for the first time, the most thorough compendium of low-glycemic diet, cooking, lifestyle information, and references has been compiled into one single source—*Glycemic Index Cooking Made Easy.*

HOW TO USE THIS BOOK

To navigate the wealth of information in *Glycemic Index Cooking Made Easy*, it's helpful to approach it as three books in one.

Part 1: "The Low-GI Plan and How It Works" contains three chapters with all the background information you'll need to understand and implement the low-GI way of cooking and eating. (Of course, the recipes stand on their own, so if you want to skip ahead to Part 2 and start cooking the low-GI way immediately, that's fine.)

Chapter 1, "Low-GI Eating—The Healthy Revolution," includes the seven guidelines of the low-GI diet, key factors that influence the glycemic index, and sources of high-quality carbohydrates in the diet. We also explain the concept of glycemic load, a formula to predict what our blood-glucose response to a meal will be. To compute this, we need to know both the *amount* of carbohydrate we eat, as well as the *type* of carbohydrate.

The second chapter, "Low-GI Eating Made Easy," enables you to set up the plan that is right for you. Just one of the advantages of a low-GI diet is the tremendous variety of foods it offers. You can eat just about anything you want—including dessert! A discussion of good fats and their importance in the diet is included. A section on

"Substituting Low-GI Foods for High-GI Foods" will help you to make healthful choices when dining out or eating at home.

"About the Recipes" gets you ready to cook in an easy and exciting new way. A quick ingredients primer gets you focused on foods that give you the biggest nutritional bang. The nutritional analyses of the recipes as well as the balance of desired nutrients in a meal, are also thoroughly explained.

In addition, each of the first three chapters will feature a "Low-GI Success Story" to inspire you to make positive changes in your own diet and life. "Your Questions Answered" boxes sprinkled throughout will give clear concise answers to tricky dietary queries.

THE COMPLETE LOW-GI COOKBOOK

Part 2 is a complete cookbook in itself. Even without glancing at Part 1, you can cook nutritious and delicious low-GI meals from the more than 200 easy recipes for breakfast, lunch, dinner, desserts, and snacks.

For those of you familiar with the revolutionary low-glycemic diet, you will already know that you can eat plenty of fruit and orange and green vegetables, plus sensible quantities of bread, pasta, noodles, breakfast cereal, rice, and whole grains—the low-GI ones of course. On the low-GI diet you can also enjoy lean meat, poultry, fish, shellfish, eggs, and low-fat dairy foods such as milk, cheese, and yogurt. And you will also know that legumes play a starring role because they have the lowest GI of all.

For those of you who have just picked up this book, you will discover that the low-GI diet is not low-fat or low carb or high protein. It's the safe, delicious, and satiating weight-loss plan that gets an approving nod from nutritionists all around the world. We like to describe it as a carbohydrate-controlled diet because it is based on choosing low-GI carbs that are slowly digested and absorbed, producing only gentle rises in your blood glucose and insulin levels. Lowering your insulin levels is not only a key ingredient in weight loss, but also the secret to long-term health.

Two reasons the low-GI diet is so easy to live with long-term are that there are no special foods to buy and you can enjoy three balanced meals a day, including a dessert or indulgence at dinner and snacks in between, if you wish. So, to keep making it easy for you, that's how we have organized the chapters in our cookbook.

Breakfast

Lunch, Brunch, and Small Dishes

Soups, Side Salads, and Vegetables

Pasta and Grains

Fish and Shellfish

Chicken, Pork, Beef, and Lamb

Desserts and Sweet Treats

If you're pleasantly surprised to see recipe chapters for pasta and desserts, get used to it. Low-GI cooking is all about variety, smart food choices, moderation, and enjoyment.

The recipes are generally quick and easy to make, and full of flavorful ingredients. The preparation and cooking times are listed for each recipe. If a dish is rich in particular micronutrients, we have identified them for you in the recipe introduction. We have also included "Cook's Tips," with information on recipe shortcuts, preparation hints, and shopping tips. The recipes in this book use common household measurements. All cups and spoon measures are level. Our recipes use large eggs with an average weight of 2 ounces. All herbs used in the recipes are fresh unless otherwise stated.

Each of the recipes in this book is accompanied by a nutritional analysis. We have chosen recipes that will give you a healthy balance of all the nutrients your body needs. We have analyzed the recipes and the nutrient profile includes the energy (calories), carbohydrate, protein, fat, and fiber content per serving. For a thorough explanation of the role each nutrient plays in the low-GI diet, turn to page 34.

LOW-GI INFORMATION AT A GLANCE

The final part of the book, "Low-GI Information Resources," will become your standard reference for years to come. To keep making low-GI eating easy every day and every meal, turn to the section called "Your Low-GI Diet Foods" (page 359). Here's where we explain what to stock in your pantry, refrigerator, and freezer.

And, of course, the final essential component to the Low GI way of living is movement. In Appendix B, "Get Moving!," you'll delight in activity ideas to help you stay motivated and make physical activity a natural part of your schedule. The low-GI diet deals not only with what goes in your mouth (energy intake), but with physical activity (energy output). This is the critical side of the energy equation. Because low-GI foods actually increase the body's energy levels, you'll find yourself *wanting* to exercise more! You will have not only the desire but the physical tools to change your body shape for life.

Exercising while you lose weight will help you maximize fat loss and minimize lean muscle loss. This means you get leaner faster. Throughout *Glycemic Index Cooking Made Easy,* we have included "Activity Tips" to help you stay on track.

More energy. Less hunger. No desires to overeat. Whether you're brand new to the low-GI diet or have already realized some of its incredible health benefits, *Glycemic Index Cooking Made Easy* is your complete guide for a lifetime of healthy eating.

Dilled Pasta Salad with Smoked Salmon (*recipe on page 242*)

THE
LOW-GI PLAN
AND
HOW IT WORKS

Chapter 1

LOW-GI EATING— THE HEALTHY REVOLUTION

The dreaded "D" word! It's out there everywhere. "Diet" discussions proliferate on TV, radio, magazines, newspapers, and the Internet. You hear the chatter in the office, at church, at the mall, the soccer match, after the holidays, and before bathing suit season. You see the ads on billboards. You can't go anywhere these days without people talking about what they're eating—or, more accurately, not eating. The quest to drop those pounds—fast—is almost a national mania.

Yet, you may not be surprised to learn that even with all these diets (not to mention gimmicks, schemes, pills, and potions), the number of overweight and obese people in our society is actually climbing. The reason is simple: Diets don't work.

DIETS ON THE DEFENSIVE

Perhaps it's happened to you. You've lost weight on a particular diet only to gain the weight you worked so hard to lose (or even more) right back. Don't blame yourself. Blame the diet for doing the damage.

At best, a weight-reducing "diet" will reduce your calorie intake. At worst, it will change your body composition for the fatter. The reason? Many diets teach you to reduce your carbohydrate intake to bring about quick weight loss. The weight you lose, however, is mostly water (that was trapped or held with stored carbohydrates) and eventually muscle (as it is broken down to produce glucose). Once you return to your former way of eating, you regain a little bit more fat. With each desperate repetition of a diet, you lose more muscle. Over the course of years, the resulting change in body composition to less muscle and more fat makes it increasingly difficult to lose weight.

Eating the low-GI way is markedly different from radical weight loss diets. That's because low-glycemic foods have the unique ability to keep you feeling fuller for longer and to maximize your engine revs (metabolic rate) during active weight loss.

And, as we all know, the higher your metabolic rate, the easier your weight loss. By slowing down digestion and absorption of carbohydrates, the low-GI diet steadies both your blood glucose and insulin levels, stopping the roller-coaster ride that spells hunger and bingeing. And by bringing down insulin, your body will burn more body fat.

SCIENCE SUPPORTS THE GLYCEMIC INDEX

The Glycemic Index concept was first developed in 1981 by a team of scientists led by Dr. David Jenkins, a professor of nutrition at the University of Toronto, Canada, to help determine which foods were best for people with diabetes. Jenkins was one of the first researchers to investigate how real foods behave in the bodies of real people.

Jenkins' approach attracted a great deal of attention because it was so logical and systematic. When scientists, using Jenkins' technique, began to study the actual blood sugar responses to different foods in hundreds of people, they found that many starchy foods (such as some types of bread and potatoes) were digested into sugar and entered the bloodstream very quickly and that many sugar-containing foods, such as fruit and even some cookies, were not responsible for high blood sugars. This new information was revolutionary.

Over the next 25 years, medical researchers and scientists around the world, including the authors of this book, tested the effect of many foods on blood sugar levels and developed a new concept of classifying carbohydrates based on their glycemic index.

Tested foods are ranked against pure glucose—the substance that produces the greatest rise in blood sugar levels. The glycemic index of pure glucose is set at 100, and every other food is ranked on a scale from 0 to 100, according to its effect on blood sugar levels.

Low GI 55

Medium GI 56–69

High GI > 70

Today, we know the GI values of hundreds of different foods that have been tested following the standardized method.

We believe that choosing low-GI foods is one of the most important dietary choices you can make for lifelong health, energy, and weight control. As well as identifying your best low-GI choices, the guidelines that follow give you a blueprint for healthy eating for life.

THE SEVEN GUIDELINES OF THE LOW-GI DIET

1. Eat Seven or More Servings of Fruits and Vegetables Every Day

Being high in fiber, and therefore filling, and low in fat (apart from olives and avocado, which contain "good" fats), fruits and vegetables play a central role in the low-GI diet. They are also bursting with vitamins, minerals, antioxidants, and phytochemicals that will give you the glow of good health. Aim to eat at least two servings of fruits and five servings of vegetables daily, preferably of three or more different colors. A serving is about one medium-size piece of fruit, ½ cup of cooked vegetables, or 1 cup of raw vegetables.

Most vegetables have very little carbohydrates, so they do not have a GI. The potato, however, has a high GI, so if you are a big potato eater, try to replace some with low-GI alternatives such as corn, sweet potatoes, and yams. As for green and salad vegetables, you can eat them freely, so pile your plate high and remember that variety is the key.

Most fruits have a low GI, the lowest being apples, citrus (such as oranges and grapefruit), and stone fruits (such as peaches and nectarines). However, there's no need to limit high-GI fruits such as watermelon or cantaloupe, because even a large serving of these healthy fruits contains very few carbohydrates.

2. Eat Low-GI Breads and Cereals

The type of breads and cereals you eat affects the GI of your diet the most. Mixed grain breads, sourdough, traditional rolled oats, bulgur wheat, pearl barley, pasta, noodles, and certain types of rice are just a few examples of low-GI cereal foods. One of the easiest and most important changes you can make to lower the overall GI of your diet is to choose a low-GI bread. Most people need at least four servings of grains a day, and very active people need more. A serving is 2 slices of bread or ½ cup of rice or pasta.

3. Eat More Legumes, Including Beans, Chickpeas, and Lentils

Whether you buy dried beans, chickpeas, or lentils and cook them yourself at home—or opt for convenient, time-saving canned varieties—you are choosing one of nature's lowest-GI foods. These nutritional "power packs" are high in fiber, low in calories, and provide a valuable source of protein, carbohydrates, B vitamins, folate, iron, zinc, and magnesium. Enjoy them at least twice a week for meals or snacks.

4. Eat Nuts More Regularly

Although nuts are high in fat (averaging around 50 percent), it is largely unsaturated fat. They make a healthy substitute for snacks such as cookies, cakes, pastries, potato chips, and chocolate. They also contain relatively few carbohydrates, so most do not have a GI. The exceptions are cashews and peanuts, which are low-GI. Nuts contain a variety of antioxidants and are also one of the richest sources of vitamin E—in fact, a small handful of mixed nuts provides more than 20 percent of your recommended daily intake.

5. Eat More Fish and Shellfish

Fish and shellfish do not have a GI because they are a source of protein, not carbohydrates. Increased fish consumption is linked to a reduced risk of coronary heart disease, improvements in mood, lower rates of depression, better blood fat levels, and enhanced immunity. The likely protective components are the omega-3 fatty acids. Our bodies only make small amounts of these fatty acids, so we rely on our diet, especially fish and shellfish, to obtain them. One to three meals of fish each week is a good habit to get into to start reaping all the health benefits.

The richest sources of omega-3 fats are oily fish such as Atlantic and smoked salmon and swordfish. However, canned salmon, sardines, mackerel, and, to a lesser extent, tuna are also good sources. Look for canned fish packed in water, olive oil, canola oil, tomato sauce, or brine. Drain well before using.

Due to the risk of high levels of mercury in certain species of fish, the Food and Drug Administration (FDA) recently advised that although pregnant women,

YOUR QUESTIONS ANSWERED

Why are diets that disregard widely accepted nutritional guidelines so fashionable right now?

Several best-selling books have been published promoting high-protein diets and generating a lot of publicity. But the fact is: Diets that limit major food groups do not work over the long haul.

nursing mothers, women planning a pregnancy, and young children can consume a variety of fish as part of a healthy diet, they should avoid the consumption of certain species. Shark, swordfish, king mackerel, and tilefish should not be consumed, because these long-lived, larger fish contain the highest levels of mercury. Pregnant women should select a variety of other fish—shellfish, canned fish such as light tuna, smaller ocean fish, or farm-raised fish. The FDA says you can safely eat up to 12 ounces of cooked fish per week, with a typical serving size being 3 to 6 ounces.

6. Eat Lean Red Meats, Poultry, and Eggs

These protein foods do not have a GI because they are not sources of carbohydrates. Red meat, however, is the best source of iron you can get. Good iron status can increase your energy levels and improve your exercise tolerance. We suggest eating lean red meat two or three times a week. A serving size of about 3½ ounces is okay in a healthy diet. Accompany it with a salad or vegetables. A couple of eggs or about 4 ounces of skinless chicken provide options for variety once or twice a week.

7. Eat Low-Fat Dairy Products

Milk, cheese, ice cream, yogurt, buttermilk, and custard are the richest sources of calcium in our diet. By replacing full-fat dairy foods with reduced-fat, low-fat, or fat-free versions, you will reduce your saturated fat intake and actually boost your calcium intake.

SOURCES OF CARBOHYDRATES

Carbohydrates mainly come from plant foods, such as cereal grains, fruits, vegetables, and legumes (such as lentils and beans).

Cereals and grains are the major source of energy and protein for many of us these days, but they weren't part of the diet that we evolved over millions of years. Archaeological findings of life 15,000 years ago herald the beginnings of our use of cereal grains for food. As populations increased, resources of mammals, fish, and birds became depleted and the demand on agriculture increased. Over the past 10,000 years, we have increasingly relied upon cereals for food. Our ancestors began processing cereals by grinding them between stones, which yielded small amounts of coarse meal. Later, we began to mill cereals using high-speed rolling machines, which yielded tons of fine white flour.

There are many nutritional implications of this change to our diets, one of which has been an increase in the glycemic index of the foods we eat. Modern cereal processing methods transform the low-GI carbohydrates of cereal grains to high-GI foods. In order to eat a low-GI diet, we need to rely less on processed cereal products and more on whole grain cereals.

Milk products also contain carbohydrates in the form of milk sugar or lactose, which is the first carbohydrate we eat as infants. Some foods contain a large amount of carbohydrates (cereals,

The Impact of Insulin

The pancreas is a vital organ near the stomach, and its main job is to produce the hormone insulin for carbohydrate metabolism. Carbohydrates stimulate the secretion of insulin more than any other component of food. Eating low-GI foods slows carbohydrate absorption so the pancreas doesn't have to work as hard.

If the pancreas is overstimulated over a long period of time, it may become "exhausted," and genetically susceptible people may develop type 2 diabetes. And even if you don't have diabetes, too-high insulin levels can be dangerous. Medical experts now believe that high insulin levels are one of the key factors responsible for heart disease and hypertension. Since insulin also influences the way we metabolize foods, it helps determine whether we burn fat or carbohydrates to meet our energy needs, and ultimately determines whether we store fat in our bodies.

Can people with diabetes eat as much sugar as they want?

Research shows that moderate consumption of refined sugar (about 8 teaspoons a day) doesn't compromise blood sugar control. This means you can choose foods that contain refined sugar or even use small amounts of table sugar. Try to spread your sugar budget over a variety of nutrient-rich foods that sugar makes more palatable. Remember, sugar is concealed in many foods—a can of soft drink contains about 40 grams of sugar.

Most foods containing sugar do not raise blood sugar levels any more than most starchy foods. Golden Grahams (GI 71) contain 39 percent sugar, while Rice Chex (GI 89) contain very little sugar. Many foods with large amounts of sugar have GI values close to 60—lower than white bread.

Sugar can be a source of enjoyment and help you limit your intake of high-fat foods, but the blood sugar response to a food is hard to predict. Use your own blood sugar monitoring as a guide.

potatoes, legumes, and corn are good examples), while other foods, such as string beans, broccoli, and salad greens,

have very small amounts of carbohydrates. You can eat these foods freely, but they can't exclusively provide anywhere near enough carbohydrates for a high-carbohydrate diet. And as nutritious as they can be, plain green salads aren't meals by themselves and should be complemented by a carbohydrate-dense food such as bread and a small portion of legumes or other low-fat protein.

The following selected foods are high in carbohydrates and provide very little fat. Eat lots of them, but spare the butter, margarine, and oil when you prepare them. For a complete list of low-GI diet pantry essentials, turn to Appendix A on page 359.

THE BEST LOW-FAT, HIGH-CARBOHYDRATE CHOICES

- **Breads and cereal grains.** These include rice, wheat, oats, barley, rye, and anything made from them (whole grain bread, pasta, and breakfast cereal). One of the most important changes you can make to lower your diet's glycemic index is to choose a low-GI bread. Some good choices include:

  chapati (chickpea flour-based)

  pumpernickel

  sourdough

  stone-ground 100% whole wheat flour and sprouted wheat

  tortillas (corn-based)

  whole grain breads

Key Factors That Influence the Glycemic Index

Cooking Methods

Cooking and processing increase the glycemic index of a food because they increase the amount of gelatinized starch in the food. Here's what happens: When a food is exposed to water, the swelling (gelatinization) of starches increases, as does the food's surface area. That, in turn, increases the food's enzymatic activity, which increases the glycemic index. Cornflakes, rice cakes, and popcorn are all good examples of foods that have higher GI values when they're processed.

Physical Form of the Food

An intact fibrous coat on a food, such as that on whole grains and legumes, acts as a physical barrier (it takes longer for enzymes to break through the food's fibrous layers), slowing digestion and lowering a food's glycemic index.

Type of Starch

There are two types of starch in foods, amylose and amylopectin. The more amylose starch a food contains, the lower the glycemic index. Examples of high-amylose foods include most legumes (kidney beans, chickpeas, and lentils) and several types of rice (Uncle Ben's converted, brown, and basmati). Amylopectin, on the other hand, is a larger, more branched molecule. Its bonds are broken down more easily, causing faster digestion and giving the food a higher glycemic index.

Fiber

Viscous soluble fibers, such as those found in rolled oats and apples, slow down digestion and lower a food's glycemic index. The more viscous a food is, the slower it moves through the gut, and the more slowly it gets digested.

Sugar

The amount and type of sugar will influence a food's glycemic index. For example, fruits with a high concentration of naturally occurring fructose (such as apples and oranges) have a low glycemic index. Our bodies metabolize fructose in such a way that results in a slow release of glucose, lowering the glycemic index of a food.

- **Fruits.** A few tasty examples are apples, oranges, bananas, grapes, peaches, and melons.

- **Starchy vegetables.** Foods such as potatoes, corn, and sweet potatoes help to create filling, satisfying meals.

• •

Are naturally occurring sugars better than refined sugars?

Naturally occurring sugars are those found in foods such as fruit, vegetables, and milk. Refined sugars are concentrated sources of sugar such as table sugar, honey, or molasses.

The rate of digestion and absorption of naturally occurring sugars is no different, on average, from that of refined sugars. There is wide variation within both food groups, depending on the food. For example, the glycemic index of fruits ranges from 22 for cherries to 72 for watermelon. Similarly, among the foods containing refined sugars, some have low-GI values, while others have high-GI numbers. The glycemic index of sweetened yogurt is only 33, while each Life Savers candy has a glycemic index of 70 (the same as some breads).

Some nutritionists argue that naturally occurring sugars are better because they contain minerals and vitamins not found in refined sugar. However, recent studies that have analyzed high-sugar and low-sugar diets clearly show that the diets overall contain similar amounts of micronutrients. Studies have shown that people who eat moderate amounts of refined sugars have perfectly adequate micronutrient intakes.

- **Legumes, peas, and beans.** Baked beans, lentils, kidney beans, and chickpeas are good low-GI choices.
- **Milk.** Not only is milk an excellent source of carbohydrates, it's also rich in bone-building calcium. Adults should choose low-fat or fat-free milk and yogurt to minimize fat intake.

ALL ABOUT THE GLYCEMIC LOAD

In order to predict what our blood-glucose response to a meal will be, we need to know both the amount of carbohydrates we eat and the type of carbohydrates. The concept of glycemic load was developed by researchers at Harvard University to describe this combination of carbohydrate amount and type. The glycemic load (or GL) is calculated simply by multiplying a food's GI value (the type of carbohydrates) by the amount of carbohydrates per serving and dividing by 100.

GLYCEMIC LOAD = (GI VALUE × CARBOHYDRATES PER SERVING) ÷ 100

Some nutritionists argue that the concept of glycemic load is an improvement over the glycemic index, because it provides an estimate of both the amount (the serving size) and the quality of carbohydrates (its GI value). And you may wonder: Why not consider only the glycemic load of a food when making your food choices? We recommend against this, for several reasons. If you consider only the GL, you may end up eating a diet with very little carbohydrates but lots of fat, especially saturated fat, and excessive amounts of protein.

How Much Carbohydrates?

FOOD	PERCENTAGE OF CARBOHYDRATES PER 100 GRAMS
Apple	12
Baked beans	11
Banana	21
Barley	61
Bread	47
Cookie	62
Corn	16
Cornflakes	85
Flour	73
Grapes	15
Ice cream	22
Milk	5
Oats	61
Orange	8
Pasta	70
Pear	12
Peas	8
Plum	6
Potato	12–17
Raisins	75
Rice	79
Split peas	45
Sugar	100
Sweet potato	17
Water cracker	71

Essentially, you'd be eliminating most carbohydrate foods from your diet, which we don't advocate. The low risk of disease associated with the lowest glycemic load—evidence supported by large, long-term studies out of Harvard University— was associated with the consumption of low-GI foods, not with a low-carbohydrate intake. Carbohydrate content alone showed absolutely no relationship to disease risk. So our message is: Don't aim for a very low-carb diet. Rather, use the GI to compare foods of a similar nature— as we do in the table "Substituting Low-GI Foods for High-GI Foods" starting on page 28.

HOW TO USE THIS BOOK

To navigate the wealth of information in *Glycemic Index Cooking Made Easy* it's best to approach it as three books in one.

Part 1, "The Low-GI Plan and How It Works," contains information you'll need to understand and implement the low-GI way of cooking and eating. (Of course, the recipes stand on their own, so if you want to skip ahead to Part 2 and start cooking the low-GI way immediately, that's fine.)

Chapter 2, "Low-GI Eating Made Easy," enables you to set up the plan that is right for you. Just one of the advantages of a low-GI diet is the tremendous variety of foods it offers. You can eat just about anything you want—including dessert! A table titled "Substituting Low-GI Foods

Food manufacturers are showing increasing interest in having the GI values of their products measured. Some are already including the GI value of foods on food labels. As more and more research highlights the benefits of low-GI foods, consumers and dietitians are writing and telephoning food companies and diabetes organizations asking for GI data. This symbol has been registered in several countries, including the United States and Australia, to indicate that a food has been properly GI tested—in real people, not in a test tube—and also makes a positive contribution to nutrition. You can find out more about the program at www.gisymbol.com.au.

As consumers, you have a right to information about the nutrients and physiological effect of foods. You have a right to know the GI value of food and to know it has been tested using appropriate standardized methodology.

for High-GI Foods" will help you to make healthful choices when dining out or eating at home.

"About the Recipes," Chapter 3, gets you ready to cook in an easy and exciting new way. An ingredients primer gets you focused on foods that give you the biggest nutritional bang. The nutritional analyses of the recipes, as well as the balance of desired nutrients in a meal, are also thoroughly explained.

Throughout the first few chapters, the "Low-GI Success Story" features will inspire you to make positive changes in your own diet and life. And "Your Questions Answered" boxes provide clear, concise answers to tricky dietary queries.

THE COMPLETE LOW-GI COOKBOOK

Part 2 is a complete cookbook with more than 200 easy recipes for breakfast, lunch,

dinner, desserts, and snacks.

The preparation and cooking times are listed for each recipe. If a dish is rich in particular micronutrients, we have identified them for you in the recipe introduction. We have also included "Cook's Tips," ● with information on recipe shortcuts, preparation hints, and shopping tips. The recipes in this book use common household measurements. All cups and spoon measures are level. Our recipes use large eggs with an average weight of 2 ounces. All herbs used in the recipes are fresh unless otherwise stated.

Each of the recipes is accompanied by a nutritional analysis. We have chosen recipes that will give you a healthy balance of all the nutrients your body needs. We have analyzed the recipes, and the nutrient profile includes the calories, carbohydrates, protein, fat, and fiber content per serving. For a thorough explanation of the role each nutrient plays in the low-GI diet, turn to Chapter 3.

LOW-GI INFORMATION AT A GLANCE

Finally, in Part 3, "Low-GI Information Resources," turn to Appendix A, "Your Low-GI Diet Foods," where we explain what to stock in your pantry, refrigerator, and freezer.

And, of course, the final essential component to the low-GI way of living is movement. In Appendix B, "Get Moving," our activity ideas will help you stay motivated and make physical activity a natural part of your schedule. The low-GI diet deals not only with what goes in your mouth (energy intake), but with physical activity (energy output). This is the critical side of the energy equation. Exercising while you lose weight will help you maximize fat loss and minimize lean muscle loss. This means you get leaner faster. Throughout *Glycemic Index Cooking Made Easy*, we have included "Activity Tips" with this logo ⊗ to help you stay on track.

LOW-GI SUCCESS STORY

Marianne

AGE: 30

HEIGHT: 5'6"

WEIGHT: 198 pounds, pre-pregnancy (clinically defined as "obese")

BACKGROUND: Married with a 3-year-old daughter, Marianne is a stay-at-home mom who is pregnant for the second time. She doesn't smoke or drink alcohol, and for exercise she walks and plays with her daughter. During the third trimester of her last pregnancy, Marianne was diagnosed with pre-eclampsia (a toxemia accompanied by high blood pressure, water retention, and protein in the urine). Her daughter was born two weeks early by C-section.

This pregnancy, Marianne suffers from gestational diabetes, which was diagnosed in her seventh month of pregnancy. She takes no medications other than prenatal vitamins.

Nutritional assessment by dietitian Johanna Burani, MS, RD, CDE

Marianne is grossly underconsuming in all food categories except starches. Her caloric intake is meeting only about two-thirds of her current needs. She should try to eliminate all processed foods high in sodium (such as canned soups) and should increase her dairy foods to at least 24 ounces of milk or the equivalent.

Along with increasing her milk intake, Marianne needs to increase her protein sources by adding 6 ounces of high-quality protein (poultry, fish, eggs, meats, and so on) proportioned throughout the day (three meals plus a bedtime snack). She also needs to increase her vegetable portions at both lunch and dinner, and include condiments to help provide the required 35 percent calories from fat.

GI-specific counseling:

Marianne should try to replace her current cereal and cracker choices with whole grain options, substitute high-GI fruits (watermelon and pineapple) with low-GI options (apples, cherries, grapefruit, peaches, and so on), and replace the baked potato with noodles or long-grain rice. Those changes will help produce lower-GI meals that will help regulate Marianne's blood sugar levels for the duration of her pregnancy.

Marianne's "BEFORE" diet:

BREAKFAST: 2 cups dry cereal, 4 ounces fat-free milk, 4 ounces orange juice

SNACK: 2 cups watermelon

LUNCH: Bowl of chicken noodle soup, 6 saltines, 1 piece of string cheese, butterscotch candy, 1 cup unsweetened canned peaches, water

SNACK: 2 cups watermelon

DINNER: Large baked potato with sour cream, small baked chicken cutlet, sliced cucumber, water

LATE-NIGHT SNACK: 1/2 bag popcorn, water

Marianne's "Before" Nutritional Analysis:

CALORIES: 1,400

CARBOHYDRATES: 237 g (70%)

PROTEIN: 59 g (17%)

FAT: 19 g (13%)

GI: 73

. . . .

Marianne's NEW, LOW-GI MENU:

BREAKFAST: 2 slices 100% stone-ground whole wheat toast, 2 pats butter, 1 egg, 8 ounces 2% milk

SNACK: Small bran muffin, 1 cup low-fat plain yogurt

LUNCH: Roast beef (2 ounces) sandwich with 2 slices sour-dough bread, a tomato and cucumber salad topped with 2 tablespoons salad dressing, 4 ounces unsweetened canned peaches, water

SNACK: 1 ounce potato chips, 4 ounces apple juice

DINNER: 1 cup spaghetti with marinara sauce, a 2-ounce meatball, 1 cup asparagus tips, 2 pats butter, medium orange, water

SNACK: 8-ounce glass of 2% milk, 3 graham cracker squares, 1 tablespoon natural peanut butter (no added salt)

Marianne's "After" Nutritional Analysis:

CALORIES: 2,100

CARBOHYDRATES: 236 g (45%)

PROTEIN: 101 g (19%)

FAT: 84 g (36%)

GI: 46

Marianne's winning results:

Marianne delivered a full-term healthy baby girl by C-section and gained a total of 17 pounds throughout her pregnancy. Her blood sugar remained within the normal ranges without the need of medical insulin, and her blood pressure was also stable and within normal ranges without medication.

Marianne's comments:

"I'm so relieved the pregnancy turned out so well. I was worried about the gestational diabetes, but we were able to control it with my diet. That's why I'm anxious to get on a permanent meal plan—it's the best way I can think of to prevent my getting type 2 diabetes."

LOW-GI EATING MADE EASY

Although there are bad diets, no individual food is bad, especially when it comes to the glycemic index. Eating the low-GI way means eating a variety of foods—possibly a wider variety than you are already eating. (For a complete at-a-glance reference for stocking your pantry, turn to Appendix A, "Your Low-GI Diet Foods.")

Usually we eat a combination of carbohydrate foods, such as sandwiches and fruit, pasta and bread, cereal and toast, potatoes and corn. The glycemic index of a meal consisting of a mixture of carbohydrate foods is a weighted average of the glycemic index of those foods. The weighting is based on the proportion of the total carbohydrates contributed by each food. Studies show that when a food with a high glycemic index is combined with a food with a low glycemic index, the complete meal has an intermediate glycemic index.

A rule of thumb:

HIGH-GI FOOD + LOW-GI FOOD = INTERMEDIATE-GI MEAL

As with calories, the GI value is not precise. The glycemic index gives you a guide to help you lower the glycemic index of your day, and just one simple change can make a big difference. Look at the following ideas for the meals in your day and see how you could lower the glycemic index of your diet.

BREAKFAST BASICS

1. Include some fruit

Fruit contributes fiber and, more important, vitamin C, which helps your body absorb iron. Fruits may be fresh, cooked, packed in water or juice, or loose-pack frozen.

The lowest-GI fruits and juices are:

apple juice	apricots, fresh or dried
apples	blueberries

(continued on page 19)

The Benefits of High Fruit and Vegetable Intake

Five million years ago, the ancestors of the first hominids lived in the rain forests of Africa. Their diet was based on fruits, nuts, berries, and insects supplemented with animal food. Although the tables turned and animal food began to dominate as humans evolved, we inherited the need for large amounts of the substances found in fruit and vegetables to promote good health. In fact, there's overwhelming evidence that fruits and vegetables play an important role in preventing disease, especially cancer. The evidence is stronger for vegetable consumption and for raw, rather than cooked, foods.

Scientists have been researching the protective factors in fruits and vegetables for many years. Here are some of the key players:

- Carotenoids. Among the most well-known phytochemicals, carotenoids are found in yellow and orange fruits and vegetables, as well as in dark green leafy vegetables. They are heart-healthy and may help to prevent certain cancers.
- Lycopene. This chemical gives tomatoes and pink grapefruit their red pigment, and has strong anti-cancer and antioxidant properties.
- Indoles. Found in cruciferous vegetables such as broccoli, cauliflower, cabbage, and Brussels sprouts, indoles may reduce breast cancer risk.
- Flavonoids and genistein. Especially prevalent in soy foods, these phytochemicals help to prevent tumor formation.
- Vitamin C. This antioxidant vitamin abounds in many types of produce, including strawberries, oranges, grapefruit, broccoli, and green peppers.
- Vitamin E. This antioxidant vitamin plays a role in heart health; good food sources include vegetable oils, nuts, and seeds.
- Selenium. A mineral often grouped with antioxidants, selenium may be cancer protective.

These protective factors may work by:
- Binding with and diluting cancer-causing substances in the gut
- Stimulating detoxifying enzymes
- Inhibiting the formation of nitrosamines
- Altering the metabolism of hormones

It's more than likely that it is the combined effect of these substances that is responsible, rather than any one component. So don't be tempted to take a multivitamin supplement to replace a high intake of fruits and vegetables—you won't find all of the protective substances in a pill.

Ten Quick, Low-Fat, Low-GI Breakfast Ideas

1. Spread raisin toast with low-fat cream cheese and top with sliced apple or peach
2. Toast a slice of 100% stone-ground whole wheat bread, then melt a 1-ounce slice of low-fat cheese on it
3. Sprinkle oatmeal with cinnamon, brown sugar, and apple slices or chunks
4. Whip up a low-fat milkshake
5. Mix a sliced peach and $\frac{1}{4}$ cup of raspberries into a container of light plain yogurt
6. Top a bowl of All-Bran and fat-free milk with canned pear slices
7. Spread 1 tablespoon natural peanut butter and 2 teaspoons spreadable fruit on 2 slices of sourdough toast
8. Team a cup of Mother's oat bran and fat-free milk with $\frac{3}{4}$ cup berries
9. Toast a whole wheat pita and top with 2 tablespoons cottage cheese or light ricotta and nectarine, plum, or pear slices
10. Prepare a cup of steaming hot chocolate (made with fat-free milk) with sourdough toast and apple butter

cherries

grapefruit

grapefruit juice

grapes

melon

oranges

peaches or nectarines

pears

plums

strawberries

2. Try some breakfast cereal

Cereals are important as a source of fiber, vitamin B, and iron. When choosing processed breakfast cereals, look for those with a high fiber content. Some of the lowest GI cereals are:

Complete bran flakes

Kellogg's All-Bran with Extra Fiber

Kellogg's Bran Buds with Psyllium

Kellogg's Special K

Multi-Bran Chex

natural or toasted muesli

oatmeal (cooked, with fat-free milk)

Mother's Oat Bran Hot Cereal

raw oat bran or rice bran

The Benefits of Soy

Scientists believe that soybeans and products made from them, such as tofu, protect Japanese, Chinese, and other Asian populations from developing the high rates of heart disease and breast cancer that normally plague Western populations. In many Asian countries, people eat soy—a staple food—in many forms, including soy milk, soy sauce, soy flour, tofu, and tempeh. Research suggests that soy foods help to reduce high blood lipid levels.

Some studies suggest that the isoflavones in soybeans are responsible for reducing the risk of breast cancer; they're thought to counteract the action of estrogen in premenopausal women. Some women, especially those who are overweight, are thought to produce too much estrogen, which stimulates the growth of abnormal breast tissue. Soy products are one of the best dietary sources of these isoflavones—or phytoestrogens, as they are often called.

Soybeans have one of the lowest GI values of any food. When you add them to meals and snacks, you reduce the overall glycemic index of your diet and gain important health benefits.

Here are a few ways to incorporate more soy into your diet:

- Use canned soybeans in place of other beans in any recipe.
- Drink soy milk—it comes in plain, vanilla, chocolate, and cappuccino flavors.
- Use "okara"—the drained soybean pulp that is the by-product of soy milk—as a thickener in baking.
- Cut firm tofu into cubes; marinate them in soy sauce, ginger, and garlic; and add them to stir-fries. Or thread them onto kebabs for grilling.
- Include soybean oil or light, low-sodium soy sauce in your stir-fries.
- Use silken tofu as a base for cheesecakes, creamy sauces, smoothies, and salad dressings.
- Substitute soy flour for half a cup of wheat flour in baked goods.
- Use roasted soy nuts in granola and salads, or eat them as a snack in place of peanuts (look for unsalted or lightly salted products).

3. Add milk or yogurt

Low-fat milk and yogurt can make a valuable contribution to your daily calcium intake when you include them at breakfast. Both have a low glycemic index, and lower-fat varieties have just as much, or more, calcium as whole milk.

4. Then add some bread or toast, if you'd like

The lowest-GI breads are:

chapati (Baisen)

Healthy Choice Hearty 7 Grain

Natural Ovens 100% Whole Grain

Are You Really Choosing Low Fat?

There's a trick to food labels that it is worth being aware of when shopping for low-fat foods. These food labeling specifications guidelines were enacted by the United States Department of Agriculture (USDA) in 1994:

FREE: Contains a tiny or insignificant amount of fat, cholesterol, sodium, sugar, or calories; less than 0.5 g of fat and sugar per serving

LOW-FAT: Contains no more than 3 g of fat per serving

REDUCED/LESS/FEWER: These diet products must contain 25 percent less calories, sodium, sugar, or fat of a nutrient than the regular product

LIGHT/LITE: These diet products contain one-third fewer calories than, or half the fat of, the original product

LEAN: Meats claiming this contain less than 10 g of fat, 4 g of saturated fat, and 95 mg of cholesterol per serving

EXTRA LEAN: These meats have less than 5 g of fat, 2 g of saturated fat, and 95 mg of cholesterol per serving

Natural Ovens Happiness Cinnamon Pecan Bread with Raisins

Natural Ovens Hunger Filler

100% stone-ground whole wheat

rye

sourdough

sourdough rye

whole grain pumpernickel

100% stone-ground whole wheat pita

LIGHT LUNCH IDEAS

1. Base your light meals on carbohydrates such as cooked dried beans and whole grains like bulgur.

2. Include some high-protein foods, such as:

boiled ham

fresh turkey or chicken breast

hard-boiled egg or vegetable omelet

natural, no-salt-added peanut butter and all-fruit jelly or fruit spread

(continued on page 24)

Tony

AGE: 60

HEIGHT: 5'3"

WEIGHT: 190 pounds

BACKGROUND: Tony is married, works as a full-time school administrator, and doesn't smoke or drink alcohol. For exercise, he walks for at least one hour every day. Tony has just been diagnosed with type 2 diabetes and was sent to dietitian Johanna Burani, MS, RD, CDE, to see whether dietary changes could control his diabetes so medication wouldn't be necessary. Tony also suffers from borderline high blood pressure.

Nutritional assessment by dietitian Johanna Burani, MS, RD, CDE

The best strategy to address Tony's multiple medical problems (diabetes, hypertension, obesity) all at once is to correct his diet. He would need to decrease his fat and sodium intake and increase his carbohydrates in the form of fruits, vegetables, and whole grains, and eat minimally processed foods. He should consume his daily calories in three meals and one or two snacks. He should attempt to drink 64 ounces of water throughout the day.

Tony needs to reduce his fat from his current 55 percent of calories to less than 30 percent. He needs to include three or four servings of fruit with meals and snacks. He needs to follow some brown-bag lunch guidelines and identify the proper portion sizes for evening entrees, with an emphasis on low-fat choices.

GI-specific counseling:

Although Tony's carbohydrate foods fall into the "intermediate-GI" category, those foods contribute a paltry 22 percent of his caloric intake on an average day. His high-fat foods are making him feel full. He'll still feel full if he replaces these calorically dense foods with low-GI carbohydrates, but will be consuming less than half the calories.

Tony's "BEFORE" diet:

BREAKFAST: A small pastry or muffin, and coffee throughout the morning

LUNCH: He usually skips lunch on workdays; an occasional business lunch would consist of tuna steak, roll, coleslaw, french fries, and Diet Coke

DINNER: Four hot dogs; tossed salad dressed with oil, vinegar, and bacon bits; small piece of Italian bread; diet iced tea; and coffee

SNACK: Glass of fat-free milk

Tony's "Before" Nutritional Analysis:

CALORIES: 2,700

CARBOHYDRATES: 149 g (22%)

PROTEIN: 154 g (23%)

FAT: 163 g (55%)

GI: 67

. . . .

Tony's NEW, LOW-GI MENU:

BREAKFAST: ¾ cup Raisin Bran, 8 ounces fat-free milk, coffee, ½ cup unsweetened canned peaches

LUNCH: Roasted turkey breast (2 ounces) sandwich on 2 slices multigrain bread, 1 cup cantaloupe, water or decaf diet beverage

SNACK: 1 cup light yogurt

DINNER: 1½ cups fettuccine with marinara sauce, 3-ounce breaded pork cutlet pan-fried in 1 tablespoon olive oil, 1 cup spinach, ½ cup natural applesauce, water

SNACK: 8-ounce glass fat-free milk, 1 oatmeal cookie

Tony's "After" Nutritional Analysis:

CALORIES: 1,500

CARBOHYDRATES: 211 g (55%)

PROTEIN: 86 g (22%)

FAT: 39 g (23%)

GI: 43

Tony's winning results:

Tony reached his initial goal weight of 160 pounds after five months of eating low-GI meals and snacks. He takes no medications for either diabetes or high blood pressure. At my recommendation, he will maintain this weight for the next two to three months, at which time we'll design a new meal plan and exercise program to promote further gradual loss of another 10 to 20 pounds.

Tony's comment:

"I've never felt better in my life!"

reduced-fat cheese

roast beef, lean (see page 27)

small can of tuna, salmon, or sardines

3. Include starches such as:

chili, vegetarian

corn

lentil soup

minestrone

mixed bean salad

100% whole grain bread or toast

pasta

pasta salad

pea soup

pita bread

pumpernickel bread

raisin toast

ravioli

rice salad

sourdough rye bread

steamed rice

tabbouleh

whole grain bread roll

4. Always include a hearty portion of vegetables. Here are some suggestions:

beets

broccoli

cabbage, shredded

carrot, grated

cauliflower florets

YOUR QUESTIONS ANSWERED

What are some possible side effects of a high-protein diet?

Some high-protein diets are harmful for elderly people and anyone with high blood pressure or diabetes. High-protein, high-fat diets can lead to high cholesterol and heart disease, and increase the risk of heart attck. These diets also lack fiber, which may lead to constipation. What's more, some high-protein diets can reduce the intake of important vitamins, minerals, fiber, and trace elements.

celery sticks

chard

corn

cucumber

eggplant

mushrooms

onions

parsley and other fresh herbs

pepper strips

salad greens

shallots

snow peas

spinach

sprouts

tomatoes, cherry, grape, or plum

tomatoes, sun-dried

zucchini

Learn from the Italians

During the low carbohydrate diet craze, twirling a plateful of spaghetti was a big no-no. But pasta ranks low on the GI scale (an average GI value of 40 on a scale of 100), so it's fine to include moderate portions in low-GI meals.

Most pasta is made from semolina (finely cracked wheat), which is milled from very hard wheat with a high protein content. A stiff dough, made by mixing the semolina with water, is forced through a die and dried. There is very little disruption of the starch granule during this process, and the strong protein-starch interactions inhibit starch gelatinization. The dense consistency also makes the pasta resistant to disruption in the small intestine and contributes to the final low GI value—even pasta made from fine flour (instead of semolina) has a relatively low GI value. There's some evidence that thicker pasta has a lower GI value than thin types because of its dense consistency and perhaps because it cooks more slowly. (It's also less likely to be overcooked.) The addition of egg to fresh pasta lowers the GI value by increasing the protein content: Higher protein levels slow stomach emptying because only about 60 percent of the protein gets broken down; the rest goes into storage as fat.

Italians eat their pasta al dente, which literally means "to the tooth." It must be slightly firm and offer some resistance when you're chewing it. Not only does al dente pasta taste better than soft, soggy pasta, but it also has a lower GI value, because overcooking pasta increases starch gelatinization (or swelling) and boosts its glycemic index.

5. And round it off with fruit. Refer to the Breakfast list of fruits (starting on page 17), if you wish.

MASTERING LOW-GI DINNERS

Just one of the advantages of a low–GI diet is the tremendous variety of foods it offers. You can eat just about anything you want—including dessert! Let the following ideas jump-start your menu-planning creativity.

1. First, choose the carbohydrates

Which will it be? A new potato or sweet potato? Basmati or Uncle Ben's Original Converted Rice? A type of pasta? A grain, such as cracked wheat or barley? Chickpeas, lentils, or beans? Or a combination? Could you add some bread or corn?

barley	rice
couscous	sweet potatoes
pasta or noodles	tortillas
polenta	

Ten Low-GI Lunches on the Go

1. Pita with hummus and tomatoes or broccoli
2. Pasta with pesto, sun-dried tomatoes, and part-skim ricotta cheese
3. Grilled ham, cheese, and tomato sandwich on sourdough rye
4. Melted cheese and tomato sandwich on 100% stone-ground whole wheat bread
5. 1 cup light yogurt, 1½ cups fresh fruit salad, 2–3 graham crackers
6. Large mixed salad with beans, olives, and sunflower seeds
7. Chunky vegetable soup with barley and beans; a piece of fruit
8. Veggie burger with salsa and grilled vegetables on 100% whole wheat sandwich bun
9. Smoked salmon and avocado slices on pumpernickel bread
10. A fruit smoothie and high-fiber blueberry oat bran muffin

2. Add lots of fresh, frozen, or canned vegetables

Remember to aim for at least five servings a day. Include a large tossed salad every day, and eat a wide variety of other vegetables, whether raw or cooked (with something green included!).

artichokes	eggplant	
asparagus	fennel	
beans	leeks	
bok choy	mushrooms	
Brussels sprouts	okra	
cabbage	onions	
carrots	pea pods	
cauliflower	peas	
celery	peppers	
radishes	tomatoes	
salad greens	zucchini	
squash		

3. Now, just a little protein for flavor and texture

Remember, you don't need much—some slivers of beef to stir-fry, a sprinkle of tasty cheese, strips of ham, a dollop of ricotta cheese, a tender chicken breast, slices of salmon, a couple of eggs, or a handful of nuts.

4. Think twice about using any fat

Check that you are using a healthy type (monounsaturated or polyunsaturated), such as canola or olive oil.

Ten Low-GI Dinner Ideas

1. Spaghetti with meatballs and a large mixed salad
2. Fish fillet stuffed with fresh herbs, tomatoes, and onions, baked in foil; serve with whole grain bread roll, steamed vegetables, or large mixed salad
3. Stir-fried shrimp, scallops, beef, or chicken and vegetables over basmati rice or lo mein noodles
4. Grilled steak with grilled vegetables and an ear of corn
5. Omelet with ham, cheese, vegetables, beans, or salsa filling; serve with rice pilaf and asparagus spears
6. Spinach or cheese tortellini, fresh tomato sauce, and steamed garden vegetable medley
7. Chicken or tuna casserole with mixed vegetables and new potatoes
8. Meat or vegetarian lasagna served with a large mixed salad
9. Barbecued chicken; steamed corn; tomato, onion, and cucumber salad
10. Beef, chicken, or bean soft corn tortilla topped with salsa, served with a large mixed salad

DAIRY FOODS

Cheese

American, low-fat

Cheddar, low-fat

cottage cheese, low-fat

feta, low-fat

goat cheese, low-fat

ricotta, part-skim

Milk products

milk, fat-free or 1%

soy milk, enriched

yogurt, fat-free or low-fat

FISH

All fresh and canned fish are good options. Aim for two fish dinners a week, as suggested by the American Heart Association.

LEAN MEATS

Beef

flank

loin cuts (such as tenderloin and sirloin)

round cuts (including top round, ground round, bottom round)

T-bone and porterhouse steaks

Pork

center and loin cuts (such as center cut ham pork chops, loin chops, sirloin roast, tenderloin roast, and Canadian bacon)

Lamb

leg roast

loin chops

Veal

leg roast

scallopine

breast

Poultry

skinless chicken and turkey breasts

LEGUMES

beans (black, cannellini, chickpeas, great Northern, kidney, navy, or others)

lentils

split peas

dessert, why not simply serve a bowl of seasonal fruit?

apples	oranges
apricots	papaya
bananas	peaches
blueberries	pears
cantaloupe	persimmons
cherries	plums
grapefruit	prunes
grapes	quinces
honeydew	raspberries
kiwi	rhubarb
mandarins	star fruit
mangoes	strawberries
nectarines	

DESSERTS: A LOW-GI FINISH

Although often overlooked, desserts can make a valuable contribution to your daily calcium and vitamin C intake when they are based on low-fat dairy foods and fruits. Recipes incorporating fruit for sweetness will have more fiber and lower GI values than recipes with sugar. What's more, desserts are usually carbohydrate rich, which means they help top up our satiety center, signifying the completion of eating and reducing the tendency for late-night nibbles.

If you don't have time to prepare a

SUBSTITUTING LOW-GI FOODS FOR HIGH-GI FOODS

We believe that the most appropriate and practical way to put the GI theory into practice is simply to substitute low-GI foods for high-GI foods, which lowers your diet's overall glycemic index.

As we mentioned previously, some of the richest sources of carbohydrates include bread, crackers, cookies, breakfast cereals, rice, pasta, and potatoes. Choosing low-GI varieties of these foods from the table on page 29 will significantly lower the glycemic index of your diet.

Substituting Low-GI Foods for High GI-Foods

HIGH-GI FOOD	LOW-GI ALTERNATIVES
BREAD	
Fluffy, light, smooth-textured white or whole wheat (made from enriched wheat flour)	Dense breads containing a lot of whole grains; sourdough and stone-ground flour breads (types that don't contain any enriched wheat flour)
RICE	
Short-grain sticky (Chinese or Italian), jasmine, gluten-free, quick-cooking brown rice	Long-grain basmati, imported Japanese, Uncle Ben's converted, long-grain white, brown rice
POTATOES	
Instant mashed, red- and white-skinned baking varieties	Sweet potato, yam, new potatoes (these have a moderate glycemic index)
PASTA	
Overcooked (mushy) pastas or noodles	All pastas or noodles cooked al dente
GRAINS	
Gluten-free corn, millet, tapioca	Barley (cracked), bulgur wheat (cracked wheat), buckwheat, buckwheat groats, corn (canned)
LEGUMES	
All legumes are low-GI. Some examples are: beans (including baked), chickpeas, lentils	
CEREALS	
Most processed cold breakfast cereals, as well as quick and instant cooked types (such as oatmeal)	Rolled oats, semolina, muesli, granola, All-Bran with Extra Fiber, All-Bran Buds, Grape-Nuts, Special K, oat bran
CRACKERS	
Most crackers (Saltines, Triscuits), rice cakes	Ryvita, multigrain and five-grain Wheat Thins, Wasa crispbreads
FRUIT	
Mango, pineapple, dates, watermelon, raisins	Apples, pears, citrus fruits, cherries, peaches, plums

Joyce

AGE: 64

HEIGHT: 5'6"

WEIGHT: 227 pounds (clinically defined as "obese")

BACKGROUND: Joyce is an unmarried professional full-time cook. She neither smokes nor drinks alcohol and walks every day for 20 minutes (when she isn't feeling sick). Joyce has a number of health problems: She suffers from high blood pressure and is taking multiple medications to control her diabetes. She also injects insulin twice a day (total of 111 units) and takes one oral agent as well. Her blood sugar numbers range above 330, indicating poor control. Joyce's cholesterol is also high, though she takes no medications for that condition.

Nutritional assessment by dietitian Johanna Burani, MS, RD, CDE

Because Joyce is morbidly obese and carries her excess fat abdominally, her body is resistant to insulin; even though she is taking large doses, her sugar control remains unsatisfactory. Joyce will need to reduce her caloric intake (specifically her fat calories) and balance her diet with more vegetables and low-fat dairy foods.

GI-specific counseling:

Joyce's carbohydrate choices consist predominantly of low- or intermediate-GI foods, which is a good start. By balancing her meals and snacks with more whole grains, vegetables, and low-fat dairy foods, and reducing her fat calories, she will start losing some weight and become less insulin-resistant, without feeling hungry. Her low-GI food choices will simultaneously help lower her weight, blood sugars, blood pressure, and cholesterol levels and give her more energy.

Joyce's "BEFORE" diet:

BREAKFAST: Fried egg, 2 slices of whole wheat toast with margarine, coffee with 2% milk

SNACK: 8-ounce glass of apple juice

LUNCH: Baked fish, ½ cup hash brown potatoes, creamed spinach, apple, water

DINNER: 2 slices of pizza, a handful of chips, 2 bologna slices, apple, water

LATE-NIGHT SNACK: Handful of pretzel nuggets

Joyce's "Before" Nutritional Analysis:

CALORIES: 2,200

CARBOHYDRATES: 235 g (42%)

PROTEIN: 87 g (15%)

FAT: 106 g (43%)

GI: 56

Joyce's NEW, LOW-GI MENU:

BREAKFAST: 1⅓ cups All-Bran with Extra Fiber, 8 ounces fat-free milk, small apple

LUNCH: 1 cup noodles, 4-ounce broiled chicken breast, 1 cup green beans, tossed salad dressed with 1 teaspoon olive oil and vinegar, 3 ounces cherries, water

DINNER: ⅔ cup Uncle Ben's Original Converted rice, 4-ounce lemon sole, 1 cup steamed broccoli and cauliflower florets, 1 tablespoon light margarine spread, 1 cup grapes, water

SNACK: 8 graham cracker squares and 1 cup light yogurt

Joyce's "After" Nutritional Analysis:

CALORIES: 1,700

CARBOHYDRATES: 224 g (53%)

PROTEIN: 90 g (21%)

FAT: 47 g (26%)

GI: 43

Joyce's winning results:

In the past six years, Joyce has lost 47 pounds and has been able to maintain a weight of 180. Her blood pressure and cholesterol levels have normalized. She is taking one insulin injection a day, having reduced her insulin requirement by 85 percent. Her blood sugars are all within the normal range.

Joyce's comments:

"It's so nice to have energy again. And I have more time on my hands now to work on my hobbies, since I go to the doctor less often."

Is it better to eat complex carbohydrates instead of simple sugars?

There are no big distinctions between sugars and starches in either nutritional terms or when it comes to GI values. Some sugars such as fructose (fruit sugar) have a low glycemic index. Others, such as glucose, have a high glycemic index. The most common sugar in our diet, ordinary table sugar (sucrose), has a moderate glycemic index.

Starches can fall into both the high- and low-GI categories too, depending on the type of starch and what treatment it has received during cooking and processing. Most modern starchy foods (such as bread, potatoes, and breakfast cereals) contain high-GI carbohydrates.

What our research has shown is that you don't have to eliminate sugar completely from your diet. However, it is important to remember that sugar alone won't keep the engine running smoothly, so don't overdo it. A balanced diet contains a wide variety of foods.

MAKING THE CHANGE

Some people change their diet easily, but for the majority of us, change of any kind is difficult. Changing our diet is seldom just a matter of giving up certain foods.

A healthy diet contains a wide variety of foods, but we need to eat them in appropriate proportions. If you are considering changes to your diet, keep these guidelines in mind:

1. Aim to make changes gradually

2. Attempt the easiest changes first

3. Break big goals into a number of smaller, more achievable goals

4. Accept lapses in your habits

5. If you feel like you need some extra help, seek out some professional assistance from a dietitian

Chapter 3

ABOUT THE RECIPES

Now that you can distinguish between low- and high-GI foods, how about some recipes to put your knowledge into practice and turn mealtimes into healthy and delicious events? The recipes we've chosen aren't gourmet—they're just delicious, low-GI, and super easy to make. (We know that you probably don't have a lot of time to cook!) And they're full of healthy ingredients—available in any supermarket—such as fish and shellfish, legumes, whole grains, olive oil, fresh fruit, and vegetables.

Our recipes are formatted to make your cooking experience as pleasant and efficient as possible. Starting with the head note, we share ideas for serving suggestions or valuable information about nutrients in the dish.

At a glance, you check the preparation time and cooking time so you'll know before you begin how long the dish will take to make. We also list the times required for marinating, soaking, chilling, and other steps that don't require your direct involvement. This makes it so easy to break a recipe into several easy stages. The ingredients lists are intentionally as short as possible and the recipe directions are numbered so it's always easy to find the next step you need.

Cook's Tips are included with many of the recipes to help you build your skills and become more kitchen efficient. Whether it's toasting nuts, soaking beans, or selecting fish, we'll give you the facts.

Of course, we understand that first and foremost, you and your family's tastebuds have to be tempted. We think our recipes will do the trick. Ricotta Blueberry Hotcakes, Sweet Corn and Mushroom Omelet, Black Bean Soup, Tortellini and Ham Salad, Mediterranean Lasagna, Grilled Fish Kebabs, Thai Chicken Curry, Pork with Creamy Mustard Sauce and Red Cabbage, Beef Fajitas, Raisin Bread and Butter Pudding, and more than 200 other delectable dishes are sure to please.

RECIPE NUTRITION INFORMATION

Our recipes are based on a dietary philosophy that emphasizes:

- Low-GI carbohydrates, with carbohydrates meeting 40 to 50 percent of calorie requirements

- Monounsaturated fats and omega-3 fats, with 30 to 35 percent of calories coming from fat

- A moderate level of protein providing 15 to 20 percent of calories

We've included nutrition information with each recipe, including the calories, carbohydrates, protein, fat, and fiber content per serving.

Calories

In keeping with our dietary philosophy, we recommend the following levels of macronutrients for various energy requirements. (These energy levels are an approximate guide only, and assume good health status and a moderate level of activity.)

An average energy requirement for young to middle-age men:

2,400 calories, made up of 90 to 120 grams protein, 80 to 95 grams fat, 250 to 300 grams carbohydrates

An average energy requirement for young to middle-age women and older men, and a reduced energy intake for younger men:

2,000 calories made up of 75 to 100 grams protein, 70 to 80 grams fat, 210 to 250 grams carbohydrates

An average energy requirement for older women, a reduced energy intake for young to middle-age women, and a low energy intake for men:

1,500 calories made up of 55 to 75 grams protein, 50 to 60 grams fat, 150 to 200 grams carbohydrates

A low energy intake for young to middle-age women:

1,200 calories made up of 45 to 60 grams protein, 40 to 45 grams fat, 125 to 150 grams carbohydrates

Carbohydrates

Most of our recipes have a carbohydrate base, but the emphasis is always on low GI because the slow digestion and absorption of these foods will fill you up, trickle fuel into your engine at a more useable rate, and keep you satisfied for longer. The actual amount of carbohydrates consumed at each meal may be relevant to those with diabetes and those who monitor their blood glucose levels.

We've used moderate amounts of refined sugar (medium GI) in our recipes for healthy desserts and sweet treats. The World Health Organization says that "a moderate intake of sugar-rich foods can provide for a palatable and nutritious diet." So enjoy refined sugar, using it

(continued on page 36)

YOUR QUESTIONS ANSWERED

What's wrong with a low-carbohydrate diet?

There is little scientific evidence to back up or refute low-carbohydrate diets. One reason for the popularity of low-carbohydrate diets for weight loss is that initial loss is rapid. Within the first few days, the scales will be reading 4–7 pounds lower. That's a really encouraging sign to anyone trying to lose weight. The trouble is that most of that weight loss isn't body fat, but muscle glycogen and water.

When carbohydrates are no longer being supplied in sufficient amounts by your diet, the body uses its small carbohydrate reserves (muscle glycogen) to fuel muscle contraction. One gram of carbohydrates in the form of muscle and liver glycogen binds 4 grams of water. So when you use up your total reserves of 500 grams of glycogen within the first few days, you also lose 4 pounds of water, for a total loss of $5\frac{1}{2}$ pounds, none of it fat. Conversely, when you return to normal eating, the carbohydrate reserves will be rapidly replenished along with the water, which is why there is an instant weight gain.

People who have followed low-carbohydrate diets for any length of time observe that the rate of weight loss plateaus off, and they begin to feel rather tired and lethargic. That's not surprising because the muscles have little in the way of glycogen stores. Strenuous exercise requires both fat and carbohydrates in the fuel mix. So, long-term, these low-carbohydrate diets may discourage people from the physical exercise patterns that will help them keep their weight under control.

Our good advice is that the best diet for weight control is one you can stick to for life—one that includes your favorite foods, that accommodates your cultural and ethnic heritage, and, perhaps most important, that you can incorporate into your current lifestyle. This diet can vary somewhat in total carbohydrates, protein, and fat. At the present time, there is more scientific evidence supporting the use of bulky, higher-carbohydrate, low-GI, low-fat diets for weight loss. But the bottom line is that the type of carbohydrates and the type of fat are critical. Choosing low-GI foods will not only promote weight control but will also reduce blood sugar levels after eating, increase satiety, and provide bulk and a rich supply of micronutrients.

judiciously to make nutritious foods more palatable. Just be mindful of sugar in liquid form (such as soft drinks and fruit juices) because they are easy to overconsume.

Protein

Sufficient protein in the diet is important for weight control because, compared to carbohydrates and fat, protein makes us feel more satisfied immediately after eating and reduces hunger between meals. Protein also increases our metabolic rate for 1 to 3 hours after eating. This means we burn more energy by the minute compared with the increase that occurs after eating carbohydrates or fats. Even though this is a relatively small difference, it may be important in long-term weight control.

There is evidence that we evolved on much higher protein intakes than we eat today, although there's insufficient evidence yet to suggest that we need to greatly increase our protein intake. Protein foods are a critical source of some nutrients such as iron (from red meat)

and omega-3 fats (from fish and seafood). Most people consume 15 to 20 percent of energy as protein, which is in line with current guidelines. The protein content of these recipes varies according to the main ingredients; the entrees based on meat, fish, or legumes are higher in protein than recipes based entirely on vegetables.

Fat

Forget what you've been told about low fat and learn the new fat message—it's not all bad. The type of fat is more important for your health than the total amount. Most of us need to eat more of certain types of fat for optimal health. These fats include the omega-3 fats found in fish and seafood, and omega-neutral monounsaturated fats found in olive and canola oils. You'll find we have incorporated the "good" fats in our recipes by using nuts, oily fish, avocado, olives, and olive oil.

It is important, however, to remember that an increase in fat intake will result in an increase in calorie intake unless you also reduce the amount of another nutrient, such as carbohydrates.

Weighing In

What's the weight of the meat you're buying? Start noticing the weight that appears on the butcher's scales or package label and consider how many servings it will give you. With a food such as steak, which is basically all edible meat, 3–5 ounces per serving is sufficient. One pound is enough for four portions. Choose lean cuts of meat, and trim away the fat before cooking or before you put it away. Alternate meat or chicken with fish once or twice a week.

Margarine: Friend or Foe?

You'll notice that in some of the meals, we suggest using reduced-fat margarine spread. As you may know, many margarines are sources of trans fats, which can raise cholesterol levels and have been implicated in increased risk of heart attacks and possibly even breast cancer. Luckily, not all margarine is created equal! Some products now on store shelves clearly boast that they are trans-fat free (look for those). Here are some other guidelines to follow to avoid these unhealthy fats:

- Buy margarine spread by the tub, not stick margarine
- Look for "light," "low-fat," "nonfat," or "fat-free" on the label
- Make sure the first ingredient says "liquid," such as "liquid canola oil" or "liquid safflower oil"
- Try a vegetable spread containing plant stanol esters

Because of this, we feel that a higher-fat diet will not suit everyone. In particular, those people who have a big appetite and like to eat a large volume of food could control their weight more easily on a low-fat, high-carbohydrate diet. Low-fat, high-carbohydrate foods are less energy dense than higher-fat foods, which means that it is possible to eat a larger volume of them while still eating within calorie requirements.

If you are trying to lose weight, and sometimes struggle with hunger, try to stick to the lower fat intakes for the various energy levels recommended above. For example, for a young to middle-age woman on a reduced-calorie intake of about 1,500 calories, aiming for around 50 grams of fat per day allows a more generous amount of carbohydrates in the diet at 200 grams per day.

Fiber

A diet rich in fruits and vegetables will be naturally high in fiber. The typical American diet contains about 20 grams of fiber a day, which falls far short of the recommendation that we should eat 30 to 40 grams every day. The daily fiber requirements of children and adolescents are estimated as their age in years plus five: This gives the number of grams of fiber recommended per day.

Most of the recipes in this book are high in fiber, providing an average of 5 grams of fiber per serving. This means they will not only keep you regular but will also help lower your blood glucose and cholesterol levels and reduce your risk of many chronic diseases.

Note: Recipes have been analyzed using nutrient analysis software, FoodWorks® (Xyris Software), based on Australian and New Zealand food composition data.

Jim

AGE: 49

HEIGHT: 5'4"

WEIGHT: 285 pounds

BACKGROUND: Jim is a computer programmer and an avid outdoor photographer. Living alone, his 12-hour-plus workday leaves little time or energy to prepare a healthy evening meal or to think about breakfast or lunch food for the next day. Neither a drinker nor a smoker, Jim's only exercise is photographic walks on the weekends. He was diagnosed with type 2 diabetes at age 44, has high blood pressure, elevated cholesterol, and, with a BMI of 42, is clinically considered to be severely obese.

Nutritional assessment by dietitian Johanna Burani, MS, RD, CDE

Jim knew he needed to improve his health. By focusing on weight-loss strategies, Jim agreed, his other health concerns would improve. He would need to increase his daily calories—especially fruits, vegetables, and dairy foods. He should significantly reduce his caffeine intake and choose water as his most-consumed beverage throughout the day.

GI-specific counseling:

The big eye-catcher here is the amount of caffeine Jim consumes between his coffee and Diet Cokes (almost 5,000 mg, or nearly nine times the amount nutritionists consider an acceptable daily intake). In such high amounts, caffeine can have a hyperglycemic effect on blood sugar levels. Although virtually calorie-free (he deliberately chose *diet* soda and drank his coffee black), Jim's beverages were putting him on a blood sugar roller coaster, much as eating high-GI foods would. Because he wanted to lose weight, as soon as he felt hungry, he would just drink more caffeine. This quieted his hunger, albeit for a short time. Jim actually was just setting himself up for a spike in blood sugar followed by a crashing low. He was spinning his wheels.

Jim's "BEFORE" diet:

BREAKFAST: 2 eggs over easy, 2 thin slices buttered white toast, 8 ounces orange juice, 3 mugs black coffee throughout the morning

LUNCH: Commercially prepared frozen dinner, small green salad, 2 tablespoons ranch dressing

DINNER: Commercially prepared frozen dinner, 2 cups Brussels sprouts, 1½ tablespoons margarine spread (Throughout the course of the day, Jim also drank 4 liters of Diet Coke and admits that the food diary above represents a "very good day.")

Jim's "Before" Nutritional Analysis:

CALORIES: Approximately 1,500

CARBOHYDRATES: 155 g (42%)

PROTEIN: 81 g (22%)

FAT: 58 g (36%)

GI: 69

Jim's NEW, LOW-GI MENU:

BREAKFAST: 2 slices whole grain pumpernickel, 1 egg over easy, 2 clementines, water

LUNCH: 2 ounces whole wheat pita, ½ cup tuna salad (store bought), handful cherry tomatoes, apple, water

SNACK: 1 cup light fruited yogurt, 2 oatmeal cookies, water

DINNER: Commercially prepared frozen dinner (looked for lowest sodium and highest fiber options), 2 cups broccoli, apple, water

SNACK: 4 ounces fat-free milk, apple cinnamon snack bar (Jim decided to eliminate all diet soda and enjoys one 16-ounce mug of coffee throughout the morning.)

Jim's "After" Nutritional Analysis:

CALORIES: 1,900

CARBOHYDRATES: 250 g (54%)

PROTEIN: 104 g (22%)

FAT: 50 g (24%)

GI: 44

Jim's winning results:

After eight months of revamping his diet, Jim has lost 55 pounds (BMI of 35). He is two-thirds of the way to achieving his goal weight of 200 pounds. He now takes only one of his two diabetes medications, and his HbA1c has come into the normal range (4.5). His last blood pressure check measured 110/70, and his lipid profile was almost completely normal. He is hoping his doctor will decrease or even eliminate his blood pressure and cholesterol medications as he approaches his goal weight.

Jim's comments:

"I never thought I could get through a day without lots of caffeine. I have so much more energy now that I've taken to climbing stairs during work hours."

Pan-Fried Lamb and Greens Salad with Tzatziki *(recipe on page 316)*

part 2

THE
RECIPES

Chapter 4

BREAKFAST

Make breakfast a priority. It's the most important meal of your day, recharging your brain and speeding up your metabolism after an overnight "fast." These delicious morning meals—filled with high-fiber grains, fresh dairy, and fruit—will nourish your body and sustain you through the early part of your busy day. With our tips for advance preparation and minimum fuss, you can wake up to Apricot and Muesli Muffins, Breakfast Pockets, French Toast with Berry Compote, Ricotta Blueberry Hotcakes, and more.

ORANGE MUESLI

Serves 2

Muesli, which means "mixture" in German, was developed as a health food in the late 1800s. Prepared with a variety of low-GI natural ingredients, this convenient dish is still a smart way to start the day.

SOAKING TIME: OVERNIGHT   PREPARATION TIME: 5 MINUTES

1	cup rolled oats
¼	cup raisins
1	cup orange juice
1	apple, unpeeled and grated
2	tablespoons low-fat plain yogurt
¼	cup blueberries
4	strawberries, sliced

1. The night before, place the oats, raisins, and orange juice in a bowl. Cover and leave in the refrigerator overnight.

2. In the morning, add the apple and yogurt and mix well. Serve in 2 bowls topped with the blueberries and strawberries.

Per serving: 345 calories, 68 g carbohydrates, 8 g protein, 4 g fat, 7 g fiber

THREE-GRAIN MUESLI

(photo on page 49) *Makes 32 (2-ounce) servings*

This recipe makes a large batch that can be used for meals or snacks on the run. Store the muesli in an airtight container for up to a month.

PREPARATION TIME: 10 MINUTES   COOKING TIME: 25 TO 35 MINUTES

COOLING TIME: 30 MINUTES

7½ cups rolled oats
2   cups rye or barley flakes (or use extra oats)
½   cup sesame seeds
1⅓ cups sliced almonds
1   cup wheat germ
1½ cups mixed dried fruit, such as peaches, pears, apricots, apples
2   cups raisins
½   cup pumpkin seeds
1   cup sunflower seeds

1. Preheat the oven to 350°F. Spread half the rolled oats and half the rye or barley flakes on a large ungreased baking sheet. Bake for 10 to 15 minutes, stirring several times, until the oats are golden brown (take care they don't burn). Spread onto a large plate or tray to cool. Repeat with the remaining oats and rye or barley.

2. Put the sesame seeds and almonds on the pan and bake for 3 minutes, stirring occasionally, or until toasted and golden. Allow to cool for 30 minutes.

3. Combine the toasted oats, rye or barley, sesame seeds, and almonds with the wheat germ, dried fruit, raisins, pumpkin seeds, and sunflower seeds. Mix well.

Per serving: 235 calories, 30 g carbohydrates, 7 g protein, 10 g fat, 5 g fiber

Recipe: Dr. Rosemary Stanton

NATURAL TOASTED MUESLI

Makes 12 (⅓ cup) servings

While this muesli is relatively high in fat, most of it comes from the "healthy" fats in the nuts and seeds. Serve with low-fat milk or yogurt, and fresh fruit in season.

PREPARATION TIME: 15 MINUTES   COOKING TIME: 35 MINUTES

COOLING TIME: 30 MINUTES

2½ cups rolled oats
2   cups rolled rye
½   cup raw unsalted pumpkin seeds
⅓   cup sunflower seeds
¼   cup almonds, chopped
¼   cup hazelnuts, chopped
1   cup dried apricots, chopped
1   cup raisins

1. Preheat the oven to 350°F.

2. In a large baking dish, combine the oats, rye, pumpkin seeds, sunflower seeds, and nuts. Stir to mix well.

3. Bake for 35 minutes, until lightly toasted, stirring several times during cooking.

4. Cool 30 minutes. Add the apricots and raisins. Stir to mix well.

Per serving: 304 calories, 41 g carbohydrates, 9 g protein, 12 g fat, 6 g fiber

COOK'S TIPS

Rolled rye is available in natural food stores. Rolled oats or triticale may be substituted.

Store the muesli in an airtight container in a cool, dark place for up to one month.

HIGH-TEST GRANOLA

Makes 18 (½ cup) servings

Make this recipe just once, taste it just once, and store-bought granola will be wiped off your shopping list forever!

PREPARATION TIME: 5 MINUTES   **COOKING TIME: 25 MINUTES**
COOLING TIME: 30 MINUTES

	Canola oil spray
½	cup pure floral honey
6	cups old-fashioned oats (not quick oats)
¾	slivered almonds (or any other nut, such as pecans, cashews, or walnuts), toasted
¼	cup ground flaxseed
¼	cup soy nuts
1	tablespoon ground cinnamon
1	cup dried blueberries and currants (or any other combination of dried fruit, except dates)

1. Lightly coat a large baking pan (10" x 9" x 2½") with oil spray. Add the honey. Place the pan in a cold oven. Turn oven to 350°F. Warm for 5 minutes, or until honey has melted.

2. Meanwhile, in a large bowl, combine the oats, almonds, flaxseed, soy nuts, and cinnamon. Mix well.

3. Remove the pan of melted honey from the oven. Add the oat mixture to the baking pan. Spread and turn to coat well with honey.

4. Bake for 25 minutes, or until the oats are well toasted, turning every 5 to 6 minutes. Remove from the oven. Cool 30 minutes.

5. Add the dried fruit. Store in airtight container.

Per serving: 200 calories, 31 g carbohydrates, 7 g protein, 5 g fat, 5 g fiber

APPLE 'N' OATS BREAKFAST PUDDING

Serves 4

Here is a fabulous invitation to a great day! When you taste the combination of these flavors, you'll know they were made for each other.

PREPARATION TIME: 5 MINUTES   COOKING TIME: 35 MINUTES

Canola oil spray
2   cups fat-free milk
3   tablespoons brown sugar
1   tablespoon reduced-fat margarine spread or light butter
¼   teaspoon ground cinnamon
⅛   teaspoon salt
1   medium baking apple (peeled, cored, and diced)
1   cup rolled oats
1   teaspoon vanilla extract
¼   teaspoon grated nutmeg
1   tablespoon cream (optional)

1. Preheat the oven to 350°F. Lightly coat a 1-quart baking dish with oil spray.

2. Combine the milk, sugar, margarine or butter, cinnamon, and salt in a 2-quart saucepan. Cook over high heat for 4 minutes to scald the milk.

3. Add the apple and the oats. Continue cooking on high for 1 minute. Remove from heat and stir in the vanilla.

4. Pour the mixture into the prepared baking dish. Bake for 15 minutes.

5. Remove from the oven. Stir the mixture thoroughly. Sprinkle the top with nutmeg. Return to the oven and bake for 15 minutes.

6. Serve warm with cream, if desired.

Per serving: 166 calories, 27 g carbohydrates, 8 g protein, 3 g fat, 3 g fiber

COOK'S TIP

Good baking apples are Macintosh, Cortland, Jonathan, Winesap, and Rome Beauty.

Three-Grain Muesli (*page 45*)

Mixed Grain Cereal with Dried Fruit Compote and Yogurt *(page 66)*

Fruity Quinoa Porridge *(page 67)*

French Toast with Berry Compote (*page 70*)

Buckwheat Pancakes with Berries *(page 72)*

Fiber-High Bran Muffins *(page 75)*

Fruit Compote *(page 76)*

Lentil, Spinach, and Feta Salad *(page 80)*

Curried Lentil Salad (*page 81*)

Roast Butternut Squash and Chickpea Salad *(page 86)*

Sweet Chile Tuna Salad *(page 90)*

Azuki Bean Stew *(page 93)*

Vegetable Chili Bowl *(page 94)*

Breakfast Sandwich with Spicy Tomato Salsa *(page 96)*

Scrambled Eggs with Smoked Salmon (*page 98*)

Brunch Egg Bowls *(page 104)*

TRADITIONAL SCOTTISH PORRIDGE

Serves 2

Many traditional Scottish meals are both rich in nutrients and have a low GI. Oats were once a staple of Scotland, used not only to make porridge, but incorporated in baked goods and in many dishes as a thickener. If you have never tasted old-fashioned porridge, give this recipe a try.

SOAKING TIME: OVERNIGHT   COOKING TIME: 10 TO 15 MINUTES

1   cup steel-cut oats
½   teaspoon salt
     Muesli (optional)
1   cup low-fat milk

1. The night before, combine the oats, salt, and 3 cups water in a nonstick saucepan and soak overnight (there is no need to refrigerate, except in very hot weather).

2. In the morning, put the saucepan over medium heat, bring to a boil, then reduce the heat and simmer for 10 minutes, stirring occasionally.

3. Spoon the porridge into bowls and sprinkle with a little muesli, if desired. Traditionally, the steaming bowls of porridge are served with a cup of milk on the side. Take half a spoonful of hot porridge and fill the rest of your spoon with the cold milk.

Per serving: 225 calories, 40 g carbohydrates, 10 g protein, 5 g fat, 3 g fiber

COOK'S TIP

Seek out steel-cut oats if you can, as they do taste better. You can find them in health food stores and some supermarkets. Failing this, rolled oats are almost as good. (Rolled oats are simply steamed and flattened oats—the partial cooking of these reduces the flavor but does shorten the cooking time.) If you are using rolled oats, use 1 cup oats and 2½ cups water and reduce the cooking time to 3–5 minutes. There is no need to soak the rolled oats overnight.

MIXED GRAIN CEREAL WITH DRIED FRUIT COMPOTE AND YOGURT

(photo on page 50)   *Serves 4*

For an aromatic addition, grate a bit of fresh lemon or orange peel over the compote.

PREPARATION TIME: 10 MINUTES   COOKING TIME: 15 MINUTES

⅔   cup dried apples
⅓   cup dried apricots
¼   cup pitted prunes
4   cups water, divided
1   cinnamon stick
¾   cup rolled oats
¾   cup rolled barley
6½ ounces Stonyfield Farm low-fat vanilla yogurt

1. Combine the apples, apricots, prunes, 1 cup water, and the cinnamon stick in a medium saucepan. Bring to a boil, then reduce the heat, partially cover, and simmer for 10 to 15 minutes, or until the fruit is soft. Discard the cinnamon stick and cool slightly.

2. Meanwhile, place the oats and barley in another saucepan and add 3 cups of water. Bring to a boil, then reduce the heat and simmer for 3–5 minutes, stirring frequently, until creamy.

3. Spoon the oatmeal into serving bowls, top with the fruit compote, and drizzle with some of the fruit cooking liquid. Add a dollop of yogurt and serve immediately.

Per serving: 300 calories, 65 g carbohydrates, 9 g protein, 2.5 g fat, 8 g fiber

COOK'S TIPS

Rolled barley is sold in health food stores. Rolled oats or triticale may be substituted.

   The compote can be made up to three days in advance. Refrigerate until required, then reheat, or serve cold.

FRUITY QUINOA PORRIDGE

(photo on page 51)   *Serves 4*

Quinoa (pronounced keen-wa) is a tiny, quick-cooking grain. It is rich in nutrients and has less than 5 percent fat, with no saturated fat, and a low GI of 53. Quinoa has a mild, nutty flavor and a slightly chewy texture. Look for it in larger supermarkets or health food stores.

PREPARATION TIME: 10 MINUTES   COOKING TIME: 15 MINUTES

    1   cup quinoa
2½–3 cups fat-free milk, divided
    1   apple, chopped with skin on
    ⅓   cup raisins
    1   cinnamon stick or ½ teaspoon ground cinnamon
    1   tablespoon pure floral honey

1. Put the quinoa in a sieve and rinse well under cold running water. Transfer the quinoa into a saucepan. Pour in 2 cups of the milk. Bring to a boil, then reduce the heat and simmer for 5 minutes. Add the apple, raisins, and cinnamon and simmer for 5 to 6 minutes, or until all of the liquid is absorbed. Remove the cinnamon stick, if using.

2. Serve the quinoa porridge in small bowls. Drizzle the honey over the top and serve with the remaining ½ to 1 cup fat-free milk, warmed, if desired.

Per serving: 290 calories, 54 g carbohydrates, 13 g protein, 3 g fat, 4 g fiber

BREAKFAST FRUIT LOAF

Makes 12 slices

Although it is difficult to predict the GI of baked foods containing flour, we know that fruit loaves have a lower GI because some of the flour is replaced with dried fruit. This loaf is also packed with the fiber needed for a healthy digestive system. Top with light cream cheese.

SOAKING TIME: 30 MINUTES   PREPARATION TIME: 10 MINUTES
COOKING TIME: 1 TO 1¼ HOURS

¾   cup All-Bran cereal

1⅓ cups fat-free milk

1½ cups whole wheat pastry flour

1   tablespoon baking powder

½   teaspoon salt

¾   cup raisins

⅔   cup dried apricots, chopped into small pieces

¼   cup pitted prunes, chopped into small pieces

⅓   cup dark brown sugar

4   tablespoons pure floral honey

1. Put the cereal in a bowl, pour the milk over it, and soak for 30 minutes. Preheat the oven to 350°F.

2. Sift the flour, baking powder and salt into a bowl. Stir in the cereal mixture, along with any wheat particles left in the sieve. Stir in the raisins, apricots, prunes, sugar, and honey and mix well.

3. Spoon the mixture into a nonstick 8" x 4" x 2½" loaf pan (or brush the pan with oil to prevent sticking) and level off the top. Bake for 1 to 1¼ hours, or until the loaf is baked through and golden brown on top.

4. Allow the loaf to cool a little in the pan before turning it out onto a wire rack to cool completely. The loaf will store for several weeks if wrapped in aluminum foil and kept in an airtight container.

Per slice: 170 calories, 38 g carbohydrates, 4 g protein, 1 g fat, 4 g fiber

BREAKFAST POCKETS

Serves 2

Breakfast is the most important meal of the day. This simple egg-filled pita is loaded with nutrients and long-lasting energy. Can you think of a better way to say "Good morning" to your body?

PREPARATION TIME: 5 MINUTES   COOKING TIME: 8 MINUTES

2 strips center-cut bacon	Freshly ground black pepper
2 scallions, green part only	Canola oil spray
4 eggs	2 whole wheat pitas (2 ounces each)
Salt	4 tablespoons salsa

1. Place the bacon strips in a preheated nonstick skillet and cook over medium-high heat for 1 minute on each side (be careful of splattering). When done, remove the strips from the skillet and drain on paper towels. When cooled, crumble the bacon into a small dish.

2. Clean the skillet with paper towels and set aside.

3. Wash and pat dry the scallions. Cut them into thin horizontal slices and place in another small dish.

4. In a small mixing bowl, whisk the eggs and a pinch each of salt and pepper. Lightly coat the skillet with oil spray and preheat (avoid burning). Add the egg mixture, stirring frequently, especially around the edges, until scrambled, approximately 3 minutes. Remove the eggs to a separate dish and keep warm.

5. Reduce heat to low and warm each pita on both sides in the skillet, then cut them in half.

6. Divide the eggs, bacon, and scallions in fourths. Fill each pita pocket in this order: eggs, bacon, scallions. Top each pocket with a tablespoon of salsa. Serve immediately.

Per serving: 330 calories, 37 g carbohydrates, 20 g protein, 13 g fat, 5 g fiber

 •
COOK'S TIPS

Other lean choices are Canadian bacon or vegetable protein breakfast strips.

    Try a fruit-based salsa, like peach and chipotle, with no preservatives.

FRENCH TOAST WITH BERRY COMPOTE

(photo on page 52)   *Serves 4*

Enjoy this berry compote using your favorite mix of fresh or frozen berries—strawberries, raspberries, blackberries, blueberries, or boysenberries. Berries don't ripen once they're picked, so choose carefully—the deeply colored ones tend to be the sweetest and have the most flavor.

PREPARATION TIME: 5 MINUTES   COOKING TIME: 15 MINUTES

1   cup mixed berries
2   eggs
2   tablespoons low-fat milk
4   slices Breakfast Fruit Loaf (page 68) or whole wheat raisin bread
2   tablespoons pure maple syrup

1. Put the berries in a small saucepan and gently heat until they are warm and have softened.

2. Meanwhile, break the eggs into a flat-bottomed dish, add the milk, and whisk with a fork to combine. Add the slices of fruit loaf or bread and coat well on both sides with the egg mixture.

3. Heat a nonstick frying pan over medium heat and dry-fry 2 slices of the eggy bread for 3 minutes on each side, or until brown. Repeat with the remaining 2 slices. Cut the bread in half and serve topped with the warm berries and 2 teaspoons of the maple syrup.

Per serving: 215 calories, 37 g carbohydrates, 7 g protein, 4 g fat, 4 g fiber

● ●
COOK'S TIP

Berries are best eaten as soon as possible after you have purchased them. If you need to keep them for a day or two, here's how to minimize mold. Take them out of the container and place on a couple of layers of paper towel. Cover loosely with plastic wrap and store in the refrigerator. Don't wash them until you're ready to use them.

SOURDOUGH FRENCH TOAST WITH PEACHES

Serves 4

Sourdough and sprouted wheat breads are among the best choices for low-GI loaves.

PREPARATION TIME: 10 MINUTES   COOKING TIME: 8 MINUTES

2 eggs
1 cup low-fat milk
1 tablespoon pure maple syrup
   Pinch of grated nutmeg
   Canola oil spray
4 slices of Alvarado Sprouted Sourdough French Bread, each about ¾" thick
4 fresh peaches, sliced

1. In a shallow bowl, combine the eggs, milk, maple syrup, and nutmeg. Whisk to blend. Lightly coat a nonstick frying pan with oil spray and set over a medium heat.

2. Dip the bread in the egg mixture and turn to coat completely. Place the bread in the pan and cook for 2 to 3 minutes on each side, or until golden brown. Set aside and keep warm.

3. Lightly coat the pan with oil spray, and cook the peach slices for 1 to 2 minutes on each side, until just softened. Serve the French toast topped with the peaches.

Per serving: 226 calories, 42 g carbohydrates, 10 g protein, 5 g fat, 2 g fiber

COOK'S TIP

Sourdough and sprouted wheat breads are among the best choices for low-GI loaves.

BUCKWHEAT PANCAKES WITH BERRIES

(photo on page 53)   *Serves 4*

Buckwheat is not a cereal grain like wheat but is actually the seed of an annual that's related to sorrel and rhubarb. It has a nutty flavor and is ground into a gritty flour for making pancakes, muffins, cookies, cakes, Russian blini, and soba noodles.

PREPARATION TIME: 10 MINUTES   COOKING TIME: 10 TO 15 MINUTES

1	cup buckwheat flour
¼	cup stone-ground whole wheat flour
1½	teaspoons baking powder
2	tablespoons raw sugar
2	eggs, lightly beaten
1	cup buttermilk
1	teaspoon vanilla extract
	Canola oil spray
4	tablespoons low-fat plain yogurt
1	cup blueberries

1. In a mixing bowl, combine the flours, baking powder, and sugar. Stir to mix. Make a well in the center and pour in the eggs, buttermilk, and vanilla extract and whisk until smooth. Add a little more milk if the batter is too thick.

2. Heat a frying pan over medium heat. Coat with oil spray. Pour ¼ cup of the mixture into the pan and cook for 1 to 2 minutes each side, or until the pancake is golden and cooked. Repeat with the remaining mixture, to make 8 pancakes in total.

3. Serve 2 pancakes per person. Top with yogurt and blueberries.

Per serving: 252 calories, 39 g carbohydrates, 11 g protein, 5 g fat, 5 g fiber

 **COOK'S TIP**

Raw sugar, such as demerara or turbinado, is sold in health food stores and some supermarkets. Good-quality brown sugar may be substituted.

 **ACTIVITY TIP**

Buy a pedometer and wear it on your waistband every day. Make it your goal to reach 10,000 steps on most days.

RICOTTA BLUEBERRY HOTCAKES

Serves 4

Keep cooked hotcakes warm on a heatproof plate covered with aluminum foil in a very low oven (250°F) while cooking the remaining batter.

PREPARATION TIME: 10 MINUTES   COOKING TIME: 7 MINUTES

½   cup + 2 tablespoons reduced-fat ricotta cheese
½   cup low-fat milk
2   eggs, separated
2   tablespoons granulated sugar
1   teaspoon vanilla extract
½   cup stone-ground whole wheat flour
¾   teaspoon baking powder
¼   teaspoon salt
1   cup fresh or frozen blueberries
     Canola oil spray
6½ ounces Stonyfield Farm low-fat French vanilla yogurt

1. Place the ricotta in a large mixing bowl and mash with a fork. Add the milk, egg yolks, sugar, and vanilla. Stir with a wooden spoon to mix. In a separate bowl, mix the flour, baking powder, and salt together. Fold it into the ricotta mixture with a large metal spoon or rubber spatula until just combined. Do not overbeat.

2. In a mixing bowl with electric beaters, whip the egg whites until firm peaks form. Gently fold into the ricotta mixture, along with the blueberries.

3. Lightly coat a large nonstick frying pan with oil spray. Set over low heat. Drop ¼ cupfuls of the batter into the pan, and cook for 2 minutes, until golden underneath. Flip and cook 1½ minutes, or until the hotcakes have risen and are golden brown and cooked through. Repeat with the remaining batter, to make 8 hotcakes. Serve immediately with dollops of yogurt.

Per serving: 262 calories, 32 g carbohydrates, 15 g protein, 8 g fat, 3 g fiber

APRICOT AND MUESLI MUFFINS

Makes 12

Nothing beats muffins warm from the oven—even on a busy weekday morning. The night before, combine the dry ingredients in a mixing bowl and the wet ingredients in a covered container in the refrigerator, and also oil the muffin pan. In the morning, you'll need less than 10 minutes to mix the batter and plop it in the muffin cups. When you get out of the shower, your piping hot pastries will be ready.

PREPARATION TIME: 10 MINUTES   **COOKING TIME: 20 MINUTES**

	Canola oil spray
2	cups self-rising flour
1½	cups Natural Toasted Muesli (page 46)
1	cup (about 6 ounces) coarsely chopped dried apricots
1	teaspoon baking powder
1	cup apple juice
¼	cup pure floral honey
3	tablespoons canola oil
1	egg

1. Preheat the oven to 375°F. Lightly coat a 12-cup muffin pan with oil spray.

2. In a large mixing bowl, combine the flour, muesli, apricots, and baking powder. Stir to mix.

3. In another bowl, combine the apple juice, honey, oil, and egg. Add the reserved flour mixture and stir until just combined.

4. Spoon the batter into the prepared pan. Bake for 20 minutes, or until browned and a wooden pick inserted comes out clean.

Per muffin: 237 calories, 38 g carbohydrates, 5 g protein, 7 g fat, 4 g fiber

FIBER-HIGH BRAN MUFFINS

(*photo on page 54*)   *Makes 48*

*These small muffins pack a powerful energy punch. Top with a little
dab of peanut butter and you're ready for several hours on the fast track.*

PREPARATION TIME: 12 MINUTES   COOKING TIME: 20 MINUTES

	Canola oil spray
4	cups low-fat buttermilk
2	cups boiling water
5	teaspoons baking soda
¾	cup reduced-fat margarine spread
2	cups granulated sugar
4	eggs
2	cups rolled bran
4	cups All-Bran with Extra Fiber
5	cups whole wheat flour
1	cup walnuts, coarsely chopped
1	cup dried blueberries (or 2 cups fresh), optional

1. Preheat the oven to 425°F. Lightly coat four 12-cup muffin pans with oil spray.

2. In a mixing bowl, combine the buttermilk, water, and baking soda. Stir. Allow to cool.

3. In the bowl of an electric mixer, combine the margarine, sugar, and eggs. Beat for 2 minutes at medium speed, or until smooth.

4. Place the rolled bran and All-Bran in the bowl of a food processor fitted with a metal blade. Process until coarsely ground and pour into a large mixing bowl. Add the flour.

5. Alternately add the buttermilk mixture and margarine mixture to the dry ingredients. Fold in the walnuts and blueberries, if desired. Spoon the batter into the prepared pans.

6. Bake for 20 minutes, or until browned and a wooden pick inserted comes out clean.

Per muffin: 160 calories, 26 g carbohydrates, 4 g protein, 6 g fat, 4 g fiber

FRUIT COMPOTE

(photo on page 55)   *Serves 6*

We often sweeten recipes with honey rather than sugar. Since every species of flower has a unique nectar, honey from different types of flowers can have very different flavors and qualities. The lower-GI honeys tend to be pure floral honeys rather than a commercially blended product.

PREPARATION TIME: 10 MINUTES   COOKING TIME: 10 MINUTES

3	cups apple juice
1¼	cups dried apples
¾	cup dried pear halves
½	cup dried apricots
1	tablespoon pure floral honey
1	cinnamon stick
8	cardamom pods
½	cup pitted prunes

1. In a saucepan, combine the apple juice, apples, pears, apricots, honey, cinnamon stick, and cardamom. Bring to a boil, then reduce the heat and simmer for 10 minutes, or until the fruit has softened.

2. Remove the pan from the heat. Add the prunes, then transfer to a serving dish. Allow to cool. Cover and refrigerate until ready to serve.

Per serving: 221 calories, 52 g carbohydrates, 2 g protein, 1 g fat, 6 g fiber

ACTIVITY TIP

People who exercise are happier—being active for just 20 minutes a day helps to lift your spirits and improve your mood.

30-SECOND BREAKFAST EGGNOG

Serves 2

This recipe eliminates your "I-have-no-time" excuse for skipping breakfast. And come mid-morning, you'll be delighted with the energy your body will still be receiving from this delicious drink.

PREPARATION TIME: 30 SECONDS

1   cup raspberries, fresh or frozen
½   cup low-fat vanilla or raspberry
      yogurt
½   cup fat-free milk

2   in-shell pasteurized eggs
2   tablespoons cocoa powder
1   tablespoon pure floral honey

1. In a blender, combine the raspberries, yogurt, milk, eggs, cocoa powder, and honey.

2. Mix at high speed for 30 seconds, or until smooth. Serve immediately.

Per serving: 220 calories, 32 g carbohydrates, 13 g protein, 6 g fat, 6 g fiber

COOK'S TIP

In-shell pasteurized eggs may be safely eaten raw. They are sold in some supermarkets and health food stores.

CARROT, APPLE, AND GINGER JUICE

Serves 4

It's easy to overdo the calories when drinking fruit juice, so it is a good idea to mix a fruit with a vegetable, as we've done here. This cuts both the sweetness and the calories, while providing many of the nutrients found in whole food.

PREPARATION TIME: 10 MINUTES

2 carrots
2 apples, cored
2¼ cups fresh orange juice
½ teaspoon finely grated fresh ginger

1. If you have a juicer, juice the carrots and apples into a small pitcher. Mix in the orange juice and ginger.

2. Alternatively, use a blender to purée all the ingredients until as smooth as possible.

3. Pour the juice into 4 glasses and serve with ice, if desired.

Per serving: 90 calories, 21 g carbohydrates, 1 g protein, 0 g fat, 3 g fiber

Chapter 5

LUNCH, BRUNCH, AND SMALL DISHES

Too often, a hasty lunch eaten on the run is too high in fat and low-GI carbs, leaving us feeling sleepy and sluggish in the afternoon. Put the brakes on that destructive pattern with our lighter, yet incredibly sustaining lunches of protein, vegetables, and a small serving of carbs. On weekends, lunch morphs into brunch or a meal of several small dishes. These plates often can double as dinner appetizers. Small changes add up to big nutrition with the likes of Bean and Corn Burritos, Cheddar-Bean Chili, Asparagus Tomato Frittata, Curried Lentil Salad, and Portobello Mushrooms with Ricotta and Roasted Tomatoes.

LENTIL, SPINACH, AND FETA SALAD

(photo on page 56)   *Serves 4*

The slightly peppery-tasting French lentils are ideal for salads because they hold their shape when cooked, although they tend to take a little longer to cook than other lentils. Use brown lentils as a substitute if French are not available, but watch the cooking times as they can turn mushy if you overcook them.

PREPARATION TIME: 10 MINUTES   **COOKING TIME: 25 MINUTES**

1   cup French lentils
2   cloves garlic, flattened with the side of a knife
2   red bell peppers, quartered
5½ cups baby spinach leaves
3   ounces reduced-fat feta cheese, cubed
1   tablespoon extra-virgin olive oil
2   teaspoons balsamic vinegar
1   teaspoon sugar

1. Put the lentils and garlic in a saucepan. Cover with water and bring to a boil. Reduce the heat and simmer for 25 minutes, or until the lentils are soft (these lentils should retain their shape). Remove the garlic and drain.

2. Meanwhile, place the peppers, skin side up, under a broiler and cook until the skins are completely black. Allow to cool for 6 to 8 minutes, then remove the skins. Slice the flesh into strips.

3. Combine the lentils, peppers, spinach, and cheese in a serving bowl. Add the oil and vinegar, sprinkle with sugar, and mix well. Serve at room temperature.

Per serving: 265 calories, 23 g carbohydrates, 20 g protein, 9 g fat, 9 g fiber

 **ACTIVITY TIP**

Arrange social get-togethers that involve some activity rather than solely eating and drinking—meet for a walk, go bowling, or have a picnic in the park.

CURRIED LENTIL SALAD

(photo on page 57)   *Serves 4*

One of the keys to the low-GI cooking is to eat more legumes such as beans, chickpeas, and lentils—in fact, we recommend you have a meal that includes legumes at least twice a week. This curried lentil salad will make that easy!

PREPARATION TIME: 10 MINUTES   COOKING TIME: 20 MINUTES

1   tablespoon reduced-fat margarine spread
1   tablespoon curry powder
1½ cups French or brown lentils
     Salt
1   small red onion, thinly sliced
8   cherry tomatoes, halved
2   cups baby spinach leaves
¼   cup cilantro leaves
¼   cup mint leaves
2   tablespoons red wine vinegar
2   tablespoons extra-virgin olive oil
     Freshly ground black pepper

1. Melt the margarine in a saucepan and add the curry powder. Stir for 20 seconds, then add the lentils, stirring to coat well. Add a generous pinch of salt. Cover the lentils with water, bring to a simmer, and cook for 20 minutes, or until the lentils are soft. (Take care not to let the lentils get too dry. Add more water if necessary, but don't make them too wet.) Remove from the heat, drain, rinse, and let cool.

2. Put the cooled lentils in a large bowl with the onion, tomatoes, spinach, cilantro, and mint. Whisk together the vinegar and oil, pour over the salad, and toss well. Season to taste with salt and pepper.

Per serving: 332 calories, 29 g carbohydrates, 18 g protein, 14 g fat, 12 g fiber

Recipe: Luke Mangan

CHICKPEA AND BEET SALAD

Serves 4

*This easy combo dish contrasts sharp peppery arugula
against the sweetness of beets.*

PREPARATION TIME: 20 MINUTES

2   cans (15 ounces each) chickpeas, rinsed and drained
1   red onion, cut into thin wedges
4   cups baby arugula leaves
1   tablespoon extra-virgin olive oil
1½ tablespoons red wine vinegar
1½ tablespoons lemon juice
1   clove garlic, crushed
     Pinch of granulated sugar
     Salt and freshly ground black pepper
1   can (16 ounces) beet chunks, drained and patted dry with paper towel
4   slices Pepperidge Farm Sprouted Wheat bread

1. Place the chickpeas, onion, and arugula in a large serving bowl.

2. Whisk together the oil, vinegar, lemon juice, garlic, and sugar. Season to taste with salt and pepper.

3. Add the dressing to the salad and toss gently to combine. Add the beets and toss gently again. Serve with the bread.

Per serving: 300 calories, 50 g carbohydrates, 20 g protein, 7 g fat, 11 g fiber

THREE-BEAN AND BASIL SALAD

Serves 8

The Italian seasoning trio of olive oil, garlic, and fresh basil works its flavoring magic here on a trio of simple beans.

PREPARATION TIME: 5 MINUTES

1   can (16 ounces) cannellini beans, rinsed and drained
1   can (16 ounces) light red kidney beans, rinsed and drained
1   can (19 ounces) red kidney beans, rinsed and drained
2   cloves garlic, crushed
3   tablespoons extra-virgin olive oil
1   tablespoon lemon juice
    Salt and freshly ground black pepper
½   bunch fresh basil leaves, torn

1. Rinse all the drained beans well under cold running water. Drain.

2. Combine the beans in a large serving bowl or flat white platter.

3. In a lidded jar, combine the garlic, oil, and lemon juice; shake well. Pour over the beans. Season to taste with salt and pepper.

4. Toss in the basil leaves.

Per serving: 166 calories, 18 g carbohydrates, 8 g protein, 8 g fat, 8 g fiber

WHITE BEAN ASPARAGUS SALAD

Serves 4

A sprinkling of grated Pecorino Romano cheese perfectly complements this delightful salad. For a heartier meal, serve the salad with rosemary-grilled pork tenderloin.

PREPARATION TIME: 10 MINUTES   COOKING TIME: 2 MINUTES

12 spears asparagus
2   tablespoons red wine vinegar
2   teaspoons pure floral honey
2   teaspoons olive oil
16 cherry tomatoes, halved
1   can (14 ounces) white beans, rinsed and drained
2   tablespoons chopped parsley
    Freshly ground black pepper

1. Bring a large frying pan filled with water to a gentle simmer. Place the asparagus in the water and cook for 1 to 2 minutes, or until tender. Refresh under cold water, then chop into 1¼" lengths and let cool.

2. In a small screw-top jar, combine the vinegar, honey, and oil. Shake to mix.

3. In a serving bowl, combine the tomatoes, beans, parsley, and asparagus. Add the dressing and toss to combine. Season to taste with pepper.

Per serving: 130 calories, 21 g carbohydrates, 7 g protein, 3 g fat, 4 g fiber

VINAIGRETTE ASPARAGUS WITH EGGS

Serves 3

This is a simple, inexpensive, wholesome dish that is as pleasant to look at as it is to taste. A definite crowd-pleaser, this is a common main dish in several Mediterranean countries.

PREPARATION TIME: 2 MINUTES   COOKING TIME: 10 TO 12 MINUTES

1   bunch thin asparagus (approximately 12 ounces)
3   hard-cooked eggs, shelled and quartered
     Salt and freshly ground black pepper
1   tablespoon olive oil
½   teaspoon red wine vinegar
¼   cup grated Parmesan cheese

1. Cut or break off 2" from the bottom of the asparagus spears. Wash and place them in a steam basket with 1" of water in a saucepan. Cover and steam until tender (thin asparagus need 3 minutes—thick asparagus may require 10 to 12 minutes).

2. Meanwhile, in a small bowl lightly mash the eggs with a fork. Add salt and pepper to taste.

3. In another small bowl, whisk the oil and vinegar with salt and pepper to taste.

4. Place the cooked asparagus in a deep, oblong serving dish. Toss with the dressing and the cheese. Arrange the eggs on top and serve warm.

Per serving: 165 calories, 5 g carbohydrates, 11 g protein, 11 g fat, 2 g fiber

ROAST BUTTERNUT SQUASH AND CHICKPEA SALAD

(photo on page 58)   *Serves 6*

This sun-dried tomato dressing can also be tossed with pasta,
potatoes, or grilled vegetables.

SOAKING TIME: OVERNIGHT   PREPARATION TIME: 15 MINUTES

COOKING TIME: 50 MINUTES

1   cup chickpeas
1   butternut squash (1 pound 10 ounces), cut into large cubes (about 5 cups)
    Olive oil spray
¼   cup sun-dried tomatoes
1½ tablespoons red wine vinegar
2   tablespoons extra-virgin olive oil
2   teaspoons balsamic vinegar
2   teaspoons sugar
2   teaspoons lemon juice
1   clove garlic
    Freshly ground black pepper
2   tablespoons chopped cilantro or mint leaves

1. Soak the chickpeas overnight in a bowl of cold water.

2. The next day, drain the chickpeas and rinse. Put the chickpeas in a large
saucepan and cover with fresh water. Bring to a boil and cook for 40 to 50
minutes, or until tender. Drain and allow to cool.

3. Meanwhile, preheat the oven to 400°F. Put the squash on a baking sheet lined with parchment paper. Coat the squash with oil spray. Roast for 30 to 40 minutes, or until the squash is tender and lightly caramelized. Allow to cool.

4. While the squash is baking, combine the tomatoes and red wine vinegar in a saucepan over low heat. Allow the tomatoes to soak in the hot vinegar to soften. Transfer the tomatoes to the bowl of a food processor fitted with a metal blade. Add the oil, balsamic vinegar, sugar, lemon juice, garlic, and pepper. Process to combine (don't overprocess—the texture should remain a little chunky). Transfer to a serving platter.

5. Toss the squash and chickpeas in the dressing. Sprinkle with the cilantro or mint.

Per serving: 243 calories, 24 g carbohydrates, 9 g protein, 10 g fat, 7 g fiber

Recipe: Julie Le Clerc

COOK'S TIP

To save time, substitute already cooked canned chickpeas, rinsed and drained.

WHITE BEAN SALAD

Simple and quick, this salad has all the markings of convenience. Its nutritious ingredients guarantee a supply of fiber; minerals like potassium, iron, magnesium, and copper; vitamins A, C, and B; folic acid; and niacin.

PREPARATION TIME: 4 MINUTES

1	can (19 ounces) cannellini beans, rinsed and drained
1	can (14 ounces) diced tomatoes, drained
½	cup chopped red onion
1	tablespoon extra-virgin olive oil
½	tablespoon balsamic vinegar
2	tablespoons fresh parsley, finely chopped (5 sprigs)
1	clove garlic, minced
1	ounce crumbled blue cheese
¼	teaspoon salt
	Freshly ground pepper

1. In a medium serving dish, combine the beans, tomatoes, onion, oil, vinegar, parsley, garlic, cheese, and salt.

2. Season to taste with pepper. Toss.

3. Serve at room temperature.

Per serving: 125 calories, 17 g carbohydrates, 5 g protein, 4 g fat, 5 g fiber

 **COOK'S TIPS**

In season, 3 fresh plum tomatoes may replace the canned tomatoes.

Feta or gorgonzola cheese may replace the blue cheese, if preferred.

SALMON AND LIMA BEAN SALAD

Serves 3

Baby limas are a tasty choice in this dish, but cannellini, great Northern, or navy beans can take their place.

PREPARATION TIME: 10 MINUTES

1	can (6 ounces) pink salmon, drained
1	can (15½ ounces) lima beans, drained
½	small cucumber, sliced
½	red onion, diced
1	tablespoon olive oil
1	tablespoon lemon juice
1	clove garlic, minced
	Freshly ground black pepper

1. Place the salmon in a medium mixing bowl. Break into small chunks.

2. Add the beans, cucumber, onion, oil, lemon juice, and garlic. Season to taste with pepper. Mix well. Serve cold.

Per serving: 233 calories, 29 g carbohydrates, 18 g protein, 7 g fat, 7 g fiber

SWEET CHILE TUNA SALAD

(photo on page 59)   *Serves 2*

PREPARATION TIME: 10 MINUTES

4   iceberg lettuce leaves, shredded
¼   red bell pepper, finely chopped
1   tomato, chopped
½   red onion, finely chopped
1   can (6 ounces) tuna packed in water, drained
1   cup fried thin rice noodles
1   tablespoon mild chile sauce
     Juice of 1 lime
     Cilantro leaves

1. In a serving bowl, combine the lettuce, pepper, tomato, and onion.

2. Add the tuna, noodles, chile sauce, and lime juice. Toss to combine.

3. Garnish with cilantro leaves. Serve immediately.

Per serving: 290 calories, 20 g carbohydrates, 28 g protein, 10 g fat, 7 g fiber

TUNA AND BEAN SALAD
WITH GARLIC PITA TOASTS

Serves 4

For a lunch that will sustain you through your afternoon, pack individual portions of this satisfying salad. Combine all the ingredients in a resealable plastic container, placing the arugula on top. Don't toss until just before eating and the greens will stay crisp and fresh.

PREPARATION TIME: 10 MINUTES   TOASTING TIME: 2 TO 3 MINUTES

1	can (13 ounces) cannellini beans, rinsed and drained
1	can (6 ounces) light tuna, drained and flaked
2	ripe tomatoes, cut into thin wedges
1	small red onion, very finely sliced
1	bunch arugula, trimmed and leaves torn
2	tablespoons lemon juice
1	tablespoon extra-virgin olive oil
	Salt and freshly ground black pepper
4	small 100% whole wheat pitas
1	large clove garlic, halved

1. In a large bowl, combine the beans, tuna, tomatoes, onion, and arugula. Drizzle with the lemon juice and oil. Season to taste with salt and pepper. Toss gently to combine.

2. Toast the pitas on both sides, then rub the cut garlic clove all over one side. Break into pieces and serve with the salad.

Per serving: 340 calories, 36 g carbohydrates, 25 g protein, 8 g fat, 7 g fiber

TUNA-VEGGIE TOSS

Serves 6

To put this dish together even faster, start with leftover plain cooked pasta in a small shape such as bows or spirals. If you like, canned salmon can replace the tuna, and tarragon or cilantro can take the place of the basil. Drizzle with extra-virgin olive oil for the best flavor.

PREPARATION TIME: 10 MINUTES   COOKING TIME: 10 TO 14 MINUTES

2   cups medium pasta shells
2   cups cooked vegetables, such as zucchini, mushrooms, broccoli, or peppers, reheated if desired
1   can (6 ounces) tuna packed in water, drained
1½ tablespoons finely chopped fresh parsley
1½ tablespoons finely chopped fresh basil or 1½ teaspoons dried
1   tablespoon olive oil
1   clove garlic, minced
     Freshly ground black pepper

1. Cook the pasta according to package directions until al dente.

2. Meanwhile, combine the vegetables, tuna, parsley, basil, oil, and garlic in a large serving dish. Mix well. Season to taste with pepper.

3. Drain the pasta and add to the tuna-vegetable mixture. Toss well, and serve immediately.

Per serving: 99 calories, 10 g carbohydrates, 9 g protein, 3 g fat, 2 g fiber

AZUKI BEAN STEW

(photo on page 60)   *Serves 4*

Azuki beans are eaten widely in their native Japan. They are one of the most delicious of all dried beans and have a sweet, meaty flavor. You may want to serve this dish with steamed basmati rice or sourdough bread.

SOAKING TIME: OVERNIGHT   PREPARATION TIME: 15 MINUTES
COOKING TIME: 45 TO 50 MINUTES

1   cup dried azuki beans
1   leek, sliced
1   carrot, chopped
1   sweet potato (about 9 ounces), cubed
1   chicken bouillon cube, crumbled
2   tablespoons tomato paste
1   tablespoon Worcestershire sauce
1   teaspoon Tabasco sauce
1   cup small broccoli florets
¼   cup chopped cilantro leaves
4   tablespoons low-fat plain yogurt (optional)

1. Soak the beans overnight in a bowl of cold water.

2. The next day, drain the beans and rinse well. Put the beans in a saucepan, cover with water, and bring to a boil. Then reduce the heat and simmer for 30 to 35 minutes, partially covered (the beans should still be a little firm after this time).

3. Add the leek, carrot, sweet potato, bouillon cube, tomato paste, Worcestershire, and Tabasco. Cook for 10 minutes. Add the broccoli and cilantro. Simmer for 5 minutes, or until the broccoli is tender.

4. Serve in bowls topped with a spoonful of yogurt, if desired.

Per serving: 215 calories, 32 g carbohydrates, 14 g protein, 2 g fat, 13 g fiber

Recipe: Jill McMillan

COOK'S TIP
You may need to buy dried azuki beans from a health food store; they are not as widely available as the canned version.

VEGETABLE CHILI BOWL

(photo on page 61)   *Serves 6*

This vegetable variation of chili con carne has a lively, spicy taste and is a complete meal in itself. Serve with yogurt and Cheddar cheese for garnish, plus some crusty low-GI bread, such as sourdough, to mop up the juices.

PREPARATION TIME: 15 MINUTES   COOKING TIME: 20 MINUTES

2	tablespoons olive oil
2	onions, coarsely chopped
3	cloves garlic, minced
2	red bell peppers, halved and cut into squares
2	small zucchini, halved and cut into chunks
1	tablespoon chili powder, or to taste
1	tablespoon ground cumin
2	cans (14 ounces each) peeled tomatoes, coarsely chopped, juice reserved
1	can (15½ ounces) red kidney beans, rinsed and drained
1	can (15½ ounces) chickpeas, rinsed and drained
¼	teaspoon salt
	Freshly ground black pepper
½	cup chopped flat-leaf parsley
½	cup chopped cilantro leaves
2	tablespoons lemon juice

1. Heat the oil in a 4-quart Dutch oven over medium heat. Add the onions, garlic, and peppers and cook for 5 minutes. Add the zucchini and cook for 3 minutes.

2. Add the chili powder and cumin and stir for a minute to combine, then add the chopped tomatoes with their juice, the kidney beans, and chickpeas. Season to taste with salt and plenty of pepper.

3. Cover and cook over low heat for 8 to 10 minutes, or until the zucchini is tender. Stir in the parsley, cilantro, and lemon juice and serve.

Per serving: 215 calories, 22 g carbohydrates, 9 g protein, 8 g fat, 9 g fiber

Recipe: Margaret Fulton

CHEDDAR-BEAN CHILI

Serves 10

On busy days, it's especially helpful to be able to prepare a meal from pantry staples. Pack leftovers in plastic storage containers for microwaveable lunches at the office.

PREPARATION TIME: 10 MINUTES   COOKING TIME: 40 MINUTES

Olive oil spray
2   medium onions, coarsely chopped
2   large cloves garlic, minced
2   cans (16 ounces each) pinto beans, drained
1   can (28 ounces) crushed tomatoes in puree
½–1 tablespoon chili powder
1   teaspoon dried oregano
½   teaspoon salt
     Freshly ground black pepper
10   ounces Cheddar cheese, cut in strips

1. Coat a large Dutch oven with oil spray. Add the onions and garlic. Cook for 4 to 5 minutes, until soft (be careful not to burn the garlic).

2. Add the beans, tomatoes, chili powder, and oregano. Mix well. Cover and simmer for 30 minutes, stirring occasionally. Season to taste with salt and pepper.

3. Place the cheese strips on top of the chili. Cover and simmer for 3 to 4 minutes, or until cheese has melted. Serve hot.

Per serving: 224 calories, 22 g carbohydrates, 13 g protein, 9 g fat, 5 g fiber

BREAKFAST SANDWICH
WITH SPICY TOMATO SALSA

(photo on page 62)   *Serves 4*

*Eggs and bacon might sound like an unlikely inclusion in a healthy
cookbook. But when the bacon is cooked until crispy, so most of the fat
melts off, and the two are served with one or two vegetables, they provide a
perfect balance of carbohydrates, protein, and fat.*

PREPARATION TIME: 10 MINUTES   COOKING TIME: 10 MINUTES

SALSA:

2   tomatoes, seeded and finely chopped
¼   red onion, finely chopped
1   jalapeño pepper, seeds removed and finely chopped
     Juice of ½ lime
1   tablespoon chopped cilantro leaves
     Pinch of sugar

SANDWICH:

4   eggs, at room temperature
4   slices bacon, fat trimmed
4   whole grain English muffins, split
1   cup arugula leaves
     Cilantro leaves (optional)

1. To make the salsa: In a bowl, combine the tomatoes, onion, jalapeño,
   lime juice, cilantro, and sugar. Stir and set side.

2. To make the sandwich: Bring a large saucepan or deep frying pan of water
   to a simmer. Crack the eggs and gently slip them, one at a time, into the
   simmering water. Cook for 3 to 4 minutes, or until the egg whites are opaque

and the yolk is still quite soft (or until cooked to your liking). Carefully lift out the eggs with a slotted spoon and drain on paper towels.

3. In a medium skillet, over medium–high heat, cook the bacon until crisp. Meanwhile, toast the muffin halves.

4. To serve, layer the muffins (in this order) with a handful of arugula leaves, the bacon, a poached egg, and a spoonful of the salsa. Garnish with cilantro, if desired.

Per serving: 270 calories, 27 g carbohydrates, 23 g protein, 8 g fat, 5 g fiber

COOK'S TIP

To minimize the spreading of the egg whites when poaching eggs, break the egg into a teacup, then gently slip the egg into the water. Some cooks also like to add a dash of vinegar or lemon juice to the water before they poach the eggs. This helps the egg white to set, but may also flavor the eggs slightly.

SCRAMBLED EGGS WITH SMOKED SALMON

(photo on page 63)   *Serves 2*

This recipe makes a quick and easy light brunch or lunch. You could also serve it with a crispy green salad as an evening meal.

PREPARATION TIME: 10 MINUTES   COOKING TIME: 8 MINUTES

4   eggs, at room temperature
⅓   cup low-fat milk
     Freshly ground black pepper
1   tablespoon thinly sliced chives
1   tablespoon finely chopped dill
3½   ounces smoked salmon, chopped
1   cup baby spinach leaves, chopped
2   slices whole grain bread, toasted

1. In a small bowl, combine the eggs, milk, pepper, chives, and dill. Whisk until blended.

2. Heat a large nonstick frying pan over medium heat. Add the egg mixture and cook for 30 seconds, or until the eggs start to set around the edges. Using a wooden spatula, gently fold the eggs over, then repeat the folding process until the eggs are just cooked. The eggs should be quite soft.

3. Gently stir in the salmon and spinach until the salmon is heated through and the spinach is wilted. Serve the eggs on the toast.

Per serving: 325 calories, 21 g carbohydrates, 30 g protein, 13 g fat, 3 g fiber

COOK'S TIP

One of the most important changes you can make to lower the GI of your diet is to choose a low-GI bread. Choose whole grain, pumpernickel, sourdough, or stone-ground whole wheat bread.

SWEET CORN AND MUSHROOM OMELET

Serves 4

Omelets are an essential item in the busy cook's repertoire. For an even more flavorful filling in this dish, use baby portobello mushrooms.

PREPARATION TIME: 10 MINUTES   **COOKING TIME: 10 MINUTES**

Olive oil spray
4   ounces button mushrooms, sliced
1   can (11 ounces) corn kernels, well drained
½   cup flat-leaf parsley, finely chopped
6   eggs
4   slices Shiloh Farms Sprouted 7 Grain Bread, toasted
½   small ripe avocado

1. Lightly coat a 12" nonstick frying pan with oil spray. Cook the mushrooms on low heat for 2 minutes, or until soft.

2. Combine the mushrooms, corn, and parsley in a bowl.

3. In another bowl, whisk the eggs until lightly beaten. Pour half of the eggs into the frying pan, and cook over medium heat for 2 minutes, until almost set.

4. Sprinkle half the corn mixture over half of the omelet surface, and fold over to enclose. Cook for 2 to 3 minutes, remove to a plate, and cut the omelet in half using a nonscratch spatula. Repeat with remaining ingredients to cook another omelet. Cut it in half.

5. Spread the toast with mashed avocado and serve with the omelets.

Per serving: 286 calories, 25 g carbohydrates, 22 g protein, 17 g fat, 6 g fiber

POTATO AND CORN FRITTATA
WITH SUGAR SNAP PEAS SALAD

Serves 4

A frittata is one of the easiest meals to prepare when you want to make do with what's in the pantry and refrigerator. Virtually any combination of vegetables is possible. Here we use new potatoes, onion, and sweet corn, but peas and a little bacon are nice additions, if preferred.

PREPARATION TIME: 20 MINUTES   COOKING TIME: 20 MINUTES

SALAD:

3 cups sugar snap peas or snow peas
2½ cups broccoli, broken into small florets
12 spears asparagus, cut into 1¼" lengths
2 tablespoons lemon juice
1 tablespoon olive oil

FRITTATA:

1 tablespoon olive oil, divided
1 onion, chopped
1 clove garlic, minced
1 can (15½ ounces) new potatoes, drained and cubed
1 can (11 ounces) corn kernels, drained
6 eggs
⅓ cup low-fat milk
1 tablespoon chopped parsley
   Freshly ground black pepper

1. To make the salad: Bring a large saucepan of water to a boil. Add the peas, broccoli, and asparagus. Bring to a boil for 2 to 3 minutes, or until the vegetables are bright green and just tender. Drain and rinse under cold running water. Pat dry and transfer to a bowl. Set aside.

2. In a screw-top jar, combine the lemon juice and oil. Shake to blend.

3. To make the frittata: Heat half the oil in a large nonstick frying pan (with heatproof handle) over medium heat. Add the onion and garlic and cook for 3 minutes, or until the onion is translucent. Add the potatoes and corn. Cook for 1 to 2 minutes to heat through, then transfer the vegetables to a bowl.

4. In another bowl, combine the eggs, milk, and parsley. Season to taste with pepper. Beat lightly with a fork until blended.

5. Add the remaining ½ tablespoon oil to the frying pan, swirling the oil around to coat the base of the pan. Add the reserved vegetable mixture to the pan. Spread evenly, then pour the egg mixture evenly over the vegetables. Cover and cook over medium-low heat for 10 minutes, or until the egg mixture is partially set. Place under a broiler for 2 minutes, or until the frittata is golden brown and puffed on top.

6. Serve the frittata in wedges. Drizzle the dressing over the salad and serve.

Per serving: 325 calories, 31 g carbohydrates, 20 g protein, 13 g fat, 8 g fiber

ASPARAGUS TOMATO FRITTATA

Serves 4

Take a cue from cooks in Spain, France, and Italy, where egg preparations are often enjoyed at room temperature. Prepare a frittata in the evening for the next day's lunch. Cool to room temperature, then slice and wrap in a whole wheat tortilla or pita. Cover in plastic wrap and refrigerate.

PREPARATION TIME: 15 MINUTES   COOKING TIME: 30 MINUTES

16	thin spears asparagus, cut into 1" pieces
8	eggs
3	tablespoons grated Parmesan cheese
3	tablespoons fat-free milk
	Salt and freshly ground black pepper
½	cup sun-dried tomatoes, oil-packed, drained and diced
	Olive oil spray

1. Steam the asparagus for 2 minutes.

2. In the meantime, in a medium bowl, combine the eggs, cheese, and milk. Season to taste with salt and pepper. Beat with a fork until blended.

3. Fold the asparagus and tomatoes into the egg mixture.

4. Lightly coat a nonstick 12" frying pan with oil spray and warm it over medium heat for approximately 30 seconds.

5. Evenly pour the egg mixture into the pan. Cook over moderate heat for 5 minutes.

6. Cover and reduce heat to low. Cook for approximately 20 minutes. Periodically shake the pan and, using a spatula or fork, gently separate the sides and bottom of the frittata from the pan, allowing any liquid egg to fall to the bottom or sides.

7. When fully cooked, gently slip the frittata onto a serving dish.

Per serving: 210 calories, 7 g carbohydrates, 16 g protein, 13 g fat, 2 g fiber

COOK'S TIP

A dab of harissa (page 106) is a lively addition to the frittata.

CARROT AND THYME QUICHE

Serves 8

*Much lower in fat than a traditional cream-based quiche,
this vegetable flan is a powerhouse of vitamin A.*

PREPARATION TIME: 15 MINUTES   COOKING TIME: 45 MINUTES

Olive oil spray
2   pounds carrots
1   large onion
2½ ounces low-fat Cheddar cheese
2   cloves garlic
⅓   cup canola oil
3   eggs, lightly beaten
1   tablespoon fresh thyme leaves, or 1 teaspoon dried
1   teaspoon grated nutmeg
½   cup self-rising flour
Salt and freshly ground pepper

1. Preheat the oven to 350°F. Lightly coat a 12" round quiche or pie dish
with oil spray.

2. Grate the carrots, onion, cheese, and garlic. (Using the grating disc of your
food processor makes this step quick and easy.)

3. In a large mixing bowl, combine the canola oil, eggs, thyme, and nutmeg.
Beat until blended. Stir in the flour until combined. Add the carrot mixture.
Season to taste with salt and pepper.

4. Spoon into the prepared dish and bake for 45 minutes, until golden brown
and cooked through.

Per serving: 209 calories, 11 g carbohydrates, 8 g protein, 15 g fat, 6 g fiber

BRUNCH EGG BOWLS

(photo on page 64)   *Serves 4*

Eggs served in a tangy mixture of tomatoes, peppers—red, yellow, and green—and chiles are enjoyed throughout the Middle East. Serve as a brunch or light meal with whole grain toast.

PREPARATION TIME: 15 MINUTES   COOKING TIME: 25 TO 35 MINUTES

1	tablespoon olive oil
1	small red bell pepper, thinly sliced
1	small yellow bell pepper, thinly sliced
1	small green bell pepper, thinly sliced
2	cloves garlic, minced
1–2	small red chiles, seeded and finely chopped
1	can (14 ounces) plum tomatoes, chopped
1	teaspoon harissa (page 106, or prepared)
1	teaspoon caraway seeds, ground
½	teaspoon sweet paprika
½	teaspoon ground cumin
4	eggs
2	tablespoons chopped chives or flat-leaf parsley
4	thick slices whole grain bread, toasted

1. Heat the oil in a large frying pan over low heat. Add the peppers and gently cook for 10 minutes, or until soft.

2. Stir in the garlic and chiles and cook for 1 to 2 minutes. Add the tomatoes, Harissa, caraway, paprika, and cumin. Stir to combine well.

3. Increase the heat to medium and cook, uncovered, for 10 to 15 minutes, or until the tomatoes have reduced to a thick pulp.

4. Using the back of a spoon, make four equally spaced depressions in the tomato mixture, then carefully break 1 egg into each depression. Cover and leave to simmer for 5 minutes, or until the whites are just cooked but the yolks are still soft.

5. Sprinkle with the chives or parsley and serve immediately with the toast.

Per serving: 265 calories, 26 g carbohydrates, 13 g protein, 11 g fat, 5 g fiber

Recipe: Liz and Ian Hemphill, Herbies Spices

 **COOK'S TIP**

As an alternative cooking method, pour the tomato mixture into 4 individual ovenproof dishes. Make a slight depression in the top of the tomato mixture in each dish, then break 1 egg into each depression. Cover lightly with aluminum foil and bake in a preheated 350°F oven for 15 to 20 minutes, or until the eggs are set. Take care when serving, as the dishes will be hot.

HARISSA

*This Tunisian harissa—a paste of red chiles, various spices, and garlic—
is fairly fiery, so use with caution. For those who like their food zesty,
it really zips up mild-mannered grain, pasta, egg, and vegetable dishes.
You can replace the chiles with red-pepper flakes.*

PREPARATION TIME: 18 MINUTES

- 3 tablespoons + 1 teaspoon chopped, dried red chiles
- 3 teaspoons minced garlic
- 3 teaspoons sweet paprika
- 2 teaspoons caraway seeds
- 2 teaspoons coriander seeds
- 1 teaspoon cumin seeds, dry-roasted
- 1 teaspoon salt
- 6 mint leaves, finely chopped
- 3 teaspoons olive oil

1. Soak the chiles in 3 tablespoons hot water for 15 minutes (do not drain off the water).

2. Using a mortar and pestle, crush the garlic, paprika, caraway, coriander, cumin, salt, and mint. Then add to the soaked chiles in the bowl. Mix to combine.

3. Add the oil, a little at a time, mixing to form a thick paste (you may not need to use all of the oil).

4. Store, covered, in the refrigerator and use within 4 weeks.

Recipe: Liz and Ian Hemphill, Herbies Spices

MUSTARD-ROASTED FRUIT CHUTNEY

(photo on page 129)   *Makes 16 (¼ cup) servings*

This distinctive homemade chutney is a wonderful addition to brunch. All you need is a spoonful over a slice of lean ham off the bone, or serve with your favorite cold meats.

PREPARATION TIME: 10 MINUTES   COOKING TIME: 30 MINUTES

- 1 cup dried figs
- 1 cup dried Mission figs
- 1 cup dried pear halves
- ½ cup dried apricots
- ½ cup pitted prunes
- 1 tablespoon mustard powder
- 2 tablespoons yellow mustard seeds
- ½ teaspoon salt
- 1 cup brown sugar
- ½ cup white wine vinegar
- 1½ cups dry white wine

1. Preheat the oven to 400°F. Place the dried fruit in a roasting pan. Sprinkle with the mustard powder, mustard seeds, salt, and sugar. Add the vinegar and wine and stir gently to combine.

2. Roast in the oven, stirring and tossing occasionally, for 30 minutes, or until the fruits caramelize (check them after 20 to 25 minutes). Add extra liquid if you prefer them a little moister.

3. The vinegar and sugar preserve the fruit, so it will last for 2 weeks if stored, covered, in a clean jar or plastic container in the refrigerator.

Per serving: 160 calories, 35 g carbohydrates, 1 g protein, trace fat, 6 g fiber

Recipe: Julie Le Clerc

CORNMEAL, PEPPER, AND CHIVE MUFFINS

Serves 12

Serve these scrumptious hot breads with the low-GI Cheddar-Bean Chili (page 95).

PREPARATION TIME: 20 MINUTES   COOKING TIME: 25 TO 30 MINUTES

	Canola oil spray
1½	cups buttermilk
3	tablespoons canola oil
2	tablespoons pure floral honey
1	egg
1	can (15¼ ounces) corn kernels, drained
1	medium red bell pepper, finely diced
1	bunch chives, snipped
1½	cups self-rising flour
1	cup cornmeal
	Salt

1. Preheat the oven to 375°F. Lightly coat a 12-cup muffin pan with oil spray.

2. In a large mixing bowl, beat together the buttermilk, oil, honey, and egg. Stir in the corn, bell pepper, and chives.

3. Quickly stir in the flour, cornmeal, and a pinch of salt.

4. Spoon the batter into the prepared pan. Bake for 25 to 30 minutes, or until golden brown and a wooden pick comes out clean.

Per serving: 208 calories, 31 g carbohydrates, 6 g protein, 7 g fat, 2 g fiber

LENTIL BRUSCHETTA

Serves 8

This red lentil spread makes a delicious topping for bruschetta, or you could use it as a sandwich spread or a dip for fresh vegetables. Serve with a green salad, if desired.

PREPARATION TIME: 15 MINUTES   COOKING TIME: 20 MINUTES

- 1 cup red lentils
- 1 bay leaf
- 3 tablespoons olive oil
- 1 large red bell pepper, finely chopped
- 1 clove garlic, minced
- 1 tablespoon paprika
- 1 loaf (1 pound 7 ounces) sliced sourdough bread (about 16 slices), toasted
- ½ cup grated Pecorino Romano cheese

1. Rinse the lentils and place them in a large saucepan. Cover with plenty of water and add the bay leaf. Bring to a boil, then reduce the heat and simmer for 15 minutes, or until the lentils are very soft, skimming off any foam as they cook. Drain. Remove and discard the bay leaf.

2. Heat the oil in a frying pan and cook the bell pepper and garlic for 5 minutes, or until soft. Stir in the paprika. Remove from the heat. Mix in the lentils. (For a smooth spread, purée the mixture in a food processor.)

3. Spread the lentils onto slices of toasted sourdough bread. Arrange in a single layer on a nonstick baking sheet. Sprinkle with the cheese. Place under a broiler until the cheese has melted. Serve immediately.

Per serving (2 slices bread): 360 calories, 46 g carbohydrates, 15 g protein, 12 g fat, 7 g fiber

Recipe: Passion for Pulses

 **ACTIVITY TIP**

Use half an hour of your lunch break to get outside and take a walk. This is an easy way to fit regular exercise into a busy work schedule.

GOAT CHEESE WRAP

Serves 4

Here's a quick grab-and-run sandwich. You can prepare it the night before and seal it tightly with plastic wrap. It'll taste great the next day.

PREPARATION TIME: 10 MINUTES

4   ounces crumbled goat cheese
6   kalamata olives, coarsely chopped
¼   cup marinated sun-dried tomatoes, thinly sliced
¼   cup coarsely chopped red onion
1   teaspoon olive oil
2   teaspoons balsamic vinegar
1   cup arugula leaves (approximately 20)
8   slices (1 ounce each) low-salt boiled ham
4   corn tortillas (6" diameter)

1. In a medium bowl, combine the goat cheese, olives, tomatoes, onion, oil, and vinegar.

2. Chop the arugula leaves.

3. Arrange 2 slices of ham on each tortilla, overlapping them and placing them close to one end.

4. Spoon one-quarter of the cheese mixture on the ham. Top each tortilla with ¼ cup arugula leaves.

5. Starting at the end with the ham and cheese, completely roll up the tortilla.

6. This may be prepared and refrigerated several hours in advance or overnight.

Per serving: 300 calories, 30 g carbohydrates, 19 g protein, 11 g fat, 2 g fiber

PORTOBELLO MUSHROOMS WITH RICOTTA AND ROASTED TOMATOES

(photo on page 130)   *Serves 4*

There's nothing quite like tomatoes that have ripened in the sunshine on the vine. The next best thing is to buy tomatoes still on the vine—you will find they have developed a fuller flavor.

PREPARATION TIME: 10 MINUTES   COOKING TIME: 15 MINUTES

16	cherry tomatoes on the vine
1	tablespoon balsamic vinegar
2	tablespoons extra-virgin olive oil, divided
	Freshly ground black pepper
	Juice of 1 lemon
1	tablespoon chopped dill
4	medium portobello mushrooms, stems trimmed
½	cup low-fat ricotta cheese
4	thick slices sourdough or whole grain bread, toasted

1. Preheat the oven to 350°F. Put the tomatoes in a shallow nonstick baking pan. Drizzle with vinegar and 1 tablespoon of the oil. Season to taste with pepper. Bake for 8 to 10 minutes, or until the tomatoes are soft.

2. In a bowl, combine the lemon juice, dill, and remaining 1 tablespoon oil. Season to taste with pepper. Brush the mushrooms generously with the oil marinade, then place, stem side down, on a heated grill or in a frying pan. Cook for 3 minutes. Turn the mushrooms over. Crumble the ricotta over the top and spoon over the remaining marinade. Cook for 2 to 3 minutes, or until the mushrooms are soft.

3. Serve the mushrooms and roasted tomatoes with the toast.

Per serving: 240 calories, 21 g carbohydrates, 9 g protein, 13 g fat, 4 g fiber

 **ACTIVITY TIPS**

If possible, walk to work, or at least part of the way, or walk the children to school. Also, keep comfortable shoes at work so that you never have an excuse not to exercise.

TANGY MOROCCAN "BURGERS"

(photo on page 131)   *Serves 4 (2 burgers per serving)*

Chermoula—a robust seasoning blend of cumin, paprika, turmeric, onion, parsley, cilantro, garlic, and cayenne pepper— gives these chickpea burgers a tangy Moroccan flavor.

PREPARATION TIME: 20 MINUTES   MARINATING TIME: 20 MINUTES
COOKING TIME: 15 MINUTES

1	tablespoon + 1 teaspoon extra-virgin olive oil
1	large onion, finely chopped
1	clove garlic, minced
1	can (14 ounces) chickpeas, rinsed and drained
1	cup loosely packed fresh whole grain bread crumbs
1	egg, lightly beaten
	Freshly ground black pepper
1–2	tablespoons chickpea flour, to thicken (optional)
2	tablespoons Chermoula Seasoning Mix (page 113 or prepared)
2	tablespoons water
	Pita bread, warmed and cut into quarters
	Lettuce leaves
	Hummus
	Tabbouleh (page 232 or ready-to-serve)
	Baked Beet Salad (page 162)

1. Heat 1 tablespoon oil in a frying pan over low heat. Add the onion and garlic and cook for 5 minutes, or until golden. Put the chickpeas in a food processor and purée until they resemble bread crumbs. Add the whole grain bread crumbs, egg, and cooked onion and garlic and process for a few seconds, or until the ingredients are just combined. Season to taste with pepper. Add 1 to 2 tablespoons chickpea flour if the mixture is too wet.

2. Use 1 heaping tablespoon of the mixture to form each burger (the mixture will make 8 burgers). Mix the chermoula with water. Brush the burgers generously with the chermoula, then leave to marinate for approximately 20 minutes.

3. Heat the remaining 1 teaspoon olive oil in a nonstick frying pan or on a griddle and cook the chickpea burgers over medium heat for 4 to 5 minutes on each side, or until browned. Don't have the heat too high or they will burn, which will spoil the flavor.

4. Serve the chickpea burgers with pita bread, lettuce leaves, and separate bowls of hummus, tabbouleh, and baked beet salad. Assemble the burgers at the table.

Per serving: 220 calories, 24 g carbohydrates, 9 g protein, 9 g fat, 5 g fiber

COOK'S TIP

Chickpea flour is sold in some health food and Middle Eastern food stores. It can be replaced with triticale or millet.

CHERMOULA SEASONING MIX

Makes about ⅓ cup

Stored in an airtight container, this exotic seasoning blend can be refrigerated for up to a week.

½	onion, finely chopped
1	tablespoon ground cumin
2	teaspoons finely chopped parsley
2	teaspoons mild paprika
1	teaspoon finely chopped cilantro leaves
1	teaspoon turmeric
1	clove garlic, minced
	Pinch of cayenne pepper
	Salt and freshly ground black pepper

1. In a bowl, combine the onion, cumin, parsley, paprika, cilantro, turmeric, garlic, cayenne, and a pinch each of cayenne, salt, and pepper. Mix.

2. Set aside to allow the flavors to develop.

3. Use as a rub for meat or poultry before roasting or barbecuing.

Recipe: Liz and Ian Hemphill, Herbies Spices

SWEET POTATO CAKES
WITH ROAST TOMATO SALAD

Serves 2

Don't hold back on the tomato salad with your sweet potato cakes.
Tomatoes are an almost exclusive source of the antioxidant
lycopene, associated with a reduced risk of some cancers.

PREPARATION TIME: 25 MINUTES   COOKING TIME: 45 MINUTES

SALAD:

3   plum tomatoes, halved lengthwise
1   clove garlic, minced
2   teaspoons olive oil
    Freshly ground black pepper
12 ounces baby spinach leaves

POTATO CAKES:

1   large potato (10½ ounces), coarsely chopped
1   sweet potato (10½ ounces), coarsely chopped
    Olive oil spray
2   slices bacon, fat trimmed, chopped
1   cup rolled oats
2   tablespoons chopped parsley
    Freshly ground black pepper

DRESSING:

1   tablespoon mayonnaise
1   tablespoon low-fat plain yogurt
1   tablespoon shredded basil
2   teaspoons finely chopped chives

1. To make the salad: Preheat the oven to 400°F. Place the tomatoes, cut side up, in a shallow baking dish. Smear the cut side of the tomatoes with the garlic, drizzle with oil, and season to taste with pepper. Bake for 30 minutes, or until soft.

2. To make the potato cakes: Meanwhile, cook the potatoes in a large saucepan of boiling water for 10 minutes, or until soft.

3. Lightly coat a nonstick frying pan with oil spray and cook the bacon over medium heat until browned. Put the oats into the bowl of a food processor fitted with a metal blade. Process briefly until the oats resemble coarse bread crumbs.

4. Drain the cooked potatoes and mash them. Add the bacon, oats, and parsley. Season to taste with pepper. When cool enough to handle, shape the potato mixture into 4 patties.

5. Reheat the frying pan over medium heat. Coat with oil spray. Cook the potato cakes for 2 to 3 minutes on each side, or until browned.

6. To make the dressing: In a bowl, combine the mayonnaise, yogurt, basil, and chives.

7. To serve, place 2 potato cakes on each plate and top with a few spinach leaves, 3 of the baked tomato halves, and a dollop of mayonnaise.

Per serving: 275 calories, 38 g carbohydrates, 11 g protein, 7 g fat, 7 g fiber

BEAN AND CORN BURRITOS

Serves 4

This makes a delicious lunch to take to work. Store the bean mixture in an airtight container, and the lettuce and cheese in another. One option is to use whole wheat lavash in place of the tortillas, then assemble the meal just before eating.

PREPARATION TIME: 10 MINUTES   COOKING TIME: 5 MINUTES

1   can (11 ounces) corn kernels, drained
1   can (15½ ounces) red kidney beans, rinsed and drained
2   large ripe tomatoes, chopped
2   shallots, finely sliced
⅓   cup taco sauce
4   white corn tortillas (6" diameter)
4   large iceberg lettuce leaves, shredded
¾   cup reduced-fat cheese, grated

1. Preheat the oven to 350°F.

2. In a bowl, combine the corn, beans, tomatoes, shallots, and taco sauce. Stir to mix.

3. Wrap the tortillas in aluminum foil. Warm in the oven for 5 minutes.

4. To assemble, spread a lettuce leaf over a warmed tortilla, and top with the bean mixture and grated cheese. Fold the bottom of the tortilla over the filling, and roll up to enclose. Serve immediately.

Per serving: 434 calories, 60 g carbohydrates, 21 g protein, 12 g fat, 8 g fiber

Chapter 6

SOUPS, SIDE SALADS, AND VEGETABLES

The recipes in this chapter are like winning the dietary lottery. The wonderful side courses that add so much interest to our daily eating are primarily based on vegetables. And, as you've learned, most vegetables are so low in carbohydrates that they have no measurable effect on our blood sugar levels. They provide invaluable amounts of fiber and nutrients with loads of color, taste, and texture. Dig into So-Sweet Pepper Soup; Escarole and White Bean Soup; Tomato, Mint, and Cucumber Salad; Stuffed Eggplant; Herbed Balsamic Mushrooms; Spinach with Honey-Soy Dressing; Sweet Potatoes in Ginger, Cayenne, and Peanut Sauce; or Tuscan-style Beans with Tomatoes and Sage.

GOLDEN CARROT SOUP

(photo on page 132) *Serves 4*

Soups are wonderfully filling and full of nutrients, and, if you make them right, they provide all this with few calories—great for any weight loss program.

PREPARATION TIME: 10 MINUTES   COOKING TIME: 25 MINUTES

2   tablespoons olive oil
5   large carrots (about 2¼ pounds), chopped
1   large onion, chopped
2   cloves garlic, minced
3   bay leaves
5   cups beef or chicken broth
    Freshly ground black pepper
    Flat-leaf parsley

1. Heat the oil in a large saucepan. Add the carrots, onion, garlic, and bay leaves. Cook for 10 minutes.

2. Put the broth in another saucepan and bring to a boil. Pour the boiling broth over the vegetables and simmer for 15 minutes, or until tender.

3. Remove the pan from the heat. Remove and discard the bay leaves. Allow the soup to cool a little, then transfer to a food processor fitted with a metal blade or a blender. Purée until smooth.

4. Season to taste with pepper. If the soup is too thick, add some extra broth. Serve garnished with parsley.

Per serving: 180 calories, 17 g carbohydrates, 5 g protein, 10 g fat, 8 g fiber

Recipe: Steffan Rössner

● ●
COOK'S TIP

As a variation, garnish the soup with small bits of crispy bacon, or top with a dollop of low-fat plain yogurt.

SWEET POTATO, CARROT, AND GINGER SOUP

Serves 6

Toasted oat bran or whole grain bread is a simple, satisfying accompaniment for a hot bowlful of this soup.

PREPARATION TIME: 10 MINUTES   COOKING TIME: 20 MINUTES

2	pounds sweet potato, cut into large pieces
2	pounds carrots, cut into large pieces
4	cups chicken or vegetable broth
1	large onion, quartered
2	cloves garlic, coarsely chopped
	Peel of ½ lemon, cut in wide strips
1	can (6 ounces) evaporated fat-free milk
⅔	cup water
1½	teaspoons lemon juice
	Small piece fresh ginger (½" x 1"), finely chopped
	Salt and freshly ground black pepper
	Cilantro leaves

1. In a large saucepan or pot, combine the sweet potato, carrots, broth, onion, garlic, and lemon peel. Simmer for 15 minutes, or until the carrots are soft. Remove the lemon peel and discard.

2. Add the milk, water, lemon juice, and ginger. Cook for 5 minutes.

3. Transfer the mixture to a food processor fitted with a metal blade or a blender. Purée the soup until smooth. Season to taste with salt and pepper. Garnish with cilantro leaves.

Per serving: 183 calories, 27 g carbohydrates, 5 g protein, 5 g fat, 9 g fiber

SO-SWEET PEPPER SOUP

Who would have thought that this humble combination
of vegetables would produce such a hearty-tasting soup?

PREPARATION TIME: 15 MINUTES   COOKING TIME: 50 TO 55 MINUTES

1	tablespoon olive oil
1	medium onion, coarsely chopped
1½	large ribs celery, coarsely chopped
2	cloves garlic, minced
4	cups low-sodium vegetable broth
5	cups water, divided
1½	cups (8 ounces) cubed golden new potatoes
5	yellow bell peppers, quartered
½	teaspoon salt
⅛	teaspoon freshly ground black pepper
1	cup barley
	Homemade or commercial pesto sauce (optional)
	Grated Parmesan cheese (optional)

1. In a large, wide-based saucepan, heat the oil over medium-low heat. Add the onion and celery. Cook for 4 minutes. Add the garlic and continue to cook another 3 minutes (onions will be soft and translucent).

2. Add the broth, 2 cups water, potatoes, bell peppers, salt, and black pepper. Bring to a boil. Reduce the heat. Cover and simmer for 40 to 45 minutes, or until the potatoes are tender.

3. Meanwhile, in another saucepan bring the remaining 3 cups of water to a boil. Add the barley.

4. Reduce the heat. Cover and simmer, stirring occasionally, for 30 minutes, adding more water if needed. When the barley is cooked, drain and reserve in the cooking pan.

5. When the potatoes are cooked, pour half of the mixture into a food processor fitted with a metal blade or a blender. Purée until completely smooth and pour into the pan with the barley. Repeat with the remaining potatoes. Heat on low to keep warm and stir thoroughly.

6. Garnish with a dime-size dollop of pesto and grated cheese, if desired.

Per serving: 174 calories, 36 g carbohydrates, 5 g protein, 3 g fat, 6 g fiber

GREEN PEA SOUP WITH BACON

Serves 4

*Team a cup (a half serving) of this soothing soup with a
Goat Cheese Wrap (page 110) for a terrific meal.*

PREPARATION TIME: 10 MINUTES   COOKING TIME: 15 MINUTES

2   tablespoons olive oil
2   cloves garlic, minced
1   onion, chopped
4   cups chicken broth
3¼ cups frozen green peas, thawed
2   tablespoons chopped mint
2   tablespoons chopped parsley
    Freshly ground black pepper
2   lean slices bacon, chopped

1. Heat the oil in a frying pan over medium heat. Add the garlic and onion and
   cook for 5 minutes, or until the onion is soft, but not browned. Add the broth,
   peas, mint, and parsley. Bring to a boil, then reduce to a simmer for 8 minutes.

2. Remove from the heat. Allow to cool a little, then transfer to a food processor
   fitted with a metal blade or a blender. Purée until smooth. Season to taste with
   pepper.

3. Dry-fry the bacon in a frying pan until crispy. Ladle the soup into 4 warmed
   bowls and garnish with the bacon.

Per serving: 214 calories, 12 g carbohydrates, 12 g protein, 12 g fat, 8 g fiber

BABY PEA AND HAM SOUP

Serves 6

A post-holiday ham bone is an ideal enticement to prepare this uncomplicated soup. Offer thick slices of toasted low-GI bread for dunking.

PREPARATION TIME: 10 MINUTES   COOKING TIME: 50 MINUTES

1	large smoked ham bone
8	cups water
1½	pounds carrots (about 4 large), diced
3	large onions, finely diced
4	ribs celery, diced
3	bay leaves
1	pound frozen baby peas
½	bunch parsley, coarsely chopped
	Freshly ground black pepper

1. Place the ham bone and water in a large saucepan and bring to a boil. Remove any froth that forms on the surface. Simmer for 5 minutes, then add the carrots, onions, celery, and bay leaves.

2. Simmer gently for 40 minutes, removing any scum as it appears. Remove the bone from the water. Cut off any meat and dice. Discard the fat and skin. Remove and discard the bay leaves.

3. Return the diced ham to the pan. Add the peas, simmering gently until tender.

4. Add the chopped parsley. Season to taste with pepper. Serve hot.

Per serving: 121 calories, 15 g carbohydrates, 12 g protein, 1 g fat, 10 g fiber

· ·

COOK'S TIP

If a ham bone isn't available, add 1 teaspoon liquid smoke and about ½ cup chopped thick-sliced delicatessen ham to the soup, if desired.

MINESTRONE

(photo on page 133)   *Serves 4*

*Minestrone is absolutely delicious as a warming, hearty winter meal.
And it is worth the little extra effort and time it takes to make, as this
quantity will generously serve four for a main meal or six as a starter
and still leave leftovers for lunch. Leave out the bacon if you want a
vegetarian meal. You may like to serve it with sourdough bread.*

PREPARATION TIME: 20 MINUTES   COOKING TIME: 55 MINUTES

1	tablespoon olive oil
1	large onion, finely chopped
1	leek, thinly sliced
2	cloves garlic, minced
2	lean slices bacon, chopped
2	carrots, sliced into ¼" rounds, or finely chopped
1	can (14 ounces) Italian tomatoes, chopped
2	ribs celery, thinly sliced
1	bay leaf
6	cups chicken, beef, or vegetable broth, divided
½	cup small pasta or pasta pieces
1	can (14 ounces) cannellini beans, rinsed and drained
1	cup fresh or frozen peas
1	cup finely shredded cabbage
	Freshly ground black pepper
	Basil pesto or sun-dried tomato pesto (optional)
	Shaved Parmesan cheese (optional)

1. Heat the oil in a large heavy-based soup saucepan over medium heat. Add the
   onion, leek, and garlic. Cook for 5 minutes, or until the onion is golden and
   soft. Add the bacon and cook for 1 to 2 minutes. Add the carrots, tomatoes,
   celery, and bay leaf. Pour in 5 cups of the broth and bring to a boil, then
   reduce the heat and simmer, covered, for 30 minutes.

2. Stir in the pasta and continue to simmer for 10 to 15 minutes, or until the pasta
   is al dente. Add up to 1 cup more broth if the mixture is too thick.

3. Add the beans, peas, and cabbage. Season to taste with pepper. Stir to combine and cook for a few minutes to heat the vegetables through. Remove and discard the bay leaf.

4. Serve with a dollop of basil or sun-dried tomato pesto and a sprinkling of Parmesan cheese, if desired.

Per serving: 245 calories, 27 g carbohydrates, 13 g protein, 7 g fat, 9 g fiber

COOK'S TIP

To freeze, cool the soup to room temperature and divide among single-serve plastic containers with lids. Label with the recipe name and date using an indelible marker. Store in the freezer for up to 3 months.

BARLEY AND VEGETABLE SOUP

(photo on page 134) *Serves 4*

One of the oldest cultivated cereals, barley ranks high in nutrients and soluble fiber. This lowers its GI level and reduces the post-meal rise in blood glucose. Add to that its light, nutty flavor and al dente texture, and you have a winning base for many meals.

PREPARATION TIME: 15 MINUTES   COOKING TIME: 40 MINUTES

1	teaspoon olive oil
1	onion, chopped
4	cups vegetable broth
1	can (14 ounces) tomatoes
½	cup pearl barley
2	small carrots, chopped
1	tablespoon tomato paste
⅔	cup fresh or frozen peas
4	cups baby spinach leaves, shredded
¼	cup mixed herbs, such as parsley, basil, and oregano, coarsely chopped
	Freshly ground black pepper

1. Heat the oil in a heavy frying pan over low heat. Add the onion and cook, covered, for 5 minutes, or until the onion is soft. Add the broth, tomatoes, barley, carrots, and tomato paste. Bring to a boil, then reduce the heat and simmer for 30 minutes.

2. Add the peas and simmer for 2 to 3 minutes. Add the spinach and herbs. Simmer for 1 to 2 minutes, or until the spinach has wilted.

3. Divide the soup among 4 bowls. Season to taste with pepper.

Per serving: 170 calories, 27 g carbohydrates, 6 g protein, 3 g fat, 8 g fiber

Recipe: Penny Hunking, Energise Nutrition

HEARTY WINTER VEGETABLE SOUP

Serves 8

Lentils should be a legume staple of a busy cook's kitchen. Because they need no soaking before cooking, as dried beans do, advance planning isn't needed.

PREPARATION TIME: 5 MINUTES   COOKING TIME: 1 HOUR

4   cups chicken or vegetable broth
8   ounces dried lentils
6   ribs celery, thinly sliced
1   large leek, thinly sliced
1   large can (28 ounces) whole tomatoes
1⅔ cups canned tomato puree
     Salt and freshly ground black pepper
½   bunch flat-leaf parsley, coarsely chopped
2   ounces Parmesan cheese, shaved from the block

1. In a large pot, combine the broth and lentils. Bring to a boil, cover, and simmer for 45 minutes.

2. Add the celery, leek, tomatoes (with juice), and tomato puree. Simmer for 15 minutes.

3. Season to taste with salt and pepper. Stir in the parsley and ladle into soup bowls.

4. Sprinkle each bowl with the shaved Parmesan.

Per serving: 103 calories, 11 g carbohydrates, 8 g protein, 3 g fat, 5 g fiber

THICK VEGETABLE SOUP

Serves 8

The dried soup mix in this recipe is a combination of barley, red lentils, and split peas. Some brands also contain dried beans, in which case add another 15–20 minutes to the cooking time. This type of mix is available from supermarkets or health food stores. The cooled soup may be packed into airtight containers and frozen for up to three months. Freeze in single servings to make handy lunches.

PREPARATION TIME: 20 MINUTES   COOKING TIME: 1 HOUR 5 MINUTES

2	teaspoons olive oil
2	carrots, chopped
2	ribs celery, sliced
1	onion, chopped
8	cups vegetable broth
1	can (14 ounces) chopped tomatoes
1	cup dried soup mix
2	small zucchini, chopped
3	tablespoons chopped flat-leaf parsley

1. Heat the oil in a large saucepan over medium heat. Add the carrots, celery, and onion. Cook over medium heat for 5 minutes, stirring occasionally, until the onion has softened.

2. Add the broth, tomatoes, and soup mix. Cover and bring to a boil, then reduce the heat to medium-low. Tilt the lid slightly, and cook for 30 minutes.

3. Add the zucchini and cook for 30 minutes, until all the ingredients are tender. Serve sprinkled with parsley.

Per serving: 120 calories, 18 g carbohydrates, 7 g protein, 2 g fat, 3 g fiber

Mustard-Roasted Fruit Chutney *(page 107)*

Portobello Mushrooms with Ricotta and Roasted Tomatoes *(page 111)*

Tangy Moroccan "Burgers" *(page 112)*

Golden Carrot Soup (*page 118*)

Minestrone *(page 124)*

Barley and Vegetable Soup (*page 126*)

Soba Noodle Soup with Shrimp and Tofu *(page 151)*

Vietnamese Beef Soup (*page 152*)

Chicken, Mint, and Corn Soup *(page 155)*

Warm Vegetable Salad *(page 163)*

Sweet Potatoes in Ginger, Cayenne, and Peanut Sauce *(page 176)*

Tuscan-style Beans with Tomatoes and Sage *(page 179)*

Lima Bean and Cherry Tomato Stew *(page 180)*

Ridged Penne with Cauliflower and Pancetta *(page 196)*

Linguine with Salmon and Peas (*page 203*)

Spicy Beef and Noodles (*page 228*)

ESCAROLE AND WHITE BEAN SOUP

Serves 4

Escarole is a type of endive that grows in compact heads with dark green outer leaves and lighter leaves inside. The flavor is delightfully bittersweet. Curly endive or chicory can replace it in this recipe.

PREPARATION TIME: 20 MINUTES   COOKING AND RESTING TIME: 30 MINUTES

Salt
1   head (1 pound) escarole
    Canola oil spray
2   large cloves garlic, minced
1   medium onion, coarsely chopped
1   can (16 ounces) white beans (great Northern or cannellini)
1   cup tomato sauce
1   cup hot water
    Salt and freshly ground black pepper

2   cups vegetable, beef, or chicken broth
4   sprigs flat-leaf parsley, finely chopped
1   tablespoon chopped fresh sage or rosemary leaves or ground cumin seeds
    Grated Pecorino Romano cheese (optional)

1. Set a 6-quart pot of salted water over high heat. Bring to a boil.

2. Cut the escarole vertically in half. Remove about 1" from the bottom and cut in half horizontally. Wash the leaves thoroughly to remove all grit. Submerge the escarole in the boiling water. When the water returns to a boil, drain the escarole and set aside.

3. Coat a large Dutch oven with cooking spray and gently heat before cooking garlic and onion until soft, for 2 to 3 minutes.

4. Reduce the heat. Add the beans, tomato sauce, and water. Season to taste with salt and pepper. Mix well. Stir in the reserved escarole and broth. Cook over low heat for 15 minutes.

5. Five minutes before the soup is done, add the parsley and the sage, rosemary, or cumin.

6. Allow the soup to rest for at least 10 minutes for the flavors to blend. Sprinkle with grated cheese, if desired.

Per serving: 209 calories, 34 g carbohydrates, 10 g protein, 4 g fat, 11 g fiber

BLACK BEAN SOUP

Serves 6

This tangy, nourishing soup shows you how easy it is to incorporate legumes into your weekly meal plans. Black beans, also called turtle beans, have a mild, earthy taste when cooked. They are widely used throughout Latin America and the Caribbean.

SOAKING TIME: OVERNIGHT   PREPARATION TIME: 15 MINUTES
COOKING TIME: 1 HOUR 5 MINUTES

1	cup dried black beans
1	tablespoon olive oil
2	onions, coarsely chopped
3	slices bacon, fat trimmed, chopped
2	cloves garlic, minced
2	teaspoons ground cumin
1	teaspoon ground coriander
6	cups chicken or vegetable broth
1	pound sweet potato, cubed
2	carrots, chopped
2	bay leaves
¼	cup chopped cilantro leaves
	Freshly ground black pepper

1. Soak the beans overnight in a bowl of cold water.

2. The next day, drain the black beans, then rinse under cold water and drain again.

3. Heat the oil in a large saucepan. Add the onions, bacon, and garlic. Cook for 4 minutes, or until the onions are soft. Add the cumin and coriander. Cook for 30 seconds, or until aromatic.

4. Add the broth, sweet potato, carrots, bay leaves, and the beans. Bring to a boil, then cover and simmer over low heat for 1 hour, or until the beans and vegetables are soft.

5. Remove the bay leaves and discard. Allow the soup to cool a little, then transfer to a food processor fitted with a metal blade or a blender. Purée until smooth. Mix in the cilantro. Season to taste with pepper.

Per serving: 230 calories, 35 g carbohydrates, 13 g protein, 4 g fat, 8 g fiber

COOK'S TIPS

Although they will keep indefinitely, it's best to use legumes within 1 year of purchase. Before cooking, be sure to pick through them, taking out any small pebbles, split and withered beans, and any other foreign matter.

Don't add salt to the cooking water—it slows down water absorption, and cooking takes longer.

You can keep soaked or cooked beans in an airtight container for several days in the refrigerator.

PASTA WITH BEANS SOUP

Serves 7

Soups are a great way to enjoy a variety of flavors and nutrients with minimal preparation. This soup is no exception—and you'll have leftovers for the next day!

PREPARATION TIME: 7 MINUTES   COOKING TIME: 25 MINUTES

- 1   can (15½ ounces) light red kidney beans
- 2   fresh or canned plum tomatoes, quartered
- 1   large rib celery, preferably with leaves, sliced into 8–10 pieces
- 1   small onion, thickly sliced
- 6   large leaves fresh basil, torn into quarters
- 3   sprigs parsley, leaves only
- 1   clove garlic, coarsely chopped
- 8   cups vegetable or chicken broth
- 1½ cups small pasta (shells, elbows, ditalini)
-     Salt and freshly ground black pepper

1. Rinse and drain the beans. Place them in a 4-quart saucepan.

2. In a food processor fitted with a metal blade, combine the tomatoes, celery, onion, basil, parsley, and garlic. Pulse 8 to 10 times to coarsely chop. Add to the beans and stir to mix.

3. Add the broth and bring to a boil. Reduce the heat to medium low. Cover and cook for 15 minutes, stirring occasionally.

4. Add the pasta and mix thoroughly. Cook, uncovered, for 10 minutes, or until the pasta is done. Stir occasionally.

5. Season to taste with salt and pepper. Serve hot or warm.

Per serving: 162 calories, 32 g carbohydrates, 7 g protein, less than 1 g fat, 4 g fiber

CHUNKY VEGETABLE, CHICKEN, AND PASTA SOUP

Serves 6

Boneless, skinless chicken thighs are a wonderful addition to supermarket poultry cases. To quickly and easily remove all excess fat, lay the uncooked thighs on a tray covered with waxed paper and freeze for 30 minutes. The fat will come away easily when snipped with kitchen shears.

PREPARATION TIME: 15 MINUTES   COOKING TIME: 20 MINUTES

8   cups chicken or vegetable broth
4   large carrots, diced
2   large sweet potatoes, diced
2   large onions, diced
4   boneless, skinless chicken thighs, trimmed of all fat and sliced
1   can (15¼ ounces) corn niblets, drained
4   ounces rotini pasta
6   Brussels sprouts, cut in half
3   ribs celery, diced
4   sprigs flat-leaf parsley, coarsely chopped
    Salt and freshly ground black pepper

1. Heat the chicken or vegetable broth in a large saucepan. Add the carrots, sweet potatoes, and onions. Simmer for 10 minutes.

2. Add the chicken, corn, pasta, Brussels sprouts, and celery. Simmer gently for 10 minutes, or until the chicken is cooked.

3. Sprinkle with the parsley. Season to taste with salt and pepper

Per serving: 347 calories, 54 g carbohydrates, 23 g protein, 4 g fat, 9 g fiber

MOM'S "KICKED UP" LENTIL SOUP

Serves 5

The B vitamins, potassium, iron, and phosphorus in the lentils, combined with the antioxidants in the red wine, make a cup of this soup a healthy fill-up. And just one serving provides more than 50 percent of an adult's daily fiber requirement.

PREPARATION TIME: 12 MINUTES   COOKING TIME: 55 MINUTES

5 cups beef or vegetable broth
1 cup brown lentils, rinsed
6 medium carrots, thinly sliced
2 ribs celery, including leaves, thinly sliced
1 large onion, coarsely chopped
1 bay leaf
1 cup dry red wine
    Freshly ground black pepper
    Grated Parmesan cheese (optional)

1. In a large pot, combine the broth, lentils, carrots, celery, onion, and bay leaf. Bring to a boil, cover, and simmer for 45 minutes.

2. Add the wine and freshly ground pepper to taste. Cook over medium heat for 5 minutes. Remove the bay leaf and discard.

3. Serve hot with a sprinkle of grated cheese, if desired.

Per serving: 202 calories, 37 g carbohydrates, 10 g protein, 0 g fat, 14 g fiber

SOBA NOODLE SOUP WITH SHRIMP AND TOFU

(photo on page 135)   *Serves 4*

*Tofu, whether you buy the soft or firm variety, absorbs other flavors well
and makes a delicious addition to stir-fries and soups such as this one.*

PREPARATION TIME: 20 MINUTES   COOKING TIME: 10 MINUTES

3½ ounces soba noodles	24 large raw shrimp, peeled and deveined, with tails intact
4 cups vegetable broth	2 cups baby spinach leaves, shredded
2 tablespoons soy sauce	2 scallions, sliced on the diagonal
1 tablespoon mirin	10½ ounces silken firm tofu, cut into ¾" cubes
2 teaspoons grated fresh ginger	¼ cup cilantro leaves
2 teaspoons sugar	
1–2 small red chiles, seeded and finely chopped	

1. Cook the soba noodles in a saucepan of boiling water for 4 minutes, or until tender. Drain and set aside.

2. In a large saucepan, combine the broth, soy sauce, mirin, ginger, sugar, and chiles. Bring to a boil, then reduce the heat and simmer for 3 minutes. Add the shrimp, spinach, and scallions. Simmer for 2 minutes, or until the shrimp turn pink and are cooked.

3. Divide the noodles and tofu evenly among 4 bowls. Spoon the soup over top and serve garnished with cilantro.

Per serving: 290 calories, 23 g carbohydrates, 38 g protein, 6 g fat, 2 g fiber

• •

 **COOK'S TIPS**

Soba, Japanese buckwheat noodles, and mirin, sweet rice wine, are available in some supermarkets and in Asian food stores.

The sodium content of this recipe can be reduced by using either a homemade or a low-salt vegetable broth, and a low-sodium soy sauce.

VIETNAMESE BEEF SOUP

(photo on page 136)   *Serves 4*

Pho bo, a beef soup with rice noodles, is often referred to as Vietnam's national dish and is eaten at any time of day. A boiling broth is poured over thinly sliced raw beef and is hot enough to cook the beef. Separate aromatic seasonings such as chile and Vietnamese mint are often served on the side.

PREPARATION TIME: 20 MINUTES   COOKING TIME: 35 MINUTES

2	teaspoons olive oil
1	small onion, chopped
1½"	piece fresh ginger, thinly sliced
1	clove garlic, minced
6	cups beef broth
4	cups water
1	cinnamon stick
1	star anise
1	stalk lemongrass, lightly bruised
1	tablespoon fish sauce
1	tablespoon soy sauce
1	teaspoon sugar
1	pound flat rice noodles
7	ounces beef eye-of-round roast, very thinly sliced
1	cup bean sprouts
2	tablespoons coarsely chopped cilantro leaves
4	scallions, thinly sliced
1–2	small red chiles, to taste, seeded and very thinly sliced
½	lime, cut into wedges

1. Heat the oil in a large saucepan and add the onion, ginger, and garlic. Cook 3 minutes, or until aromatic. Add the broth, water, cinnamon, star anise, lemongrass, fish sauce, soy sauce, and sugar. Bring to a boil, then reduce the heat and simmer, uncovered, for 30 minutes.

2. Cool for 10 minutes. Strain the broth. Return the liquid to the pan and to a boil.

3. Meanwhile, put the rice noodles in a bowl and cover with boiling water. Allow to soak for 15 minutes. When the noodles have softened, gently separate them, then drain. Add to the broth. Boil for 1 minute.

4. With tongs or a skimmer, divide the noodles among 4 deep bowls. Top with the raw beef slices, bean sprouts, and cilantro. Pour on the broth. Garnish with scallions and chiles. Serve with the lime wedges for squeezing over.

Per serving: 230 calories, 30 g carbohydrates, 15 g protein, 5 g fat, 2 g fiber

Recipe: Lynne Mullins, Noodles to Pasta

 **COOK'S TIPS**

Medium flat Chinese rice noodles and fish sauce (*nam pla*) are sold in some supermarkets and in Asian food stores.

If desired, the beef slices can be simmered for 1 minute in the hot broth.

 **ACTIVITY TIP**

For all short trips that would take less than 5 minutes in the car, take the time to walk instead. Go shopping on foot and carry your bags home—a fantastic total body workout! However, if you have to drive to the nearest shopping center, park the car in the furthest parking spot and walk the rest of the way.

CHICKEN BARLEY SOUP

Serves 6

Any of the dark green leafy vegetables are powerhouses of nutrients, so feel free to replace the spinach with kale, collards, mustard greens, or chard.

PREPARATION TIME: 15 MINUTES   COOKING TIME: 1 HOUR

- 6 cups water, divided
- 1 pound boneless, skinless chicken breasts
- ½ cup pearl barley
- 1 tablespoon extra-virgin olive oil
- 1½ cups thinly sliced carrots (about 3 medium)
- 1½ cups thinly sliced celery (about 3 ribs including leaves)
- 1 small onion, chopped
- 2 cups sliced mushrooms (about 4 ounces)
- 4 cups spinach leaves, stems removed
- 1 can (15½ ounces) diced tomatoes
  Salt and freshly ground black pepper

1. Pour 4 cups cold water into a medium saucepan. Add the chicken. Bring to a boil, removing any scum that forms. Reduce the heat, cover, and poach for 25 minutes.

2. Meanwhile, bring 2 cups of water to a boil in a medium saucepan. Add the barley. Cover and simmer for 40 minutes, stirring occasionally.

3. Pour the oil in a large skillet. Add the carrots, celery, and onion and cook for 3 minutes. Add the mushrooms and cook for 3 minutes.

4. Remove the vegetables from the heat and add the barley when cooked.

5. Remove the chicken from the poaching broth. Cut into cubes. Pour the broth into the barley and vegetables. Add the chicken.

6. Add the spinach and the tomatoes, with their juice, to the soup. Bring to a boil, cover, and simmer for 10 minutes. Before serving, season to taste with salt and pepper.

Per serving: 178 calories, 19 g carbohydrates, 18 g protein, 4 g fat, 5 g fiber

CHICKEN, MINT, AND CORN SOUP

(photo on page 137)   *Serves 4*

For the sweetest flavor, buy corn on the cob with the husk intact, because the natural sugar in the kernels starts converting into starch the moment the green husk is removed. Fresh-cooked corn has a low GI of 48. Frozen kernels are a suitable substitute for fresh in this recipe.

PREPARATION TIME: 10 MINUTES   COOKING TIME: 20 MINUTES

2   ears corn on the cob
4   cups chicken broth
6   mint leaves + extra for garnish
4   boneless, skinless chicken breasts (6 ounces each)
⅔   cup snow pea sprouts
2   teaspoons julienned lemon peel
¼   teaspoon salt
     Freshly ground black pepper

1. Put the corn in a large saucepan of boiling water and cook for 10 minutes. Remove the corn. Allow to cool slightly. Cut off the kernels. Set aside.

2. Put the broth and mint leaves in a large saucepan and bring to a boil. Add the chicken, return to a simmer, and poach for 10 to 12 minutes, or until the chicken is cooked through. Just before the chicken is ready, add the reserved corn and snow pea sprouts to the hot broth.

3. Remove the chicken, slice on the diagonal, then divide among 4 bowls. Ladle the broth and vegetables into the bowls. Garnish with the lemon peel and extra mint. Season to taste with salt and pepper.

Per serving: 315 calories, 16 g carbohydrates, 39 g protein, 10 g fat, 4 g fiber

Recipe: Luke Mangan

 **COOK'S TIP**

Snow pea sprouts are available in some supermarkets. Mung bean or buckwheat sprouts may take their place.

ROAST CHICKEN, GARLIC, AND BEAN SOUP

Serves 6

For quicker preparation of this soup and other dishes calling for roast garlic, mash several heads of baked garlic at a time. Refrigerate in an airtight container for up to 1 week, or freeze small dollops in resealable plastic freezer bags. No need to thaw before using in a cooked dish.

PREPARATION TIME: 10 MINUTES   COOKING TIME: 25 MINUTES

6   unpeeled cloves garlic
1   roasted broiler-fryer chicken (3 pounds)
8   cups low-salt chicken broth
1   can (15½ ounces) light red kidney (borlotti) beans, drained
2   small ribs celery, thinly sliced
1   tablespoon fresh thyme or 1 teaspoon dried
     Grated peel of 1 lemon
     Salt and freshly ground black pepper
½   bunch flat-leaf parsley, coarsely chopped

1. Preheat the oven to 350°F.

2. Prick each clove of garlic with a sharp knife and place on a baking tray. Bake for 20 minutes. Squeeze the garlic from the skin. Mash in a small bowl with the back of a spoon.

3. Remove the skin from the chicken and cut the meat (in small pieces) from the bones. Discard the carcass.

4. In a large saucepan, combine the broth, beans, celery, thyme, lemon peel, and the garlic. Season to taste with salt and pepper. Bring to a boil. Simmer gently for 5 minutes, then add the chicken.

5. Serve with parsley scattered over the top.

Per serving: 306 calories, 8 g carbohydrates, 43 g protein, 12 g fat, 5 g fiber

BABY SPINACH SALAD

Serves 4

Keeping hard-cooked eggs in the refrigerator makes quick work of this salad. Boil half a dozen on the weekend, quick chill them in ice water, and then refrigerate to use throughout the week.

PREPARATION TIME: 20 MINUTES

4 cups baby spinach leaves
½ pint grape tomatoes, halved
2 hard-cooked eggs, horizontally sliced
1 small shallot, thinly sliced

2 strips bacon, crisply cooked and diced
1 tablespoon grated Parmesan cheese
¼ cup vinaigrette dressing

1. Wash the spinach leaves and pat dry. Trim off long stalks.

2. On a large platter, layer the spinach, tomatoes, eggs, and shallot.

3. Sprinkle with the bacon and cheese.

4. Drizzle with the dressing. Toss and serve.

Per serving: 159 calories, 5 g carbohydrates, 7 g protein, 13 g fat, 1 g fiber

CUCUMBER RAITA

Makes 4 (¼ cup) servings

This cooling and creamy side dish is perfect alongside Tandoori Chicken with Herbed Rice (page 274).

PREPARATION TIME: 5 MINUTES

1 cup low-fat plain yogurt
1 small cucumber, peeled, seeded, and finely chopped
½ bunch cilantro, chopped

1. In a serving bowl, combine the yogurt, cucumber, and cilantro. Stir to mix. Cover and refrigerate until serving.

Per serving: 38 calories, 3 g protein, 5 g carbohydrates, 0 g fiber, 1 g fat

Recipe: Carol Selva Rajah, Gourmet Asian Cuisine

TOMATO, MINT, AND CUCUMBER SALAD

Serves 6

This refreshing and crispy salad goes well with the Mediterranean Lasagna (page 199) or the Spinach and Ricotta Cannelloni (page 197).

PREPARATION TIME: 10 MINUTES

SALAD:

1 pound plum tomatoes (approximately 10)
2 tablespoons chopped fresh mint
1 pound cucumbers
15 kalamata olives
½ cup shaved Parmesan cheese

DRESSING:

3 tablespoons olive oil
3 tablespoons white wine vinegar
10 mint leaves, chopped
1 clove garlic, crushed
   Salt and freshly ground black pepper

1. To make the salad: Slice the tomatoes crosswise and sprinkle with chopped mint. Slice the cucumbers crosswise and toss in a salad bowl with the tomatoes.

2. Add the olives and sprinkle with cheese.

3. To make the dressing: In a screw-top jar, combine the oil, vinegar, mint, garlic, and a pinch each of salt and pepper. Shake to mix. Pour over the salad and serve immediately.

Per serving: 135 calories, 4 g carbohydrates, 3 g protein, 12 g fat, 3 g fiber

CELERY, WALNUT, AND LEMON THYME SALAD

Serves 6

*Lemon thyme imparts a fresh citrus-flavored accent to this dish.
If you can't locate any at your local market, simply use regular thyme and
add ½ teaspoon of grated lemon peel.*

PREPARATION TIME: 10 MINUTES

SALAD:

6   ribs celery
1   cup walnuts
6   sprigs lemon thyme leaves, stripped from stalks

DRESSING:

2   tablespoons extra-virgin olive oil
2   tablespoons apple juice
1   tablespoon lemon juice
1   tablespoon fresh thyme leaves
1   teaspoon celery seeds
    Salt and freshly ground black pepper

1. To make the salad: Wash and slice the celery ribs diagonally.

2. In a salad bowl, toss the celery with walnuts and thyme sprigs.

3. To make the dressing: In a screw-top jar, combine the oil, apple juice, lemon juice, thyme leaves, celery seeds, and a pinch each of salt and pepper. Shake to mix. Pour over the salad.

Per serving: 180 calories, 3 g carbohydrates, 3 g protein, 18 g fat, 3 g fiber

GREEN BEAN, TOMATO, AND OLIVE SALAD

Serves 6

Many vegetables, blanched just until tender, make excellent candidates for the salad bowl. This distinctive side dish goes particularly well with Garlic Shrimp with Cilantro Pasta (page 259).

PREPARATION TIME: 15 MINUTES

6 ounces green beans
1 bunch arugula
1 pint cherry tomatoes, halved
3 scallions, finely sliced
10 kalamata olives
6 basil leaves, torn
¼ cup extra-virgin olive oil
2 tablespoons wine vinegar
1 clove garlic, crushed
   Salt and freshly ground black pepper

1. Wash and trim the beans, and halve if very long. Wash the arugula, cut off the stems, and discard any bruised leaves. On a platter or in a shallow bowl, combine the beans and arugula leaves.

2. Scatter the tomatoes, scallions, olives, and basil leaves over the salad vegetables.

3. In a screw-top jar, combine the oil, vinegar, garlic, and a pinch each of salt and pepper. Shake to mix.

4. Pour the dressing over the salad.

Per serving: 110 calories, 3 g carbohydrates, 2 g protein, 10 g fat, 3 g fiber

GRILLED PEPPER, SWEET POTATO, AND HERB SALAD

Serves 4

A substantial vegetable salad such as this becomes a complete meal with grilled pork tenderloin and some crusty whole grain rolls.

PREPARATION TIME: 10 MINUTES   COOKING TIME: 25 MINUTES

2	large bell peppers, halved
4	medium sweet potatoes
1	tablespoon canola or olive oil
1	bunch flat-leaf parsley, coarsely chopped
½	bunch whole chives
	Salt and freshly ground black pepper
1	tablespoon balsamic vinegar

1. Preheat the grill to high. Place the pepper halves, skin side up, on the hot grill and cook for 10 minutes, or until black blisters appear. Place them into a paper bag. When cool, remove and discard the skin. Cut the flesh into thick slices.

2. Meanwhile, parboil the sweet potato for 10 minutes, then drain and slice diagonally. Brush each wedge with some of the oil. Place on a sheet of aluminum foil on the grill and cook, turning occasionally, for 15 minutes, or until golden brown.

3. Arrange the peppers and sweet potatoes on a platter or in a shallow bowl. Decorate with the parsley and chives. Season to taste with salt and black pepper. Drizzle with vinegar and any remaining oil.

Per serving: 166 calories, 25 g carbohydrates, 5 g protein, 5 g fat, 4 g fiber

COOK'S TIP

Choose any color of bell peppers—green, red, yellow, or orange—for this dish. The peppers can be broiled instead of grilled, if it's more convenient. The sweet potato can also be broiled.

BAKED BEET SALAD

Serves 4

Slow-roasting brings out the inherent sweetness of these ruby-red roots. The beets may be cooked, cooled, and refrigerated in their skins several days in advance of serving.

PREPARATION TIME: 5 MINUTES   COOKING TIME: 45 MINUTES

2   large beets (approximately 1 pound)
2   tablespoons lemon juice
1   tablespoon olive oil
¼   teaspoon salt
     Freshly ground black pepper
2   tablespoons finely chopped flat-leaf parsley

1. Preheat the oven to 350°F. Leaving the beets unpeeled and with 1¼" of root attached (so they don't "bleed" during cooking), wrap in aluminum foil. Place the beets in a shallow baking dish or on a baking sheet and bake for 45 minutes, or until cooked (test with a wooden skewer). When cool, peel the beets; the skins will slip off easily. Finely dice or grate the beets and spoon into a serving dish.

2. In a screw-top jar, combine the lemon juice, oil, salt, and a pinch of pepper. Shake well. Pour the dressing over the beets. Stir to combine. Serve garnished with the parsley.

Per serving: 102 calories, 11 g carbohydrates, 3 g protein, 5 g fat, 4 g fiber

WARM VEGETABLE SALAD

(photo on page 138)   *Serves 2*

This salad makes it easy to boost your vegetable intake—something we are all being urged to do. The lemon yogurt dressing is delicious with all sorts of vegetables, so try it with zucchini, sweet potato, or Hubbard squash, for a change.

PREPARATION TIME: 10 MINUTES   COOKING TIME: 3 MINUTES

SALAD:

1   large carrot, sliced
4   cauliflower florets, broken into small pieces
4   broccoli florets, broken into small pieces
20 green beans, trimmed and halved

DRESSING:

2   tablespoons low-fat plain yogurt
2   tablespoons lemon juice
2   teaspoons pure floral honey
1   teaspoon crushed garlic
    Freshly ground black pepper
2   tablespoons chopped flat-leaf parsley

1. To make the salad: Bring a saucepan of water to a boil. Add the carrot and cauliflower and cook for 2 minutes. Add the broccoli and beans and cook for 1 minute, or until crisp-tender.

2. To make the dressing: In a screw-top jar, combine the yogurt, lemon juice, honey, garlic, and a pinch of pepper. Shake to mix.

3. Drain the vegetables and refresh briefly under cold water. Pat dry, then place the vegetables in a bowl. Pour on the dressing and toss to coat. Sprinkle with parsley and serve.

Per serving: 85 calories, 13 g carbohydrates, 6 g protein, trace fat, 6 g fiber

 **ACTIVITY TIP**

Be an active role model for your family—if you exercise, your partner and children are more likely to.

MARINATED EGGPLANT SLICES WITH HERBS   *Serves 5*

This recipe can be made on the spot or in advance of a meal. You can also use one or two of these eggplant slices to slip inside a sandwich to enhance both flavor and daily vegetable consumption!

PREPARATION TIME: 10 MINUTES   SOAKING TIME: 20 MINUTES
COOKING TIME: 8 MINUTES   MARINATING TIME: SEVERAL HOURS OR OVERNIGHT

1	eggplant (approximately 1¼ pounds)
2	tablespoons coarse salt
	Canola oil spray
1	cup canned tomatoes, diced
½	cup loosely packed thyme leaves (about 15 sprigs)
¼	cup diced red onion
1	tablespoon extra-virgin olive oil
1	tablespoon lemon juice
1	large clove garlic, minced

1. Remove the stem end of the eggplant. Cut it into 15 round slices.

2. Fill a large bowl three-quarters full with water. Add the salt and the eggplant slices. Let them soak for at least 20 minutes to remove bitterness.

3. Preheat the broiler. Coat a baking sheet with cooking spray.

4. Remove the eggplant slices from the salted water. Pat them dry with paper towels and spread in a single layer on the baking sheet.

5. Broil 4½" from the heat source for 5 minutes on the first side, and 3 minutes when turned over. Remove and arrange the slices, slightly overlapping each other, on a large platter.

6. In a small mixing bowl, combine the tomatoes, thyme, onion, oil, lemon juice, and garlic. Whisk to mix.

7. Distribute the tomato-herb mixture evenly over the eggplant. Cover and let stand for several hours at room temperature before serving. You can also refrigerate overnight. Bring the dish to room temperature before serving.

Per serving: 60 calories, 7 g carbohydrates, 1 g protein, 3 g fat, 3 g fiber

HERBED BALSAMIC MUSHROOMS

Serves 3

Even though mushrooms are 90 percent water, they contain fiber, are rich in potassium, and are a good source of vitamin B_2. This recipe harmoniously combines the natural, earthy flavors of the mushrooms and the herbs.

PREPARATION TIME: 5 MINUTES   COOKING TIME: 25 MINUTES

- 1   pound small portobello mushrooms (approximately 24)
  Olive oil spray
- ½   tablespoon olive oil
- 1   tablespoon fresh rosemary, finely chopped (1–2 sprigs)
- 1   clove garlic, minced
- ½   to 1 tablespoon balsamic vinegar
- 1   tablespoon parsley, finely chopped (2–3 sprigs)

1. Preheat the oven to 450°F.

2. With a mushroom brush or damp cloth, clean the tops and bottoms of the mushrooms. Do not wash under a running faucet or submerge in water.

3. Lightly coat a jelly-roll pan with cooking spray. Place the mushrooms upside down on the pan.

4. In a small bowl, combine the oil, rosemary, and garlic. Brush the mushrooms with the oil mixture.

5. Bake for 25 minutes. Cool slightly and then slice. Place in a serving bowl. Add the vinegar and parsley. Toss and serve.

Per serving: 61 calories, 7 g carbohydrates, 3 g protein, 3 g fat, 2 g fiber

 COOK'S TIPS

Baby bella or small portobello mushrooms are less expensive and more robustly flavored than the large ones. They're also easier to wash.

The amount of balsamic vinegar required depends on the quality. The more expensive the vinegar, the denser it is, so you use less of it than a thinner product.

TOMATO AND OLIVE VINAIGRETTE

Makes 8 (2 tablespoons) servings

You may refrigerate this dressing in a screw-top jar for several days before serving. Allow to come to room temperature before dressing the salad.

PREPARATION TIME: 10 MINUTES

4 tablespoons olive oil
   Juice of 1 small lemon
1 tablespoon white wine vinegar
1 clove garlic, crushed
1 teaspoon grainy mustard

1 tablespoon finely chopped flat-leaf parsley
1 small ripe plum tomato, finely diced
4 pitted kalamata olives, pitted and finely diced

1. In small screw-top jar, combine the oil, lemon juice, vinegar, garlic, mustard, parsley, tomato, and olives. Shake well to combine.

2. Let stand 20 to 30 minutes before serving.

Per serving: 66 calories, 0 g carbohydrates, 0 g protein, 7 g fat, 0 g fiber

ROASTED SWEET POTATO

Serves 8

The simplicity of roasted sweet potatoes can turn any meal into a feast of thanksgiving.

PREPARATION TIME: 5 MINUTES   COOKING TIME: 31 MINUTES

   Olive oil spray
2 pounds sweet potatoes
1 tablespoon olive oil

½ tablespoon fresh or dried rosemary
⅛ teaspoon freshly ground black pepper

1. Preheat the oven to 375°F. Coat a baking pan with oil spray.

2. Peel the potatoes and cut into 1" cubes.

3. Microwave on high power for 6 minutes, until the outside begins to soften. Drain any liquid from the potatoes. Transfer to the baking pan.

4. Brush the potatoes with the olive oil and sprinkle with rosemary and pepper.

5. Bake for 25 minutes, or until tender. Serve immediately.

Per serving: 143 calories, 29 g carbohydrates, 2 g protein, 2 g fat, 2 g fiber

CROUTONS

Croutons made from scratch take little time and effort but are guaranteed to contain more fiber and less sodium than the store-bought variety. And they won't be hard as rocks!

PREPARATION TIME: 10 MINUTES   COOKING TIME: 10 MINUTES

Olive oil spray
4   slices stone-ground whole grain bread
2   tablespoons olive oil
2   tablespoons grated Parmesan cheese
1   clove garlic, crushed

1. Preheat the oven to 400°F. Lightly coat a baking sheet with oil spray.

2. Cut each slice of bread into 36 cubes. Toss the bread in a bowl with the oil, cheese, and garlic.

3. Spread out on theaf baking sheet. Bake 10 minutes, turning once.

4. Cool before using.

Per serving: 87 calories, 8 g carbohydrates, 2 g protein, 5 g fat, 1 g fiber

STIR-FRIED GREENS

Serves 8

The basic stir-fry technique for leafy greens can take on different ethnic flavor profiles. For instance, in place of the Asian seasonings in this version, go Italian with extra-virgin olive oil, garlic, and basil in place of peanut oil, ginger, and soy. But keep the garlic.

PREPARATION TIME: 15 MINUTES   **COOKING TIME: 5 MINUTES**

1½ pounds leafy greens
1   tablespoon peanut oil
½   tablespoon minced garlic
½   tablespoon minced fresh ginger
1   tablespoon soy sauce

1. Separate the leaves from the stalks. Rinse and pat dry. Chop coarsely.

2. Heat the oil in a wok over high heat. Add the greens and stir-fry for 2 minutes.

3. Add the garlic and ginger. Continue stir-frying for 1 to 2 minutes.

4. Sprinkle on the soy sauce and stir thoroughly. Serve immediately.

Per serving: 29 calories, 2 g carbohydrates, 2 g protein, 2 g fat, 1 g fiber

COOK'S TIP

Choose among bok choy, collard greens, chard, kale, or Savoy cabbage for the leafy greens.

SPINACH WITH HONEY-SOY DRESSING

Serves 6

The sweet nuttiness of toasted sesame and honey plays beautifully against the slightly bitter quality of the spinach.

PREPARATION TIME: 10 MINUTES   COOKING TIME: 2 MINUTES

1¼ pounds fresh spinach leaves
1   tablespoon pure floral honey, warmed
1   tablespoon soy sauce
1   teaspoon toasted sesame oil
1   teaspoon toasted sesame seeds

1. Wash, drain, and trim the spinach leaves. Place on a microwaveable dish. Cover the spinach and microwave on high for 2 minutes.

2. Remove from the microwave and carefully squeeze out all excess liquid. (Spinach will be very hot!)

3. In a screw-top jar, combine the honey, soy sauce, oil, and sesame seeds. Shake well.

4. Pour the dressing over the spinach and toss well. Serve immediately.

Per serving: 42 calories, 7 g carbohydrates, 3 g protein, 1 g fat, 3 g fiber

SLOW-ROASTED TOMATOES

Serves 6

This summer vegetable side dish also makes a terrific sauce for about 12 ounces of cooked short pasta such as rotini, penne, or shells.

PREPARATION TIME: 5 MINUTES   COOKING TIME: 25 MINUTES

2	pounds ripe tomatoes
1	tablespoon olive oil
1	tablespoon balsamic vinegar
	Freshly ground black pepper
½	tablespoon crushed garlic, or ½ teaspoon garlic powder
1	tablespoon prepared basil pesto

1. Preheat the oven to 350°F. Bring a large pot of water to a boil.

2. Place the tomatoes in a deep bowl. Cover them with the boiling water. Let stand 2 minutes. Drain and peel off the skins.

3. Cut the tomatoes in half and place, cut side up, in a large, shallow baking pan.

4. Combine the oil, vinegar, pepper, garlic, and pesto. Brush on the tomato halves.

5. Bake for 25 minutes, or until bubbling.

Per serving: 61 calories, 7 g carbohydrates, 2 g protein, 3 g fat, 2 g fiber

MEATLESS MEDITERRANEAN ROAST

Serves 6

Even the most dedicated carnivore will be forced to admit that hearty vegetables roasted to caramelized perfection are nearly as filling as meat.

PREPARATION TIME: 20 MINUTES   COOKING TIME: 40 MINUTES

1   pound sweet potatoes
3   medium zucchini
1   large red onion
2   red bell peppers
2   tablespoons olive oil
3   sprigs fresh rosemary
3   cloves garlic, halved
    Salt and freshly ground black pepper

1. Preheat the oven to 400°F.

2. Peel the sweet potatoes. Wash and pat dry. Cut into 1½" chunks. Place in a large mixing bowl.

3. Cut the zucchini into 1" thick round slices. Add to the mixing bowl.

4. Cut the onion into 8 wedges and add to mixing bowl.

5. Cut each pepper lengthwise into 12 slices. Add to the bowl.

6. Pour the olive oil over the vegetables. Add the rosemary and garlic. Season to taste with salt and black pepper. Toss to coat thoroughly.

7. Place the vegetables in a 13" x 9" baking pan. Bake for 40 minutes, or until browned and tender.

Per serving: 155 calories, 27 g carbohydrates, 3 g protein, 5 g fat, 5 g fiber

GRILLED GARLIC POTATOES

Serves 8

*Potato lovers rejoice! Eating on a low-GI plan doesn't mean giving up spuds—
it just means choosing the right kinds of spuds. Instead of high-GI white baking
potatoes, go for medium-GI new red potatoes and low-GI sweet potatoes.*

PREPARATION TIME: 10 MINUTES   COOKING TIME: 30 MINUTES

2   pounds red potatoes
2   pounds sweet potatoes
⅓   cup extra-virgin olive oil
6   cloves garlic, coarsely chopped
1   sprig fresh rosemary, stem removed and leaves chopped, or 1 tablespoon dried
    rosemary
    Salt and freshly ground black pepper
    Rosemary sprigs (optional)

1. Parboil the potatoes and sweet potatoes in plenty of boiling salted water
   for 20 minutes. Drain.

2. Preheat a lightly oiled grill or large heavy frying pan.

3. Mix the oil, garlic, rosemary, and a pinch each of salt and pepper in a large
   mixing bowl. Cut the potatoes into large chunks and toss in the oil mixture.

4. Cook on the grill or in the frying pan for 5 minutes, or until golden brown
   and crisp.

5. Serve hot in a large bowl with sprigs of fresh rosemary, if using.

Per serving: 226 calories, 29 g carbohydrates, 4 g protein, 10 g fat, 3 g fiber

SMASHED SWEET POTATO–CARROT PUREE   *Serves 5*

Don't save this recipe just for Thanksgiving dinner. Why not give your body the vitamin A, potassium, and fiber contained in both the sweet potatoes and carrots throughout the year—and delight your tastebuds at the same time?

PREPARATION TIME: 10 MINUTES   COOKING TIME: 1½ HOURS

	Canola oil spray
2	pounds sweet potatoes, ends trimmed
1	pound baby carrots
2	cups water
1	tablespoon brown sugar
3	tablespoons butter or reduced-fat margarine spread
	Salt and freshly ground black pepper
½	cup light sour cream
½	teaspoon grated nutmeg
1	tablespoon Cognac, port, or sherry wine

1. Preheat the oven to 350°F. Coat a 9" x 9" baking dish with oil spray.

2. Bake, steam, or microwave the sweet potatoes until tender. (Time will depend on the size of the potato and the cooking method. The longest cooking time is baking for 1 hour at 350°F.)

3. Place the carrots in a medium saucepan with the water, sugar, and butter or margarine. Season to taste with salt and pepper. Cook, uncovered, over medium heat for 30 minutes, or until tender, making sure all the water has evaporated. When cooked, place in the bowl of a food processor fitted with a metal blade.

4. When the sweet potatoes are cool enough to handle, scrape out the flesh with a spoon and add to the carrots in the processor.

5. Combine the sour cream, nutmeg, and Cognac, port, or sherry. Add to the vegetables and process until very smooth. Taste and add more salt and pepper, if desired. Transfer to the prepared baking dish.

6. Cover and bake until heated through. Serve steaming hot.

Per serving: 130 calories, 20 g carbohydrates, 2 g protein, 5 g fat, 3 g fiber

POTATO-GARLIC MASH

Serves 8

Garlic lovers, don't be shy. Go ahead and toss a few extra cloves into the pot.
Cooking the cloves whole tames any sharpness.

PREPARATION TIME: 10 MINUTES   COOKING TIME: 20 MINUTES

1½ pounds sweet potatoes
2   red potatoes (about 5 ounces each)
2   cloves garlic
    Salt
1   tablespoon olive oil
2   sprigs fresh oregano, chopped (stems removed if woody),
    or 1 tablespoon dried oregano
    Freshly ground black pepper

1. Peel and cut the potatoes into chunks. Place in hot water in a large saucepan, with the garlic and a large pinch of salt. Cook for 20 minutes, or until tender.

2. Drain and reserve ½ cup of the cooking water. Mash the drained potatoes and garlic with the oil and oregano, using a little of the reserved cooking water to moisten. Season to taste with salt and pepper.

Per serving: 187 calories, 31 g carbohydrates, 5 g protein, 5 g fat, 4 g fiber

MASHED CAULIFLOWER

Serves 5

It's not what you think it is (mashed potatoes), but it tastes at least as good. Watch the kids lap up this veggie and ask for seconds!

PREPARATION TIME: 5 MINUTES   COOKING TIME: 18 MINUTES

1	medium head cauliflower (approximately 6 cups florets)
1	tablespoon reduced-fat margarine spread or light butter
¾	cup thinly sliced leeks
1	clove garlic, minced
	Salt
1–2	tablespoons grated Parmesan cheese

1. Break or cut the cauliflower into small florets. Place in a vegetable steamer in a saucepan with 1" of water.

2. Cook over medium–high heat for 10 to 15 minutes, until tender. Cooking time will depend on the size of the florets.

3. While the cauliflower is steaming, melt the margarine or butter in a small skillet. Add the leeks and cook for 3 minutes. When they start browning, add the garlic and cook 1 minute. Remove from heat. Salt to taste.

4. Place all the vegetables in a food processor fitted with a metal blade. Process for 45 seconds, or until a smooth puree results.

5. Transfer to a serving dish. Sprinkle with cheese. Serve hot.

Per serving: 70 calories, 11 g carbohydrates, 4 g protein, 2 g fat, 6 g fiber

 **ACTIVITY TIP**

Gardening and do-it-yourself repairs are great ways to be more active at home when weather permits. Otherwise, do some spring cleaning (any time of the year) inside the house for a total body workout.

SWEET POTATOES IN GINGER, CAYENNE, AND PEANUT SAUCE

(photo on page 139) *Serves 6*

Savor the flavor of this robust vegetarian dish and serve with a side dish of basmati rice, or as the carb accompaniment to meat or fish.

PREPARATION TIME: 20 MINUTES   COOKING TIME: 45 MINUTES

1 tablespoon olive oil	1 can (15½ ounces) diced tomatoes
1 large onion, coarsely chopped	1 cup pineapple juice
4 cloves garlic, minced	½ cup smooth peanut butter
2" piece fresh ginger, grated	Freshly ground black pepper
3 small sweet potatoes, cubed (6 cups)	1 carrot, grated
	1 raw beet, grated
1 pound cabbage, coarsely chopped	1 banana, sliced
2 teaspoons paprika	Juice of 1 lime
1 teaspoon cayenne pepper	2 tablespoons chopped cilantro leaves

1. Heat the oil in a large, heavy-based saucepan over medium heat and cook the onion, garlic, and ginger for 2 minutes. Add the sweet potatoes and cabbage. When the vegetables start to soften, add the paprika and cayenne. Stir to coat the vegetables in the spices. Add the tomatoes and pineapple juice. Cover and simmer for 35 to 40 minutes, or until the vegetables are soft.

2. Stir in the peanut butter until well combined, adding a little water if it is too thick. Season with black pepper, then transfer to serving bowls.

3. Toss the carrot, beet, and banana in the lime juice and scatter over the vegetables. Garnish with cilantro.

Per serving: 355 calories, 39 g carbohydrates, 13 g protein, 17 g fat, 11 g fiber

Recipe: Chris and Carolyn Caldicott, World Food Café

CHICKPEA, TOMATO, AND EGGPLANT

Serves 8

This marvelous Mediterranean dish may be served with low-GI crusty bread as an entrée or as a side dish to a light main course such as grilled fish.

PREPARATION TIME: 5 MINUTES   COOKING TIME: 30 MINUTES

- 2   tablespoons olive oil
- 6   Italian eggplants, diced
- 2   large onions, diced
- 4   cloves garlic, minced
- ½   teaspoon ground cumin
- ½   teaspoon ground cinnamon
- ½   teaspoon ground coriander
-     Salt and freshly ground black pepper
- 2   cans (28 ounces each) whole peeled tomatoes
- 1   can (15 ounces) chickpeas, rinsed and drained

1. Heat the oil in a large, heavy frying pan, and gently cook the eggplants, onions, garlic, cumin, cinnamon, and coriander over a moderate heat for 10 minutes, stirring occasionally.

2. Season to taste with salt and pepper. Add the tomatoes (with juice), breaking them up with a wooden spoon. Add the chickpeas, cover, and simmer for 20 minutes.

Per serving: 137 calories, 5 g protein, 15 g carbohydrates, 6 g fat, 6 g fiber

COOK'S TIP

Italian eggplants, also known as baby eggplants, are tinier versions of the standard large variety. The skin and flesh are more delicate.

STUFFED EGGPLANT

Serves 4

Vegetables are gifts to smart low-GI eaters. Most are so low in carbohydrates that they don't spike blood sugar levels, but they do deliver pretty packages chock-full of fiber, vitamins, and minerals.

PREPARATION TIME: 10 MINUTES   COOKING TIME: 1 HOUR

½ cup pearl barley

3 cups water

2 medium eggplants, halved lengthwise
Salt

2 medium ripe tomatoes, finely diced

6 shallots, finely sliced

2 sprigs fresh oregano, or 1 teaspoon dried oregano

2 sprigs fresh marjoram, or 1 teaspoon dried marjoram

2 sprigs fresh thyme, or 1 teaspoon dried thyme

2 tablespoons olive oil

2 large cloves garlic, finely chopped

1 cup grated Parmesan cheese
Freshly ground black pepper
Extra sprigs fresh oregano, marjoram, or thyme

1. Preheat the oven to 350°F. Coat a baking dish (large enough to hold the eggplant halves in a single layer) with canola oil spray. Set aside.

2. Simmer the barley, covered, in the water for 30 minutes.

3. Meanwhile, scoop out the flesh of the eggplants, leaving a ½" shell. Sprinkle the shell with salt and turn upside down on paper towels to drain off the bitter juices. Dice the eggplant flesh. Set aside.

4. Combine the tomatoes, shallots, oregano, marjoram, and thyme.

5. Heat the oil in a large, heavy frying pan. Add the reserved diced eggplant and the garlic. Cook until the eggplant browns. Fold in the tomato mixture, barley, and cheese. Season to taste with salt and pepper.

6. Rinse the eggplant shells out with cold water and pat dry. Fill with the stuffing and bake for 30 minutes, or until tender.

7. Garnish with sprigs of fresh herbs and serve hot.

Per serving: 284 calories, 22 g carbohydrates, 12 g protein, 16 g fat, 8 g fiber

TUSCAN-STYLE BEANS WITH TOMATOES AND SAGE

(photo on page 140)   *Serves 4*

Tuscan beans can be served as a course on their own—either hot or cold—or as an accompaniment to meat dishes. Provide plenty of crusty sourdough bread to mop up the juices.

PREPARATION TIME: 15 MINUTES   COOKING TIME: 25 MINUTES

1   cup shelled fresh or frozen fava beans
2   teaspoons extra-virgin olive oil
2   cloves garlic, minced
1   can (14 ounces) Italian peeled tomatoes, chopped
1   can (14 ounces) cannellini beans, rinsed and drained
1½ teaspoons finely chopped sage, or ½ teaspoon dried sage
    Freshly ground black pepper

1. Bring a saucepan of water to a boil and blanch the fava beans in boiling water for 3 minutes. Drain and refresh under cold running water. Peel the outer skins from the beans when they are cool enough to handle.

2. Heat the oil in a saucepan over low heat and cook the garlic for 2 minutes. Add the tomatoes, beans, and sage. Simmer, covered, for 10 minutes. Stir in the fava beans and cook gently for 5 to 10 minutes, or until tender. Season to taste with pepper.

Per serving: 138 calories, 16 g carbohydrates, 8 g protein, 3 g fat, 7 g fiber

•
COOK'S TIP

Sage has a lovely fresh aroma and flavor, but it is quite intense. Use only 2 or 3 leaves so as not to overpower the other flavors in the dish. Dried sage (and dried herbs in general) has a more intense, concentrated flavor than fresh sage, so you only need to use about half the amount.

LIMA BEAN AND CHERRY TOMATO STEW

(photo on page 141)   *Serves 4*

This quick and easy stew makes a simple side dish to serve with meat or chicken, or enjoy as a light meal in itself. Top with pitted black olives, if you wish.

PREPARATION TIME: 20 MINUTES   COOKING TIME: 15 MINUTES

1	tablespoon olive oil
1	red onion, chopped
1	red bell pepper, thinly sliced
1	yellow bell pepper, thinly sliced
2	cloves garlic, minced (or more to taste)
1"	piece fresh ginger, grated
20	cherry tomatoes, halved
	Pinch of saffron threads
½	teaspoon sugar
2	cans (14 ounces each) lima beans, rinsed and drained
1	teaspoon paprika
½	teaspoon ground cinnamon
	Freshly ground black pepper
½	small bunch flat-leaf parsley, coarsely chopped
2	small pitas, warmed and sliced (optional)

1. Heat the oil in a large frying pan over medium heat. Add the onion, peppers, garlic, and ginger. Cook for 10 minutes, or until the onions are golden and soft. Stir in the tomatoes, saffron, and sugar. Cook for 5 minutes.

2. When the tomatoes are heated through, add the lima beans, paprika, and cinnamon. Stir gently. Season to taste with black pepper. Sprinkle on the parsley. Serve with pita for mopping up the juices, if desired.

Per serving: 95 calories, 8 g carbohydrates, 5 g protein, 5 g fat, 5 g fiber

OLD-WORLD VEGETABLE STEW

Serves 10

This versatile mixture of vegetables and herbs will enhance the flavors of rice, pasta, couscous, or pita. It mixes so well with so many staples, it can easily become a staple itself!

PREPARATION TIME: 12 MINUTES   COOKING TIME: 35 MINUTES

2	tablespoons olive oil
2	medium onions, thickly sliced
1	large clove garlic, minced
2	large yellow squash or zucchini, thickly sliced
1	medium eggplant (approximately 12 ounces), unpeeled and cubed
1	medium red bell pepper, sliced into 2" strips
1	medium green bell pepper, sliced into 2" strips
4	medium tomatoes, peeled and seeded, cut into eighths, or 1 can (14½ ounces) diced tomatoes, drained
1	jar (12 ounces) marinated artichoke hearts, drained and quartered
1	tablespoon fresh thyme or ½ teaspoon dried
1	tablespoon fresh oregano or ½ teaspoon dried
2	tablespoons fresh basil, minced, or ½ teaspoon dried
2	tablespoons balsamic vinegar
½	teaspoon freshly ground black pepper
2	tablespoons parsley, finely chopped

1. Heat the oil in a large saucepan. Add the onions and garlic. Cook over low heat until onions are soft.

2. Add the squash, eggplant, and peppers. Cook over medium heat for 5 minutes, stirring frequently.

3. Add the tomatoes, artichoke hearts, thyme, oregano, and basil. Mix well. Cover and simmer for 20 minutes, stirring frequently.

4. Stir in the vinegar. Cook, uncovered, for 5 minutes, stirring frequently.

5. Add the black pepper and parsley and mix thoroughly. May be served hot or at room temperature.

Per serving: 101 calories, 15 g carbohydrates, 1 g protein, 6 g fat, 4 g fiber

CRUNCHY-TOPPED LENTIL LOAF

Serves 6

Lentils are one of nature's superfoods—rich in protein, fiber, and B vitamins. All colors and types have a similar low GI. Serve this lentil loaf with a spicy tomato salsa, or pack and take on a picnic.

PREPARATION TIME: 20 MINUTES   COOKING TIME: 1 HOUR 20 MINUTES

COOLING TIME: 10 MINUTES

⅓ cup red lentils
½ cup green lentils
1½ cups chicken broth
1 bay leaf
1 teaspoon olive oil
1 onion, finely chopped
1 clove garlic, minced
4 ounces mushrooms, finely chopped
½ red bell pepper, finely chopped
½ yellow bell pepper, finely chopped
1½ cups loosely packed fresh whole grain bread crumbs
2 eggs, lightly beaten
   Grated peel and juice of ½ lemon
2 tablespoons chopped cilantro leaves
   Freshly ground black pepper

1. Wash the lentils and put into a large saucepan with the broth and bay leaf. Bring to a boil, then reduce the heat and simmer for 20 to 30 minutes, or until the lentils are soft and all the liquid is absorbed.

2. Preheat the oven to 350°F. Line an 8" x 4" x 3" loaf pan with nonstick parchment paper.

3. Heat the oil in a saucepan or large deep frying pan. Cook the onion and garlic for 2 minutes, or until the onion is soft. Add the mushrooms and peppers and cook for 2 minutes.

4. Remove the bay leaf from the lentils and discard. Add the lentil mixture to the pan, along with the bread crumbs (reserving 3 tablespoons of the bread crumbs), eggs, lemon peel and juice, and cilantro. Season to taste with black pepper and mix well. The mixture should be soft, but not runny.

5. Spoon the lentil mixture into the prepared pan, sprinkle the reserved bread crumbs over the top, and bake for 35 to 40 minutes, or until firm to the touch. Remove from the oven and allow to cool in the pan for 10 minutes before turning out.

Per serving: 165 calories, 19 g carbohydrates, 12 g protein, 4 g fat, 6 g fiber

Source: Isobel McMillan

MUNG BEAN DHAL

Serves 4

In India, dhal is a broad cooking term that refers to any cooked legume dish. Filling and flavorful, these preparations fall on the favorable low end of the GI index.

PREPARATION TIME: 10 MINUTES   COOKING TIME: 1 HOUR

1	cup dried whole mung beans
¼	teaspoon turmeric
½	teaspoon salt
1	tablespoon olive oil
½	onion, chopped
2	cloves garlic, minced
1–2	green chiles, finely chopped (remove the seeds for a milder taste)
1	bunch cilantro, leaves picked and chopped

1. Cover the beans with 3½ cups water and bring to a boil. Reduce the heat. Add the turmeric. Simmer for 40 to 50 minutes, or until the beans are tender. Add the salt and turn off the heat.

2. Heat the oil in a small nonstick frying pan over medium heat and cook the onion and garlic until brown. Add the chiles and fry for 30 seconds, then add to the saucepan with the beans. Cover and simmer for around 10 minutes, so the flavors can blend. Before serving, stir in the cilantro.

Per serving: 200 calories, 29 g carbohydrates, 11 g protein, 5 g fat, 8 g fiber

Recipe: Isobel McMillan

Chapter 7

PASTA AND GRAINS

Tired of high-protein diets that leave you starved for the comfort of pasta and the rice dishes you love? You'll find them here, only prepared the low-GI way so they fit beautifully into a healthy eating plan. When you begin with low-GI grains and rice, and cook them in the best low-GI methods, the results are nothing short of fabulous. For example, genuine Italian-style semolina pasta is made from a higher-protein wheat, so its GI is lower than soft wheat pasta. Then if it's cooked al dente, so it retains some "bite," there is less cooking time for the flour starches to swell. Less swelling translates into a lower GI—and dinners that everybody will love…such as Bowties with Creamed Mushrooms, Penne Pasta with Roasted Vegetables and Feta, Spinach and Ricotta Cannelloni, Mediterranean Lasagna, Couscous Salad, Saffron Pilaf, and more.

TORTELLINI AND HAM SALAD

Serves 10

There are unlimited variations to this basic recipe to suit anyone's preferred tastes. It can be prepared ahead of time and works well for leftovers, too. The unusually high fat content comes primarily from the heart-healthy olive oil.

PREPARATION TIME: 10 MINUTES

3	tablespoons extra-virgin olive oil
2	tablespoons red wine vinegar
1	pound cheese tortellini, cooked and drained
6	cups fresh broccoli florets, cooked
2	red bell peppers, julienned
2	cans (14 ounces each) artichoke hearts, drained and quartered
4	ounces low-sodium ham, cut into 2" strips
½	cup coarsely chopped red onion

1. Combine the oil and vinegar in a small jar. Shake well.

2. In a large serving bowl, combine the tortellini, broccoli, peppers, artichokes, ham, and onion. Pour in the dressing and toss well. Serve at room temperature.

Per serving: 208 calories, 23 g carbohydrates, 8 g protein, 8 g fat, 3 g fiber

COOK'S TIPS

Use frozen broccoli to save time. Microwave on high power for 5 minutes. Use 1½ cups roasted peppers from a jar, if preferred.

Substitute turkey or grilled chicken breast for the ham, if preferred.

RED, WHITE, AND GREEN TORTELLINI SALAD   *Serves 9*

*Tortellini hold their shape well, making this an appealing salad
to pack into brown bag lunches.*

PREPARATION TIME: 20 MINUTES

DRESSING:

⅓   cup olive oil

2   tablespoons red wine vinegar

1   tablespoon finely chopped fresh parsley

¼   teaspoon dried Italian herb seasoning

SALAD:

8   ounces cheese tortellini, cooked, cooled

8   ounces broccoli florets, steamed, cooled

1   large red bell pepper, julienned

2   ounces part-skim mozzarella cheese, cubed

2   tablespoons pine nuts, toasted

2   tablespoons grated Parmesan cheese

1   scallion, thinly sliced on diagonal
    Salt and freshly ground black pepper

1. To make the dressing: In a lidded jar, combine the oil, vinegar, parsley,
and herb seasoning. Shake well to mix.

2. To make the salad: In a large serving bowl, combine the tortellini, broccoli,
bell pepper, mozzarella, pine nuts, Parmesan, and scallion. Toss well. Season to
taste with salt and black pepper. Serve at room temperature or chilled.

Per serving: 202 calories, 16 g carbohydrates, 6 g protein, 13 g fat, 2 g fiber

 **COOK'S TIP**

To toast pine nuts (or any nuts), place in a dry heavy skillet.
Cook over medium heat, stirring frequently, for 5 minutes, or
until golden brown.

SPAGHETTI WITH SUMMER TOMATOES AND BASIL

Serves 4

Surprise! Here's a refreshing salad that serves as a sauce for spaghetti. This recipe is adapted from a small trattoria in the heart of Rome, famous for this dish.

PREPARATION TIME: 6 MINUTES   COOKING TIME: 10 MINUTES

- 1 tablespoon salt + extra to taste
- 6 ounces spaghetti
- 2 tablespoons olive oil
- 1 pound tomatoes-on-the-vine, seeds removed, sliced into bite-sized pieces
- 6 ounces fresh mozzarella cheese, cut into bite-sized cubes
- 20 fresh basil leaves, torn into small pieces

1. Bring a large pot of water to a rolling boil. Add the salt and the pasta. Stir until all strands are completely submerged. When the water returns to a boil, cook the pasta, uncovered, for 8 minutes, stirring occasionally. Do not overcook.

2. Drain the pasta and return it to the pot. Toss with the oil. Cool slightly.

3. Divide the pasta equally into 4 bowls. In each bowl, on top of the pasta, starting at the outer rim, form a large circle of tomatoes. Then, inside that, form a circle of the cheese cubes. In the center, place a small mound of basil. Sprinkle salt over the sauce, if desired. Serve immediately.

Per serving: 364 calories, 38 g carbohydrates, 15 g protein, 17 g fat, 2 g fiber

 **COOK'S TIP**

Tomatoes should be ripe but firm.

JUST-PLAIN-GOOD PASTA

Serves 4

If you like natural, earthy flavors, this simple recipe is for you. If you replace half of the spinach with arugula, the dish will have an appealing peppery bite.

PREPARATION TIME: 6 MINUTES   COOKING TIME: 12 MINUTES

- 1   tablespoon coarse salt
- 6   ounces linguine
- 10 ounces fresh spinach leaves, stems removed
    Olive oil spray
- 8   ounces mushrooms, sliced
- 1   jar (6 ounces) marinated artichoke hearts, drained and thinly sliced
- 6   whole no-salt-added canned tomatoes, cut into thin strips
- 12 large black olives, pitted and halved lengthwise
- 1   tablespoon olive oil
- ⅛   teaspoon garlic powder, or 2 cloves garlic, minced

1. Bring a large pot of water to a rolling boil. Add the salt and pasta. Stir until all strands are completely submerged. When the water returns to a boil, cook the pasta, uncovered, for 8 minutes, stirring occasionally. Do not overcook.

2. While the pasta is cooking, place the spinach in a strainer and rinse under cold water. Place the spinach in a large skillet with just the water clinging to its leaves. Cover and cook over medium heat for a few minutes, until the leaves are wilted. Remove from the pan and drain.

3. Away from the flame, coat the same pan with oil spray, add the mushrooms, and cook for 3 minutes.

4. Return the spinach to the pan and add the artichokes, tomatoes, and olives. Mix well. Drizzle the olive oil over the vegetables and stir.

5. When the pasta is cooked, drain well and add to the vegetables in the pan. Sprinkle on the garlic powder or minced garlic. Toss thoroughly. Serve immediately.

Per serving: 303 calories, 51 g carbohydrates, 10 g protein, 9 g fat, 6 g fiber

SPAGHETTI AGLIO E OLIO DELUXE

This "Garlic and Oil" pasta allows you to make a wholesome, nutritious dish from pantry staples.

PREPARATION TIME: 4 MINUTES   COOKING TIME: 13 MINUTES

2	tablespoons pine nuts (½ ounce)
8	ounces spaghetti
2	tablespoons extra-virgin olive oil
2–3	cloves garlic, minced
⅓	cup grated Parmesan cheese
	Freshly ground black pepper
	Red-pepper flakes (optional)

1. Spread the pine nuts in a small skillet. Toast on low heat for 5 minutes, then set aside to cool.

2. Cook the pasta according to the package directions.

3. While the pasta is cooking, heat the oil in a small, heavy saucepan over low heat. Add the garlic and cook for 2 to 3 minutes, stirring frequently to prevent burning. Remove the saucepan from the heat.

4. When the pasta is cooked, drain and return it to the pot. Drizzle the oil and garlic over the pasta and mix thoroughly. Add the cheese and season with black pepper to taste, mixing well.

5. Distribute the pasta among 4 plates and top with pine nuts, and pepper flakes, if desired. Serve immediately.

Per serving: 319 calories, 42 g carbohydrates, 11 protein, 12 g fat, 2 g fiber

BOWTIES WITH CREAMED MUSHROOMS

Serves 6

The creamy texture and the blend of the earthy flavors from the mushrooms and the brandy make this dish an absolute gourmet pleasure. And nobody would guess that it is low in fat!

PREPARATION TIME: 5 MINUTES   COOKING TIME: 20 MINUTES

2 tablespoons reduced-fat margarine spread or butter, divided
10 ounces mushrooms, sliced
¼ cup brandy or Marsala
½ cup vegetable broth (optional)
10 ounces bowtie pasta
½ cup evaporated fat-free milk
4 wedges light spreadable cheese
¼ cup grated Parmesan cheese
   Grated nutmeg (optional)

1. Melt 1 tablespoon of margarine or butter in a nonstick skillet. Add the mushrooms and the brandy or Marsala. Cook over high heat for 2 minutes, until the alcohol has evaporated. Cover and simmer for 20 minutes, adding vegetable broth, if needed, to moisten.

2. Meanwhile, cook the pasta according to the package directions.

3. While the pasta is cooking, mix the milk, spreadable cheese, and Parmesan in a wide pan or Dutch oven. Simmer, stirring, for 5 minutes, or until a smooth cream forms.

4. Drain the cooked pasta. Add to the cream mixture. Add the mushroom mixture. Toss well. Season with a sprinkle of nutmeg, if desired. Serve immediately.

Per serving: 269 calories, 41 g carbohydrates, 11 g protein, 6 g fat, 2 g fiber

 **COOK'S TIP**

For the mushrooms, use your favorite kind or even a blend of several kinds such as button, morels, shiitake, or chanterelles. Wedges of spreadable cheese, such as Laughing Cow or Swiss Knight, are sold in the specialty cheese case in supermarkets.

VEGETABLE AND SESAME NOODLE STIR-FRY

Serves 4

This quick supper tastes better than fatty, salty carry-out fare and is a good source of beneficial omega-3 fatty acids.

PREPARATION TIME: 25 MINUTES   COOKING TIME: 4 MINUTES

2   cups fresh linguine noodles
1   tablespoon canola oil
1   cup snow peas, coarsely chopped
1   cup green bell pepper, coarsely chopped
1   cup drained and thinly sliced baby corn
¼   cup thinly sliced shallots
1   tablespoon minced garlic
1   teaspoon minced fresh ginger
2   tablespoons teriyaki sauce
1   tablespoon toasted sesame oil
    Salt

1. Place the noodles in a large bowl and cover with boiling water. Set aside.

2. Heat the canola oil in a nonstick wok or large skillet over low heat. Increase the heat and add the snow peas, pepper, corn, shallots, garlic, and ginger. Stir-fry for 3 minutes.

3. Thoroughly drain the noodles and add to the wok. Drizzle on the teriyaki sauce and sesame oil. Season to taste with salt. Toss well. Stir-fry for 1 minute. Serve immediately.

Per serving: 162 calories, 42 g carbohydrates, 9 g protein, 9 g fat, 2 g fiber

ANGEL HAIR PASTA WITH GRILLED VEGETABLES

Serves 4

Delicate angel hair pasta cooks in a flash, but other kinds can also be used. Try linguine or thin spaghetti.

PREPARATION TIME: 15 MINUTES   COOKING TIME: 15 MINUTES

1	tablespoon olive oil
2	small Italian eggplants, cut in half lengthwise
2	large bell peppers, cut into thick strips
6	plum tomatoes, cut in half lengthwise
1	red onion, thickly sliced
	Salt and freshly ground black pepper
1	can (15 ounces) light red kidney beans, rinsed and drained
4	cloves garlic, coarsely chopped
8	ounces angel hair pasta
½	bunch basil leaves, torn

1. Brush a grill rack with the oil. Preheat the grill. Place the eggplants, bell peppers, tomatoes, and onion on the rack. Season to taste with salt and black pepper. Cook until the vegetables are golden brown, turning occasionally.

2. Transfer to a large platter. Add the beans and garlic. Toss to mix.

3. Meanwhile, bring a large pot of salted water to the boil. Cook the pasta, uncovered, for 4 to 5 minutes, or until al dente. Drain.

4. Transfer the pasta to the platter. Toss gently. Scatter on the basil leaves. Serve hot.

Per serving: 362 calories, 65 g carbohydrates, 14 g protein, 7 g fat, 11 g fiber

 COOK'S TIP

Italian eggplants, also known as baby eggplants, are tinier versions of the standard large variety. The skin and flesh are more delicate.

PENNE PASTA WITH ROASTED VEGETABLES AND FETA

Serves 4

*The pleasing briny tang of feta cheese lends a Greek flavor to this dish.
If you like, replace the sweet potatoes with zucchini or yellow summer squash.*

PREPARATION TIME: 20 MINUTES   COOKING TIME: 45 MINUTES

6 ounces sweet potato, cut into ¾" chunks
1 small eggplant, cut into ¾" chunks
1 red bell pepper, cut into 1¼" pieces
2 plum tomatoes, quartered lengthwise
1 small red onion, cut into wedges
  Olive oil spray
10 ounces penne pasta
3½ ounces reduced-fat feta cheese, crumbled
¼ cup basil leaves, shredded
1 small clove garlic, crushed (optional)

1. Preheat the oven to 350°F.

2. Spread the sweet potato, eggplant, pepper, tomatoes, and onion on 2 large baking sheets with sides. Coat lightly with oil spray. Toss the vegetables to coat. Roast for 45 minutes, or until tender and browned.

3. When the vegetables are almost ready, cook the pasta in a large saucepan of boiling water, according to the package directions, until al dente. Drain well and return to the pan.

4. Add the vegetables, feta, basil, and garlic, if using. Toss to combine. Serve immediately.

Per serving: 393 calories, 65 g carbohydrates, 18 g protein, 6 g fat, 4 g fiber

COOK'S TIP

Any short shaped pasta, such as rotini, butterflies, and shells, will work well in this recipe. Cooking time may vary with different thicknesses.

SPAGHETTI WITH STEAMED GREENS

Serves 6

The rich, nutty flavor of toasted sesame oil, popular in many Asian styles of cooking, is used as a flavorful condiment.

PREPARATION TIME: 5 MINUTES   COOKING TIME: 13 MINUTES

1	pound spaghetti
4	large zucchini, cut into lengthwise matchsticks
12	snow peas
1	tablespoon lemon juice
2	tablespoons olive oil
1	clove garlic, crushed
1	cup (packed) baby spinach leaves
8	basil leaves, torn
	Salt and freshly ground black pepper
1	tablespoon toasted sesame oil
2	tablespoons sesame seeds, toasted

1. Boil the spaghetti in a large pot of lightly salted water for 13 minutes, or until tender.

2. Meanwhile, steam the zucchini and peas until just softened and still bright green.

3. On a large platter, combine the lemon juice, olive oil, and garlic.

4. Drain the spaghetti and add to the platter. Toss with the vegetables, dressing, spinach, and basil leaves. Season to taste with salt and pepper. Drizzle with sesame oil and sprinkle with sesame seeds. Serve hot.

Per serving: 352 calories, 47 g carbohydrates, 12 g protein, 13 g fat, 15 g fiber

 COOK'S TIP

To toast sesame seeds, add to a small heated frying pan and toss continually until they begin to turn a light golden brown. Remove immediately to prevent burning, and cool.

RIDGED PENNE WITH CAULIFLOWER AND PANCETTA

(*photo on page 142*)

Serves 4

In southern Italy, traditional dishes such as this one, based on vegetables and grains, are naturally low on the GI index. Its simplicity and gutsy flavors are just right.

PREPARATION TIME: 5 MINUTES   COOKING TIME: 20 MINUTES

6   cups cauliflower florets
14 ounces dried ridged penne pasta
1   tablespoon olive oil
4½ ounces pancetta, finely diced
1   small red chile, finely chopped
1¼ cups aged Pecorino Romano or Parmesan cheese, grated
2   tablespoons coarsely chopped parsley
1   teaspoon salt

1. Cook the cauliflower in a large pot of boiling salted water for 10 minutes. Add the pasta. Cook for 8 minutes or until the cauliflower is tender and the pasta is al dente.

2. Meanwhile, heat the oil in a frying pan. Add the pancetta and chile and fry for 3 minutes, or until starting to brown.

3. Drain the pasta and cauliflower and place on a large serving plate or in individual bowls. Sprinkle with the cheese, pancetta, and chile. Add the parsley and salt. Mix well in the bowl before serving.

Per serving: 510 calories, 71 g carbohydrates, 24 g protein, 14 g fat, 6 g fiber

Recipe: Antonio Carluccio

 **ACTIVITY TIP**

Become an active person where you see every moment as an opportunity for movement. Be the person who offers to run an errand, wash the car, or walk to the local store. Every moment of activity counts in the long run.

SPINACH AND RICOTTA CANNELLONI

Serves 4

This delicious dinner dish is easy to assemble using today's wonderful convenience foods. Buy a really good-quality, ready-to-serve tomato sauce or make your own favorite tomato sauce, if you have the time.

PREPARATION TIME: 15 MINUTES   COOKING TIME: 30 MINUTES

Olive oil spray
1 package (10½ ounces) frozen spinach, thawed
1 container (15 ounces) reduced-fat ricotta cheese
2 tablespoons pine nuts, toasted (see Cook's Tip, page 187)

¼ teaspoon grated nutmeg
⅓ cup finely grated Parmesan cheese, divided
4 fresh lasagna sheets (12" x 6")
1¼ cups ready-to-serve tomato pasta sauce
Freshly ground black pepper
Torn basil leaves

1. Preheat the oven to 350°F. Coat a small baking dish with oil spray. Set aside. Put the spinach in a colander and squeeze out the excess liquid.

2. In a large bowl, combine the ricotta, pine nuts, nutmeg, and half the Parmesan. Mix with a wooden spoon. Lay one sheet of lasagna on a work surface and spoon a quarter of the ricotta mixture along the long edge of the sheet. Roll lengthwise to make a long sausage shape and place into the prepared dish, cutting the lasagna to fit if necessary. Repeat with the remaining ricotta mixture and lasagna sheets.

3. Spoon the pasta sauce over the cannelloni. Season to taste with pepper. Cover with aluminum foil. Bake for 25 to 30 minutes, or until the pasta is tender and the sauce is bubbling.

4. Serve with any extra tomato sauce over the top. Sprinkle with the remaining Parmesan and scatter on the basil.

Per serving: 470 calories, 49 g carbohydrates, 25 g protein, 18 g fat, 7 g fiber

LENTIL AND RICOTTA CANNELLONI

Serves 6

For advance preparation, cool the filling after cooking and prepare the recipe through step 5. Cover tightly with plastic wrap and refrigerate for up to 24 hours. To serve, remove the plastic wrap and bake for 35 to 40 minutes.

PREPARATION TIME: 30 MINUTES   COOKING TIME: 1 HOUR

2 teaspoons olive oil	4 fresh lasagna sheets (12" x 6")
1 small onion, finely chopped	1¾ cups reduced-fat ricotta cheese
2 cloves garlic, crushed	Pinch of grated nutmeg
1 can (14 ounces) chopped tomatoes	2 cups ready-to-serve tomato pasta sauce, divided
1 cup vegetable broth	½ cup grated reduced-fat Cheddar cheese
1 cup red lentils	
1 bunch spinach, stems trimmed	
Salt and freshly ground black pepper	

1. Preheat the oven to 400°F.

2. Heat the oil in a large saucepan. Add the onion and cook over low heat for 5 minutes, until soft. Add the garlic and stir for 30 seconds. Add the tomatoes, broth, and lentils. Bring to a boil. Reduce the heat to low and simmer for 20 minutes, covered, until the lentils are tender. Stir occasionally to prevent the mixture from sticking to the bottom of the pan.

3. Coarsely chop the spinach leaves and stir into the lentil mixture to wilt. Season to taste with salt and pepper. Cool to room temperature.

4. Meanwhile, cut each lasagna sheet crossways into three pieces. Mash the ricotta in a bowl with nutmeg until smooth. Then spread 1 cup of the tomato sauce over the bottom of a large lasagna dish.

5. Spread ¼ cup of the lentil mixture along the center of a lasagna piece. Spoon 1 heaping tablespoon of the ricotta mixture over the lentil mixture. Roll up to enclose, and place seam side down in the lasagna dish. Repeat with the remaining ingredients, fitting them snugly into the dish. Pour the remaining tomato sauce on top to cover. Sprinkle with the Cheddar.

6. Bake for 35 minutes, or until the pasta is tender.

Per serving: 339 calories, 33 g carbohydrates, 25 g protein, 11.5 g fat, 7 g fiber

MEDITERRANEAN LASAGNA

Serves 8

A crisp green salad in vinaigrette is not only a tasty side dish, it can actually help to lower blood sugar when eaten during a typical meal. Red wine vinegar, lemon juice, other acidic dressings may slow stomach emptying and carbohydrate digestion.

PREPARATION TIME: 15 MINUTES   COOKING TIME: 1 HOUR 50 MINUTES

2   tablespoons olive oil, divided
2   onions, chopped
4   cloves garlic, chopped
1   pound lean ground beef
1   can (28 ounces) whole tomatoes
1   cup water
½   cup tomato paste
½   bunch fresh oregano, leaves chopped

Salt and freshly ground black pepper
2   eggplants, cut into 1" slices
8   ounces frozen chopped leaf spinach, thawed
5   large oven-ready lasagna sheets
1   teaspoon grated nutmeg
3   ounces low-fat Cheddar cheese, grated

1. Preheat the oven to 350°F.

2. Heat 1 tablespoon oil in a large heavy saucepan over moderate heat. Add the onions and garlic and cook, stirring occasionally, for 3 minutes.

3. Add the meat and cook until it turns brown. Then add the tomatoes with juice, water, tomato paste, and oregano. Season to taste with salt and pepper. Cook, stirring occasionally, for 30 minutes.

4. Brush the eggplant slices with the remaining 1 tablespoon oil. Grill or broil until browned on each side.

5. Using a rectangular baking dish (approximately 13" x 9"), layer the ingredients. Start with half the meat sauce, then 2½ sheets of lasagna, half the eggplant slices, and all the spinach. Sprinkle with the nutmeg. Season to taste with salt and pepper. Continue layering with, in order, the remaining lasagna, eggplant slices, and meat sauce, and top with the grated cheese.

6. Bake for 40 to 45 minutes, or until golden and bubbling.

Per serving: 268 calories, 24 g carbohydrates, 21 g protein, 10 g fat, 6 g fiber

ROASTED VEGETABLE AND MUSHROOM LASAGNA

Serves 8

Soft layers of butternut squash, sweet potato, and mushrooms, with a creamy ricotta sauce, make this lasagna a memorable meal to share with family and friends.

PREPARATION TIME: 30 MINUTES   COOKING TIME: 1 HOUR   STANDING TIME: 5 MINUTES

3 cups (14 ounces) butternut squash, cut into ½" cubes

3 cups (14 ounces) sweet potato, cut into ½" cubes

2 large sprigs rosemary

3 cloves garlic, minced
Freshly ground black pepper
Olive oil spray

4 cups fat-free milk

1 large onion, sliced

¼ cup flour

1¼ cups ricotta cheese

9 ounces lasagna sheets

2 cups (7 ounces) mushrooms, sliced

1 scallion, sliced

½ cup reduced-fat Cheddar cheese, shredded

1. Preheat the oven to 400°F.

2. In a bowl, combine the squash, sweet potato, rosemary, and garlic. Season to taste with pepper. Lightly coat a baking sheet with oil spray. Place the vegetables on the sheet. Bake for 20 minutes, or until tender.

3. In a saucepan, combine the milk and onion over medium heat. Heat until just below boiling point. Turn off the heat and let sit for 10 minutes. Mix the flour with a little water, then add to the milk, bring to a simmer, and cook, stirring, for 5 minutes, or until thickened. Stir in the ricotta.

4. Coat a lasagna dish with oil spray. Add a layer of lasagna sheets, then a quarter of the sauce, a quarter of the baked squash and sweet potato, and a quarter of the mushrooms and scallions. Continue until all the lasagna sheets, vegetables, and sauce are used (you will end up with four layers). Sprinkle with the Cheddar.

5. Bake for 35 to 45 minutes, or until golden and bubbling. Let stand for 5 minutes before cutting.

Per serving: 300 calories, 44 g carbohydrates, 18 g protein, 5 g fat, 4 g fiber

Recipe: Michelle Trute, Cooking with Conscience

LUSCIOUS LENTIL LASAGNA

Serves 8

Here is a power-packed lunch or dinner entrée that may just become a standard in your menu repertoire. Lasagna? Easy to make? This one is.

PREPARATION TIME: 20 MINUTES   COOKING TIME: 1 HOUR 45 MINUTES

RESTING TIME: 15 MINUTES

Olive oil spray
1½ cups vegetable broth
½ cup lentils, washed
½ tablespoon olive or canola oil
½ cup coarsely chopped scallions
1 large clove garlic, minced
1 can (15 ounces) diced tomatoes

1 cup tomato sauce
9 ounces oven-ready lasagna sheets
16 ounces reduced-fat ricotta cheese
12 ounces part-skim mozzarella cheese, shredded
¼ cup grated Parmesan cheese

1. Preheat the oven to 350°F. Lightly coat a 13" x 9" baking dish with oil spray.

2. Bring the broth to a boil in a small saucepan. Add the lentils, cover, and simmer for 30 minutes, stirring occasionally.

3. Meanwhile, place the oil in a heated skillet. Add the scallions and garlic. Cook for 3 minutes, or until translucent. Remove from the heat.

4. When the lentils are cooked, pour them and any remaining liquid into the skillet with the scallions and garlic. Add the tomatoes and the tomato sauce. Stir well. Return the skillet to the heat, cover, and simmer for 30 minutes.

5. Meanwhile, soften the noodles in a bowl with hot water for 7 to 8 minutes.

6. In the prepared baking dish, layer as follows: Spread 1 to 2 tablespoons of the lentil-tomato sauce on the bottom of the pan. Cover with 4 lasagna sheets, overlapping, ½ cup ricotta, one-quarter of the lentil-tomato sauce, ¾ cup mozzarella, and 1 tablespoon Parmesan.

7. Repeat with 3 more layers. Cover with aluminum foil. Bake for 30 to 40 minutes. Allow to rest, covered, for 15 minutes before serving.

Per serving: 405 calories, 41 g carbohydrates, 26 g protein, 15 g fat, 6 g fiber

RED, WHITE, AND GREEN PAN PASTA-CRUST "PIZZA"

Serves 4

Have you ever seen a cholesterol-free pizza? When you make this recipe, you'll be looking at one. Good for vegetarians, good for kids, good for everyone.

PREPARATION TIME: 10 MINUTES   COOKING TIME: 15 MINUTES

6	ounces penne pasta
1	tablespoon olive oil
6	cups shredded zucchini (about 4 medium)
¼	cup sun-dried tomatoes (about 4 halves)
1	clove garlic, minced
1	tablespoon extra-virgin olive oil

1. Cook the pasta according to the package directions. Remove from heat 1 minute before the recommended cooking time, to keep the pasta slightly undercooked. Drain and place pasta in a large mixing bowl.

2. Meanwhile, heat the olive oil in a medium skillet over medium-high heat and cook the zucchini, sun-dried tomatoes, and garlic for 5 minutes. Stir frequently.

3. Add the vegetables to the pasta and toss.

4. Coat a 10" skillet with the oil and heat. Pour in the pasta mixture and press down firmly to make it compact. Cook, uncovered, for 6 minutes on medium heat.

5. Remove from the heat. Wearing oven mitts, place a large flat plate over the skillet and flip it over, allowing the "pizza" to loosen onto the plate. Carefully slide it back into the skillet and continue cooking for another 3 minutes, occasionally pressing down firmly on the pasta.

6. When it's done, use the plate again to remove the "pizza" from the pan. May be served warm or at room temperature.

Per serving: 249 calories, 39 g carbohydrates, 8 g protein, 8 g fat, 4 g fiber

LINGUINE WITH SALMON AND PEAS

(photo on page 143)   *Serves 4*

If you are a fan of the "meal in a bowl," then this recipe is just right for you. It's also packed with sustaining low-GI carbs, vegetables, and protein for that perfect satiety factor. Best of all, it's on the table in around 30 minutes.

PREPARATION TIME: 15 MINUTES   COOKING TIME: 17 MINUTES

12 ounces linguine
7   ounces salmon fillets, skinned
1   tablespoon extra-virgin olive oil
2   cups fresh or frozen peas
1   cup fish or vegetable broth
2   tablespoons chopped flat-leaf parsley
    Freshly ground black pepper
    Juice of 1 lemon, or to taste
1   teaspoon grated lemon peel, or to taste

1. Bring a large saucepan of water to a boil and cook the pasta until al dente.

2. Meanwhile, carefully check the salmon for any bones, then cut it into bite-size pieces. Heat the oil in a large, deep frying pan until the oil is shimmering, then add the salmon pieces and cook gently for 5 minutes, or until the salmon changes color and is cooked through, being careful not to brown it.

3. Add the peas, broth, and parsley. Cook for 1 to 2 minutes. Season to taste with plenty of pepper, then add the lemon juice and peel, to taste, stirring gently to combine all the ingredients.

4. When the pasta is cooked, drain well and add to the sauce, tossing lightly to coat. Serve immediately.

Per serving: 520 calories, 66 g carbohydrates, 34 g protein, 13 g fat, 8 g fiber

TOMATO FETTUCCINE WITH SALMON AND BABY SPINACH

Serves 4

Canned salmon is a convenient and very rich source of valuable omega-3 fatty acids. You'll want to develop the habit of keeping some on the pantry shelf at all times.

PREPARATION TIME: 10 MINUTES   COOKING TIME: 10 MINUTES

1   tablespoon extra-virgin olive oil
1   large red onion, cut into thin wedges
⅓   cup capers, drained and patted dry with paper towel
2   cloves garlic, crushed
4   large ripe tomatoes, chopped
⅓   cup vegetable broth
1   pound fresh fettuccine
4   cups baby spinach leaves
2   cans (7½ ounces each) red salmon, bones and skin removed, broken into large pieces
2   tablespoons lemon juice
     Salt and freshly ground black pepper

1. Heat the oil in a large frying pan over medium heat. Add the onion, capers, and garlic. Cook, stirring often, for 6 to 7 minutes, or until the onion softens. Add the tomatoes and stir for 1 minute. Add the broth and increase the heat to high. Bring to a boil, then remove from the heat.

2. Meanwhile, cook the pasta in a large saucepan of salted water for 2 to 3 minutes, or until tender. Drain well and return to the pan.

3. Add the spinach leaves and onion mixture to the pasta. Toss well until combined and the spinach starts to wilt. Add the salmon and lemon juice. Toss gently and season with salt and pepper to taste. Serve immediately.

Per serving: 476 calories, 45 g carbohydrates, 33 g protein, 15.5 g fat, 7 g fiber

 **COOK'S TIP**

Most types of pasta have a similar GI, so spaghetti or fusilli,
for example, could also be used in this recipe.

FETTUCCINE WITH VEGETABLES AND SAUSAGE

Serves 4

Leftover grilled chicken breasts or pork tenderloin may replace the sausages for a change of pace.

PREPARATION TIME: 5 MINUTES   COOKING TIME: 25 MINUTES

12	ounces spinach fettuccine
2	teaspoons olive oil, divided
2	large onions, coarsely chopped
2	cloves garlic, coarsely chopped
4	ribs celery, thickly sliced (retain the tender leaves for garnish)
1	large can (28 ounces) whole peeled tomatoes
3	tablespoons tomato paste
6	sprigs thyme, finely chopped, or 1 teaspoon dried thyme
6	sprigs oregano, finely chopped, or 1 teaspoon dried oregano
	Salt and freshly ground black pepper
¼	cup capers, drained and patted dry with paper towel
10	black olives, pitted
4	sweet Italian sausages, cooked and sliced

1. Boil 3 quarts of salted water, add the fettuccine, and stir until the water returns to a boil. Let boil, uncovered, until the pasta is cooked and al dente.

2. Drain, toss with 1 teaspoon oil, and keep warm.

3. Meanwhile, heat the remaining 1 teaspoon olive oil in a large heavy pan over moderate heat. Cook the onions and garlic for 3 minutes, stirring, then add the celery, tomatoes with juice, tomato paste, thyme, and oregano. Season to taste with salt and pepper. Simmer gently for 15 minutes.

4. Add the capers, olives, and sausages and simmer for 5 minutes.

5. Toss the sauce with the pasta and serve immediately, garnished with the small, young celery leaves.

Per serving: 325 calories, 41 g carbohydrates, 15 g protein, 18 g fat, 9 g fiber

FETTUCCINE WITH SMOKED TURKEY AND PINE NUTS

Serves 6

Suppers just don't get any easier than this. A warm noodle dish with a sprightly oil and vinegar dressing is particularly refreshing on a summer evening.

PREPARATION TIME: 5 MINUTES   COOKING TIME: 10 MINUTES

Salt
8   ounces spinach fettuccine
2   tablespoons pine nuts
4   tablespoons olive oil
4   tablespoons balsamic vinegar
1   clove garlic, crushed
    Freshly ground black pepper
8   ounces smoked turkey breast, thinly sliced
½   bunch flat-leaf parsley, finely chopped
2   small chile peppers, seeded and thinly sliced

1. Bring a large pot of salted water to a boil. Add the noodles and cook, stirring occasionally, until tender. Refresh under cold running water.

2. Meanwhile, cook the pine nuts in a heavy frying pan over medium heat, stirring constantly, until golden brown.

3. In a lidded jar, combine the oil, vinegar, and garlic. Shake to combine. Season to taste with pepper.

4. On a large platter, combine the noodles, pine nuts, turkey, parsley, chiles, and dressing. Toss gently to mix.

Per serving: 359 calories, 29 g carbohydrates, 17 g protein, 20 g fat, 4 g fiber

TOFU AND VEGETABLE NOODLES

Serves 4

The noodles in this dish are minimally cooked by soaking and stir-frying so they still have some resistance to the tooth. This keeps the GI lower because overcooking pasta increases starch gelatinization (or swelling) and boosts its glycemic index.

PREPARATION TIME: 10 MINUTES   MARINATING TIME: 4 HOURS

COOKING TIME: 10 MINUTES

⅓ cup soy sauce

¼ cup oyster sauce

¼ cup hoisin sauce

2 cloves garlic, crushed

14 ounces firm tofu, drained and cut into 1" pieces

1 pound fresh fettuccine noodles

1½ tablespoons olive oil, divided

1 yellow onion, cut into thin wedges

1 red bell pepper, cut into thin strips

7 ounces baby eggplant, thinly sliced lengthwise

1 can (8 ounces) bamboo shoot slices, drained

2 tablespoons water

1. In a shallow glass dish, combine the soy, oyster, and hoisin sauces, and the garlic. Add the tofu and toss gently to coat. Cover and refrigerate for 4 hours, turning once.

2. Place the noodles in a large heatproof bowl and cover with boiling water. Allow to soak for 5 minutes, then drain well.

3. Meanwhile, heat 2 teaspoons of the oil in a wok or large skillet over high heat. Add the onion, bell pepper, and eggplant. Stir-fry for 2 to 3 minutes, or until the vegetables are almost tender. Toss in the bamboo shoots. Add the water, cover, and cook for 1 to 2 minutes. Transfer the vegetables to a bowl.

4. Wipe out the wok. Add the remaining oil and heat over high heat. Drain the tofu, reserving the marinade. Stir-fry the tofu for 2 to 3 minutes, or until golden. Add the vegetables, the reserved marinade, and the noodles. Toss for 1 to 2 minutes, or until well combined and heated through. Serve immediately.

Per serving: 381 calories, 44 g carbohydrates, 19 g protein, 14 g fat, 6 g fiber

MARINATED GRILLED CHICKEN NOODLE SALAD

Serves 4

With a contemporary recipe like this, it's easy to prepare restaurant-quality (only healthier!) meals at home in minutes.

PREPARATION TIME: 20 MINUTES   MARINATING TIME: 15 MINUTES
COOKING TIME: 10 MINUTES

1	tablespoon canola oil
2	cloves garlic, finely chopped
2	strips lemon peel, finely chopped
¼	teaspoon red-pepper flakes, or 1 whole dried chile, finely chopped
1	pound chicken tenders
8	ounces angel hair pasta
½	bunch fresh cilantro, coarsely chopped

1. Combine the oil, garlic, lemon peel, pepper flakes, and chicken in a bowl. Set aside to marinate for 15 minutes.

2. Preheat the grill. Cook the chicken for 6 minutes, or until golden brown. Cut into bite-size cubes (about 1").

3. Meanwhile, cook the pasta in boiling salted water according to package directions. Drain.

4. Toss the cilantro and chicken pieces with the noodles. Serve immediately.

Per serving: 336 calories, 42 g carbohydrates, 36 g protein, 2 g fat, 3 g fiber

Couscous Salad (*page 233*)

Indonesian Fried Rice *(page 234)*

Fragrant Bulgur Wheat with Lemon Dressing *(page 235)*

● 211

Sushi Rolls *(page 238)*

Grilled Fish Kebabs (*page 240*)

● 213

Dilled Pasta Salad with Smoked Salmon (*page 242*)

Bulgur-Stuffed Snapper in Tomato-Orange Sauce *(page 250)*

Salmon with Bean Salsa and Mixed Greens Salad (*page 252*)

Tuna Poached in Tomato and Fennel with Chile Chickpea Mash (*page 254*)

Trout with Barley Risotto *(page 258)*

Scallops with Arugula Spaghetti *(page 263)*

Fresh Mussels with Fettuccine *(page 264)*

Breaded Chicken on Roast Sweet Potato Salad (*page 270*)

Pork with Honey-Glazed Apples *(page 283)*

Pork Vindaloo (*page 284*)

Beefburgers with Salsa *(page 305)*

CHINESE CHICKEN WITH SNOW PEAS AND RICE NOODLES

Serves 8

If you're just becoming acquainted with the versatility and nutritional benefits of tofu (soybean curd), this recipe is a wonderful introduction. Teamed with favorites like chicken, broccoli, and pungent Asian seasonings, your family will ask for it again and again.

PREPARATION TIME: 15 MINUTES   COOKING TIME: 10 MINUTES

5   packages (4½ ounces each) rice noodles, soaked in boiling water
3   tablespoons light soy sauce
1   tablespoon hoisin sauce
1   tablespoon oyster sauce
1   tablespoon rice wine (mirin)
5   ounces firm tofu, diced
1   tablespoon canola oil
1   pound chicken tenderloins, sliced into thin strips
2   cloves garlic, finely chopped
10 ounces broccoli florets
¼   cup vegetable or chicken broth
3   ounces snow peas
1   tablespoon sesame seeds, toasted (see Cook's Tip, page 195)

1. Cook the rice noodles according to package directions.

2. Meanwhile, in a large mixing bowl, combine the soy, hoisin, and oyster sauces and rice wine. Stir to mix. Add the tofu and toss gently to mix.

3. Heat the oil in a large wok. Stir-fry the chicken and garlic for 3 minutes. Remove from the wok and set aside.

4. Add the broccoli and broth to the wok. Cover and simmer for 3 minutes. Add the snow peas and cook for 1 minute.

5. Drain the noodles. Add to the wok with the tofu and marinade and the reserved chicken. Toss to warm the noodles. Serve hot, sprinkled with sesame seeds.

Per serving: 530 calories, 40 g carbohydrates, 24 g protein, 8 g fat, 6 g fiber

ROTINI WITH CHICKEN AND CARAMELIZED ONIONS

Serves 6

It's worth taking the time to roast the pepper and remove its skin before adding it to the pasta, as this makes it sweeter. The skin can be a little bitter and tough. To save time, you can replace the fresh pepper with jarred or delicatessen roasted peppers.

PREPARATION TIME: 15 MINUTES   COOKING TIME: 35 MINUTES

2   tablespoons olive oil, divided
2   red onions, cut into thin wedges
2   teaspoons sugar
1   red bell pepper
2   boneless, skinless chicken breasts (about 10½ ounces), thinly sliced
4   scallions, sliced
2   teaspoons crushed garlic
1   cup evaporated low-fat milk
1   cup chicken broth
2   tablespoons sun-dried tomato pesto or tomato paste
12 ounces dried rotini pasta
½   cup shredded basil
    Freshly ground black pepper

1. To make the caramelized onions, heat 1 tablespoon of the oil in a frying pan and add the onions and sugar. Cook over medium-low heat, stirring occasionally, for 10 minutes, or until the onions are soft and golden brown. Take care to keep the heat low enough so the onions do not burn. Remove to a bowl and cover to keep warm.

2. Cut the bell pepper into quarters lengthwise and remove the stem and seeds. Lay the pieces, skin side up, on a baking sheet lined with aluminum foil. Place under a broiler and cook for 7 minutes, or until the skin is blackened and

blistered. Using tongs, place the hot pieces of pepper in a plastic freezer bag. Twist to seal and put aside to cool slightly. When cool, remove the skin and slice the flesh into strips.

3. Meanwhile, heat the remaining 1 tablespoon oil in a large frying pan. Add the chicken and cook for 4 to 5 minutes, or until the chicken is browned and cooked through. Add the scallions and garlic and cook for 1 minute. Stir in the milk, broth, pesto or tomato paste, and pepper strips. Bring to a boil, then reduce the heat and simmer for 1 to 2 minutes. Remove the chicken mixture to a bowl and cover to keep warm.

4. While the chicken is cooking, cook the pasta in a large pot of boiling water until al dente. Drain and return it to the pot. Stir in the chicken mixture and caramelized onion and heat through. Stir in the basil and season to taste with black pepper.

Per serving: 390 calories, 50 g carbohydrates, 23 g protein, 10 g fat, 4 g fiber

SPICY BEEF AND NOODLES

(photo on page 144)   *Serves 4*

Fans of spicy hot food will adore this fiery Asian dish, but milder palates can adapt it by reducing or eliminating the chile sauce.

PREPARATION TIME: 10 MINUTES   COOKING TIME: 15 MINUTES

2	tablespoons canola oil, divided
½	cup cashew nuts
1	pound beef rump steak, thinly sliced
2–3	tablespoons Chinese chile garlic sauce
24	green beans, trimmed and cut into 1" pieces
12	ears baby corn, halved
¼	cup beef broth
½	cup chopped cilantro leaves
1	pound fresh fettuccine

1. Heat 1 teaspoon oil in a wok or frying pan over medium heat. Stir-fry the cashews for 1 to 2 minutes, or until brown. Remove and set aside.

2. Heat the remaining oil in the wok. Stir-fry the beef, in batches, for 3 minutes each batch, or until brown. Return all the beef to the wok, then add 2 table-spoons of chile garlic sauce, beans, corn, and broth. Stir-fry for 4 minutes, or until the vegetables are tender.

3. Stir in the cilantro and reserved cashew nuts. Add the noodles to the wok and stir to combine. Heat through and serve. Add up to 1 tablespoon more chile garlic sauce, if desired.

Per serving: 684 calories, 61 g carbohydrates, 37 g protein, 32 g fat, 7 g fiber

MEDITERRANEAN PASTA SAUCE

Makes 10 (½ cup) servings

Vary this stand-by sauce with different colors of peppers and basil, oregano, or fennel if you like.

PREPARATION TIME: 15 MINUTES   COOKING TIME: 20 MINUTES

¼ cup olive oil
1   large onion, chopped
1   medium green bell pepper, diced
2   tablespoons minced garlic
1   can (28 ounces) tomatoes, seeded
12 large cured black olives, pitted and sliced
1   cup quartered jarred artichoke hearts

1. In a large saucepan, heat the oil over medium-low heat. Add the onion, pepper, and garlic. Cook for 2 minutes, or until the onion becomes translucent.

2. Add the tomatoes and olives. Bring to a boil. Reduce the heat and simmer for 15 minutes.

3. Add the artichoke hearts just before removing from the heat.

Per serving: 87 calories, 7 g carbohydrates, 0 g protein, 6 g fat, 2 g fiber

RAW TOMATO–BASIL SAUCE

Makes 6 (½ cup) servings

*This summer classic is fabulous served with a short shaped
pasta, bruschetta, or grilled zucchini and eggplant.*

PREPARATION TIME: 15 MINUTES   STANDING TIME: 20 TO 30 MINUTES

1	pound ripe plum tomatoes, seeded and chopped
3–4	cloves garlic, slivered paper-thin
	Large bunch fresh basil
⅓	cup grated Parmesan cheese
2–3	hot chiles (optional)
½	cup olive oil

1. Place the tomatoes and garlic in a medium bowl.

2. Wash and pat dry the basil. Remove the stems and tear into small pieces
(do not cut with a knife). Add to the bowl.

3. Sprinkle the Parmesan and chiles, if using, over the tomatoes and toss.
Drizzle with the oil and mix well.

4. Cover and allow to sit at room temperature for 20 to 30 minutes for the flavors
to blend.

Per serving: 168 calories, 5 g carbohydrates, 3 g protein, 16 g fat, 1 g fiber

SAFFRON PILAF

Serves 6

This assertively flavored, yet delicate rice dish is always in good company with grilled fish, roast chicken, or a bean ragout.

PREPARATION TIME: 5 MINUTES   COOKING TIME: 12 MINUTES

STANDING TIME: 5 MINUTES

1½ cups basmati rice
½   teaspoon saffron threads
1   tablespoon boiling water
1   tablespoon olive oil
3   scallions, sliced
½   red bell pepper, chopped
2   cloves garlic, minced
2½ cups chicken broth
½   cup frozen peas, thawed
¼   cup raisins
¼   cup slivered almonds, toasted (see Cook's Tip, page 187)

1. Rinse the rice under cold water and drain.

2. Place the saffron threads in a small bowl and pour the boiling water over top. Set aside to allow the color to infuse.

3. Heat the oil in a large saucepan. Cook the scallions, pepper, and garlic for 2 minutes. Add the broth, rice, and saffron with the water. Bring to a boil. Reduce the heat to low. Cover and simmer for 10 to 12 minutes, stirring occasionally, or until the rice is just tender.

4. Remove from the heat and stir in the peas, raisins, and almonds. Cover and set aside for 5 minutes before serving.

Per serving: 270 calories, 48 g carbohydrates, 6 g protein, 6 g fat, 2 g fiber

TABBOULEH

Serves 4

Bulgur wheat grains are cracked but otherwise remain virtually intact. Our bodies need whole grains such as these, with their higher levels of fiber, vitamins, minerals, and phytochemicals. And, by the way, the nutty flavor and chewy texture are delicious!

PREPARATION TIME: 5 MINUTES   SOAKING TIME: 30 MINUTES

1   cup bulgur wheat
1   cup finely chopped flat-leaf parsley
4   scallions, finely chopped
1   tomato, finely chopped
2   tablespoons lemon juice
2   tablespoons olive oil
¼   teaspoon salt
    Freshly ground black pepper

1. Put the bulgur wheat in a bowl. Cover with boiling water and soak for 20 to 30 minutes.

2. Drain well and roll the grains in a clean, lint-free kitchen towel to squeeze out the excess water. Transfer to a mixing bowl. Add the parsley, scallion, and tomato.

3. In a screw-top jar, combine the lemon juice, oil, salt, and a pinch of pepper. Shake well. Pour over the bulgur mixture. Toss lightly to combine.

Per serving: 263 calories, 33 g carbohydrates, 6 g protein, 10 g fat, 8 g fiber

 COOK'S TIP

Tabbouleh will keep for 2 days, covered, in the refrigerator.

COUSCOUS SALAD

(photo on page 209)   *Serves 6*

Although couscous has a medium-GI, combining it with chickpeas, as we have done here, gives the overall meal a low GI. This couscous salad is delicious as a meal in itself or served as an accompaniment for chicken or meat dishes.

PREPARATION TIME: 15 MINUTES

SALAD:

- 1   cup couscous
- 1   cup canned chickpeas, rinsed and drained
- ½   small bunch flat-leaf parsley, chopped
- ½   small bunch cilantro leaves, chopped
- 1   tablespoon ground cumin
- ½   red bell pepper, chopped
- ½   green bell pepper, chopped
- 1   cup chopped mixed dried fruit
- 2   tablespoons pistachio nuts
- 2   tablespoons pine nuts, toasted (see Cook's Tip, page 187)

DRESSING:

- 2   tablespoons extra-virgin olive oil
  Juice of 1 lemon
  Freshly ground black pepper

1. To make the salad: Make the couscous according to the package directions—you should end up with about 2 cups cooked couscous. Make sure the cooked couscous is quite dry.

2. Put the couscous in a large serving bowl. Add the chickpeas, parsley, cilantro, cumin, peppers, dried fruit, pistachios, and pine nuts.

3. To make the dressing: In a screw-top jar, combine the oil and lemon juice. Season to taste with black pepper. Shake well to blend. Pour over the couscous salad and toss to coat.

Per serving: 245 calories, 25 g carbohydrates, 6 g protein, 13 g fat, 5 g fiber

COOK'S TIP

For dried fruits, choose among apricots, dates, currants, figs, or raisins.

INDONESIAN FRIED RICE

(photo on page 210) *Serves 4*

Nasi goreng—Indonesian-style fried rice—is great as a light lunch using leftover cooked rice. Make sure you use one of the lower-GI rices such as basmati, brown, or wild rice. Uncle Ben's converted long grain rice is also a good choice.

PREPARATION TIME: 10 MINUTES   COOKING TIME: 10 TO 15 MINUTES

5	eggs, at room temperature, divided	4	cups cooked basmati rice
1	teaspoon canola oil	1	tablespoon oyster sauce
1	large onion, finely chopped	2	tablespoons soy sauce
2	cloves garlic, minced		Chopped parsley or scallions
1	tablespoon grated fresh ginger		

1. Bring a large saucepan or deep frying pan of water to a simmer. Carefully crack 4 of the eggs and gently slip them, one at a time, into the simmering water. Poach for 3 to 4 minutes, or until the eggs are cooked to your liking. Lift out with a slotted spoon and drain on paper towels.

2. Heat a nonstick frying pan over medium heat. In a small dish, lightly beat the remaining egg with a fork. Add to the pan and stir-fry until the egg is scrambled. Remove and set aside.

3. Heat the oil in the pan and add the onion, garlic, and ginger. Lightly fry for 3 to 5 minutes, or until the onion is soft. Add the cooked rice and toss well. Pour in the oyster sauce and soy sauce and toss to coat the rice. Stir in the scrambled egg.

4. Spoon the rice into 4 bowls or plates and top each with a poached egg. Sprinkle with chopped parsley or scallions.

Per serving: 365 calories, 58 g carbohydrates, 14 g protein, 8 g fat, 2 g fiber

Recipe: Jill McMillan

COOK'S TIPS

To obtain 4 cups cooked rice you will need 1⅓ cups raw rice.

The GI of rice varies according to the variety and its proportion of the more slowly digested amylose starch.

FRAGRANT BULGUR WHEAT WITH LEMON DRESSING

(photo on page 211)   *Serves 4*

Bulgur wheat is used extensively in Middle Eastern cooking and not only has a low-GI (48) but is delicious and takes only minutes to prepare. Try this salad as an accompaniment to chicken or pan-fried marinated tofu slices, for a vegetarian meal.

PREPARATION TIME: 15 MINUTES   STANDING TIME: 17 MINUTES

SALAD:

1   cup bulgur wheat
1   cup boiling water
1   tablespoon olive oil
1   tablespoon finely chopped lemongrass
1   tablespoon grated fresh ginger
    Grated peel of ½ lemon
    Grated peel of ½ lime
1   tablespoon lemon juice

1   tablespoon lime juice
2   tomatoes, chopped
4   scallions, thinly sliced on the diagonal
12 spears asparagus, blanched, cut on the diagonal into 1" pieces
    Freshly ground black pepper
2   tablespoons chopped parsley

DRESSING:

1   cup low-fat plain yogurt
1   tablespoon lemon juice

2   tablespoons chopped chives

1. To make the salad: Put the bulgur wheat in a bowl and pour the water over it. Stir well, then cover with aluminum foil (or plastic wrap or a plate) and steam for 15 minutes, or until all of the water has absorbed.

2. Heat the oil in a nonstick frying pan over medium heat. Add the lemongrass and ginger and fry for 2 minutes. Add the lemon and lime peels and juices. Add the bulgur wheat and mix well. Transfer to a serving bowl and add the tomatoes, scallions, and asparagus and toss to combine. Season to taste with pepper. Sprinkle with the parsley.

3. To make the dressing: Combine the yogurt, lemon juice, and chives in a bowl and mix to combine, adding a little more lemon juice if it is too thick. To serve, drizzle the yogurt mixture over the bulgur wheat salad.

Per serving: 275 calories, 38 g carbohydrates, 12 g protein, 6 g fat, 8 g fiber

Recipe: Jill McMillan

ROASTED SWEET POTATO, BASMATI RICE, AND PARMESAN PILAF

Serves 6

*Grilled pork chops or roasted pork is a heavenly match
for this robust rice and vegetable combination.*

PREPARATION TIME: 10 MINUTES   COOKING TIME: 40 MINUTES

2 pounds sweet potatoes, cubed
8 cloves garlic, halved
9 sprigs fresh rosemary, divided
2 tablespoons olive oil, divided
4 cups chicken or vegetable broth

2 cups basmati rice
   Salt and freshly ground black pepper
1 cup grated Parmesan cheese

1. Preheat the oven to 400°F.

2. Place the sweet potatoes, garlic, and 3 sprigs of rosemary on a baking sheet. Sprinkle with 1 tablespoon of the olive oil. Toss to coat. Roast until just golden, approximately 20 minutes. Remove from the oven.

3. Heat the broth to boiling.

4. Heat the remaining 1 tablespoon oil in a large, heavy saucepan and stir in the rice. Coat the rice with oil and cook for 2 minutes, stirring.

5. Add the sweet potato and garlic to the rice. Season to taste with salt and pepper. Discard the rosemary sprigs. Add the broth and turn down the heat to simmering.

6. Cover and cook gently for 15 minutes, until all the broth is absorbed and the rice is cooked through. Stir in the Parmesan.

7. Divide the pilaf among 6 large pasta bowls. Decorate each with a fresh rosemary sprig.

Per serving: 444 calories, 76 g carbohydrates, 12 g protein, 10 g fat, 5 g fiber

Chapter 8

FISH AND SHELLFISH

The facts are in about the link between health and increased seafood consumption, and there's nothing fishy about them. Eating more seafood is linked to a roster of body benefits from reduced risk of coronary heart disease to enhanced immunity. And contrary to the rumors (probably started by the butcher's wife!), fish and shellfish are *not* difficult to prepare at home. In fact, fish fillets require virtually no prep work and cook in a flash. *Sea* for yourself with Grilled Fish Kebabs, Cod Fillets with Sun-dried Tomato Marinade, Seared Tuna with Basmati Rice and Red Pepper Coulis, Salmon with Bean Salsa and Mixed Greens Salad, and Garlic and Parsley Scallops with Fettuccine.

SUSHI ROLLS

(photo on page 212)

(photo on page 212)

Makes 4 rolls

Short- or medium-grain rice is excellent for sushi making. Long-grain rice would make the rolls too dry. Sushi rolls make a perfect light lunch or, cut into twice as many pieces, a delightful dinner appetizer.

PREPARATION TIME: 20 MINUTES　　**STANDING TIME: 10 MINUTES**
COOKING TIME: 15 MINUTES

- 1　cup sushi rice or short- or medium-grain rice
- ¼　cup Japanese rice vinegar
- 1　tablespoon sugar
- 4　sheets nori, toasted
  - Soy sauce
  - Wasabi
  - Pickled ginger

SALMON FILLING:

1¾ ounces smoked salmon, sliced
½　avocado, thinly sliced

TUNA FILLING:

- 1　can (3 ounces) tuna in water, drained
- 1　tablespoon low-fat mayonnaise
- ½　small cucumber, seeds removed, cut into long strips

1. Cook the rice in a large saucepan of boiling water for 13 to 15 minutes, or until the rice is tender. Drain the rice, without rinsing it, and place in a large bowl. Add the rice vinegar and sugar and stir into the rice. Cover with plastic wrap and let cool for 10 minutes.

2. Run a bamboo sushi mat under water and shake off the excess water. Place 1 nori sheet on the sushi mat, rough side up and with the long end of the sheet closest to you. Using wet hands, place a quarter of the rice on the nori sheet and firmly pat down the rice to cover the sheet, leaving 1½" at the top of the sheet. Make a slight indent in the rice 1½" from the bottom of the sheet, closest to you. Repeat with the other 3 nori sheets.

3. To make the salmon-filled rolls: Place half the smoked salmon and half the avocado in the indent along the rice. Using the bamboo mat, firmly roll up the sushi. Remove the mat. Using a wet knife, cut the roll into thick slices. Repeat to make a second roll.

4. To make the tuna-filled rolls: Combine the tuna with the mayonnaise. Place half the cucumber strips and half the tuna in the indent along the rice and roll up the sushi. Repeat to make a second roll.

5. You may like to serve the sushi rolls with accompaniments such as soy sauce for dipping (mix a little wasabi into the soy sauce for extra flavor) and pickled ginger.

Per salmon roll: 315 calories, 49 g carbohydrates, 11 g protein, 9 g fat, 6 g fiber

Per tuna roll: 280 calories, 47 g carbohydrates, 16 g protein, 3 g fat, 3 g fiber

COOK'S TIP

Nori (dried seaweed sheets), wasabi (Japanese "horseradish"), and bamboo sushi mats can be purchased in Asian food stores and some specialty kitchen equipment stores.

GRILLED FISH KEBABS

(photo on page 213)   *Serves 2*

Here the fish and vegetables are threaded onto long metal skewers and then marinated in a spicy yogurt mixture before grilling. You may also like to serve with accompaniments such as Saffron Pilaf (page 231), Cucumber Raita (page 157), and Mung Bean Dhal (page 184).

PREPARATION TIME: 20 MINUTES   MARINATING TIME: 30 MINUTES
COOKING TIME: 10 MINUTES

MARINADE:

1   cup low-fat plain yogurt
½   onion, finely chopped
2   teaspoons grated fresh ginger
2   cloves garlic, minced
1   teaspoon ground coriander
2   tablespoons lemon juice
1   tablespoon garam masala
1   teaspoon paprika
1   teaspoon chili powder, or to taste
2   tablespoons tomato paste

KEBABS:

14   ounces firm whitefish steak, cut into 16 chunks, about 1" each
1   large red onion, cut into 8 wedges
½   red pepper, cut into 6 pieces, about 1" square
½   green pepper, cut into 6 pieces, about 1" square
4   lemon wedges

1. To make the marinade: In a bowl, combine the yogurt, onion, ginger, garlic, coriander, lemon juice, garam masala, paprika, chili powder, and tomato paste. Stir to mix well.

2. To make the kebabs: Allow 4 fish chunks, 2 onion wedges, and 3 squares of pepper (a mix of red and green looks good) for each skewer. Thread them onto the skewers in the following order: pepper, fish, onion, fish, pepper, fish, onion, fish, pepper. Place in a shallow dish that is long enough to hold the skewers. Coat the skewers with the marinade mixture, cover, and refrigerate for 30 minutes to allow the flavors to develop.

3. Heat a grill and cook the skewers for 5 minutes on each side, or until the fish is cooked through and the vegetables are slightly charred on the edges.

4. Serve the fish skewers with lemon wedges for squeezing over.

Per serving (2 kebabs): 470 calories, 60 g carbohydrates, 34 g protein, 9 g fat, 4 g fiber

Recipe: Carol Selva Rajah, Gourmet Asian Cuisine

DILLED PASTA SALAD
WITH SMOKED SALMON

(photo on page 214)   *Serves 6*

*This special-occasion salad makes a light meal for 4 or an exquisite
starter for 6. If serving as a main meal, accompany with a cucumber
salad tossed with an oil and vinegar dressing.*

PREPARATION TIME: 15 MINUTES   COOKING TIME: 10 MINUTES

DRESSING:

⅓ cup extra-virgin olive oil
3 scallions, thinly sliced
   Juice of ½ lemon
½ cup chopped dill leaves
   Freshly ground black pepper

SALAD:

9 ounces penne pasta
5¼ ounces smoked salmon, cut into strips
6 cherry tomatoes, halved, or quartered if large
6 scallions, thinly sliced on the diagonal
1 small red onion, cut into thin rings, slices separated
1 cup low-fat plain yogurt (optional)

1. To make the dressing: In a food processor fitted with a metal blade, combine the oil, scallions, lemon juice, and dill. Purée until smooth. Season to taste with pepper.

2. To make the salad: Cook the pasta in a pot of boiling water until al dente. Drain and rinse under cold running water until cool. Drain well and place in a serving dish. Pour over the dressing, then add the smoked salmon, tomatoes, scallions, and onion rings. Toss gently to coat the pasta in the dressing. Serve with a dollop of yogurt, if desired.

Per serving: 315 calories, 33 g carbohydrates, 13 g protein, 14 g fat, 3 g fiber

Recipe: Loukie Werle, Trattoria Pasta

COOK'S TIPS

Penne is a finely ridged pasta. Ridged or ribbed pastas tend to hold on to more sauce than smooth pastas.

Avoid overcooking your pasta—not only does al dente pasta taste better, but it has a lower GI than pasta that has been cooked for too long.

SEARED SALMON FILLETS
WITH WHITE BEAN PUREE

Serves 8

Many of us know that fish high in omega-3 fatty acids, such as salmon, may help ward off heart disease. But studies have also found it beneficial in alleviating high blood pressure, arthritis, and certain cancers.

PREPARATION TIME: 5 MINUTES   COOKING TIME: 17 MINUTES

PUREE:

1   can (15½ ounces) cannellini beans, rinsed and drained
2   cloves garlic, crushed
1½ tablespoons lemon juice
4   sprigs fresh thyme leaves, or 1 tablespoon dried thyme
2   teaspoons olive oil
     Salt and freshly ground black pepper

SALMON:

1   tablespoon olive oil + extra for garnish
2   cloves garlic, halved
4   salmon fillets
1   bunch arugula

1. To make the puree: In the bowl of a food processor fitted with a metal blade, combine the beans, garlic, lemon juice, thyme, and oil. Purée until smooth. Season to taste with salt and pepper. Place in an ovenproof or microwaveable bowl. Cover and warm through in a low oven or on low power in the microwave.

2. To make the salmon: Preheat a stovetop griddle or a heavy frying pan. Heat the oil with the garlic for 1 minute on the griddle or pan. Add the salmon and cook for approximately 5 to 8 minutes, turning once, until the fish is opaque.

3. Place a large spoonful of puree in the center of heated plates, arrange arugula on top, and finish with the cooked fillets. Drizzle a little extra oil around the plate and serve immediately.

Per serving: 307 calories, 9 g carbohydrates, 43 g protein, 11 g fat, 6 g fiber

OCEAN PERCH ON ROASTED VEGETABLES   *Serves 6*

This nearly one-dish meal needs only a side serving of basmati rice to complete it.

PREPARATION TIME: 15 MINUTES   COOKING TIME: 30 MINUTES

6	ocean perch fillets (5 ounces each)
	Freshly ground black pepper
3	tablespoons olive oil, divided
3	medium zucchini, thickly sliced
6	ripe medium tomatoes, quartered and seeded
2	medium red onions, cut into wedges
1	large red bell pepper, thickly sliced
1	large green bell pepper, thickly sliced
4	large cloves garlic, coarsely chopped
8	sprigs fresh thyme, or 2 tablespoons dried thyme leaves
	Salt
½	bunch fresh basil, leaves finely sliced
3	tablespoons balsamic vinegar

1. Preheat the oven to 450°F.

2. Season the fish with black pepper and brush with 1 tablespoon olive oil.

3. In a large baking dish, combine the zucchini, tomatoes, onions, bell peppers, garlic, thyme, and the remaining 2 tablespoons olive oil. Spread in one layer. Season to taste with salt and black pepper.

4. Bake for 18 to 20 minutes, stirring occasionally. Reduce the oven to 350°F. Arrange the fillets over the vegetables and roast for 6 to 9 minutes, or until the fish flakes easily.

5. Transfer the fillets carefully to a warm plate and cover.

6. Arrange the vegetables on 6 warm plates and sprinkle with the basil leaves and a drizzle of balsamic vinegar. Top with the fillets.

Per serving: 239 calories, 7 g carbohydrates, 29 g protein, 10 g fat, 5 g fiber

COOK'S TIP

You can also use trout for this recipe.

GRILLED HALIBUT WITH WHITE BEAN SALSA *Serves 8*

The white bean salsa can be made ahead of time and kept in the refrigerator until you are ready to serve it. For a change, try it with grilled chicken, or as a light meal on its own with Alvarado Street Bakery 100% sprouted sourdough bread.

PREPARATION TIME: 15 MINUTES   COOKING TIME: 10 MINUTES

SALSA:

13 ounces canned white beans, rinsed and drained

2 ripe tomatoes, finely chopped

3 shallots, thinly sliced

⅓ cup cilantro leaves, shredded

1½ tablespoons lime juice

1 tablespoon extra-virgin olive oil
Salt and freshly ground black pepper

HALIBUT:

4 halibut steaks (3½ ounces each)

1 teaspoon olive oil
Salt and freshly ground black pepper

SALAD:

4 cups mixed salad leaves (mesclun)

2 tablespoons Tomato and Olive Vinaigrette (page 166)

1. To make the salsa: In a small bowl, combine the beans, tomatoes, shallots, cilantro, lime juice, and extra-virgin olive oil. Toss lightly to combine. Season to taste with salt and pepper.

2. To make the halibut: Preheat a grill on medium-high. If you don't have a grill, use a heavy frying pan.

3. Brush both sides of the fish with olive oil and season to taste with salt and pepper. Grill the fish for 4 minutes on each side, or until the fish is opaque and flakes when tested with a fork.

4. Meanwhile, to make the salad: In a large bowl, toss the salad leaves with the vinaigrette.

5. Serve the fish with the salsa and salad.

Per serving: 273 calories, 11 g carbohydrates, 33 g protein, 17.5 g fat, 7 g fiber

SEARED TUNA WITH BASMATI RICE AND RED PEPPER COULIS

Serves 6

Coulis is the French term for a thick puree served as a sauce. The red pepper coulis in this recipe is delicious served over a frittata or grilled vegetables.

PREPARATION TIME: 10 MINUTES   COOKING TIME: 35 MINUTES

4   large red bell peppers
1   can (28 ounces) whole peeled tomatoes, drained and seeded
    Salt and freshly ground black pepper

1½ cups basmati rice
2   tablespoons olive oil
4   cloves garlic, halved
6   tuna steaks (about 6 ounces each)
    Juice and grated peel of 1 lemon

1. Halve and seed the bell peppers. Bake, broil, or grill them, skin side up, until black and blistered. Place in a paper bag and let cool before removing skin. Transfer to a food processor fitted with a metal blade. Add the tomatoes. Purée until smooth. Season to taste with salt and black pepper. Transfer to a small saucepan and keep warm.

2. Bring a large pot of salted water to a boil and cook the rice for 11 minutes.

3. Meanwhile, heat the oil in a large, heavy frying pan. Toss in the garlic and heat through. Add the steaks. Sear each side quickly. Reduce the heat to medium. Allow to cook, unturned, for 6 to 8 minutes, until cooked through.

4. Drain the rice when cooked and transfer to a serving platter. Arrange the tuna on the bed of rice. Keep warm.

5. Remove the garlic from the pan and discard. Add the lemon juice to the pan juice. Heat through. Season to taste with salt and black pepper. Pour the pan juices over the tuna. Sprinkle with the lemon peel.

6. Spoon the red pepper coulis around the serving platter. Serve immediately.

Per serving: 439 calories, 48 g carbohydrates, 42 g protein, 9 g fat, 5 g fiber

 **COOK'S TIP**

You may grill the tuna steaks if you prefer.

COD FILLETS WITH SUN-DRIED TOMATO MARINADE

Serves 6

If you crave good food fast, get in the swim. Seafood cooks very quickly, and when prepared in a savory marinade like this one, there's no danger of it drying out.

PREPARATION TIME: 5 MINUTES   MARINATING TIME: 30 MINUTES
COOKING TIME: 15 MINUTES

Olive oil spray	Freshly ground black pepper
1 cup sun-dried tomatoes in oil (reserve the oil)	2 pounds cod fillets
Juice and grated peel of 1 lemon	Steamed basmati rice
2 cloves garlic, coarsely chopped	Flat-leaf parsley

1. Lightly coat a shallow baking dish with oil spray.

2. In the bowl of a food processor fitted with a metal blade, combine the sun-dried tomatoes with ¼ cup of the reserved oil, the lemon juice and peel, and garlic. Blend to a smooth consistency. Season to taste with pepper.

3. Place the cod in the prepared dish. Top with the tomato mixture. Cover with aluminum foil. Allow to marinate for 30 minutes. Preheat the oven to 350°F.

4. Bake, covered, until the fish flakes easily, approximately 15 minutes. Serve on a bed of basmati rice, with the marinade spooned over the top. Decorate with a few sprigs of parsley.

Per serving: 281 calories, 11 g carbohydrates, 34 g protein, 12 g fat, 3 g fiber

GRILLED COD WITH WARM BEAN SALAD

Serves 4

Tilapia, orange roughy, and catfish are also good options for this dish.

PREPARATION TIME: 10 MINUTES   COOKING TIME: 8 MINUTES

- 2 cans (15½ ounces each) light red kidney beans, divided, ½ cup liquid reserved
- 1 cup chicken or vegetable broth
- 3 cloves garlic, crushed
- 2 large ripe tomatoes, coarsely chopped
- 2 bunches arugula, coarsely chopped + extra leaves for garnish
- 1 bunch shallots, finely sliced
- ¼ bunch flat-leaf parsley, finely chopped
- 3 tablespoons lemon juice
  Salt and freshly ground black pepper
- 1 tablespoon olive oil
- 4 cod fillets (4 ounces each)

1. In a bowl, mash ½ cup of the beans with the reserved liquid from the can.

2. Place the mashed beans, broth, garlic, tomatoes, chopped arugula, shallots, parsley, lemon juice, salt and pepper (to taste), and the remaining whole kidney beans in a large saucepan. Warm the bean mixture, covered, over a low heat for 10 minutes.

3. Meanwhile, preheat the grill or stovetop grill pan and brush with olive oil. Grind black pepper over the cod fillets and cook for 8 minutes, turning once.

4. Serve the warm bean salad as a bed for the cod fillets, and garnish with extra arugula leaves.

Per serving: 309 calories, 21 g carbohydrates, 33 g protein, 10 g fat, 11 g fiber

BULGUR-STUFFED SNAPPER IN TOMATO ORANGE SAUCE

(photo on page 215)

Serves 4

This recipe is equally good using any whole fish. If you like, wrap it in aluminum foil and cook on the grill rather than in the oven.

PREPARATION TIME: 20 MINUTES   MARINATING TIME: 2 HOURS (OPTIONAL)

COOKING TIME: 40 MINUTES

FISH AND STUFFING:

Olive oil spray

1   cup bulgur wheat

1   cup boiling water

2   tablespoons olive oil

½   red onion, finely chopped

2   cloves garlic, minced

½   zucchini, finely chopped

½   red bell pepper, finely chopped

4   sun-dried tomatoes, coarsely chopped

2   tablespoons finely chopped basil

1   tablespoon lemon juice

½   teaspoon dried oregano

Freshly ground black pepper

4   small whole snappers (12 ounces each)

MARINADE:

1   can (14 ounces) crushed tomatoes

Juice and grated peel of 1 orange

½   cup torn basil + whole leaves for garnish

½   teaspoon dried oregano

Freshly ground black pepper

1. To prepare the fish and stuffing: Coat a large baking dish with oil spray. In a bowl, combine the bulgur and water. Allow to steam for 10 minutes, or until all the water is absorbed.

2. Meanwhile, heat the oil in a frying pan over medium heat. Lightly cook the onion and garlic for 3 minutes, or until the onion is soft. Add the zucchini and bell pepper and cook for 2 to 3 minutes. Add the tomatoes, basil, lemon juice, and oregano. Season to taste with black pepper. Add the bulgur and mix well to combine.

3. Stuff the fish with some of the bulgur mixture. Place the fish in the prepared baking dish. The leftover stuffing can be served cold with the fish or reheated in the oven for 10 minutes.

4. To make the marinade: In a bowl, combine the tomatoes, orange juice and peel, basil, and oregano. Season to taste with black pepper. Stir to mix. Pour the marinade over the stuffed fish. Refrigerate for 2 hours to allow the flavors to develop, or cook immediately if preferred.

5. Preheat the oven to 400°F. Cover the dish with aluminum foil. Bake for 30 to 40 minutes, or until the fish flakes easily when tested with a fork. Garnish with the extra basil leaves. Serve the fish with the remaining bulgur stuffing.

Per serving: 515 calories, 39 g carbohydrates, 51 g protein, 15 g fat, 9 g fiber

SALMON WITH BEAN SALSA
AND MIXED GREENS SALAD

(photo on page 216)   *Serves 4*

In a traditional Mediterranean diet, fish would be included once or twice a week. We now know that eating fish regularly will help reduce the risk of heart disease, so aim for two or three servings a week.

PREPARATION TIME: 15 MINUTES   COOKING TIME: 20 TO 30 MINUTES

SALMON:

	Olive oil spray
4	salmon fillets
1	lemon, halved
½	bunch cilantro, chopped
	Freshly ground black pepper

SALSA:

1	can (15½ ounces) three-bean mix, rinsed and drained
1	small red onion, finely chopped
6	sun-dried tomatoes, chopped
½	bunch cilantro, chopped
1	tablespoon olive oil
1	tablespoon chopped black olives
1	red chile, finely chopped (remove the seeds for a milder taste)
2	teaspoons balsamic vinegar

SALAD:

1	tablespoon olive oil
2	teaspoons balsamic vinegar
1	teaspoon Dijon mustard
1	teaspoon pure floral honey
6	cups mesclun (mixed salad leaves)

1. To make the salmon: Preheat the oven to 350°F. Coat a baking dish with oil spray. Put the salmon fillets in the dish, squeeze the lemon juice over top, sprinkle on the cilantro leaves, and season to taste with plenty of pepper. Cover with aluminum foil and bake for 20 to 30 minutes for medium to well-done (or if you prefer your salmon rare, bake for 15 minutes).

2. Meanwhile, to make the salsa: In a bowl, combine the beans, onion, tomatoes, cilantro, oil, olives, chile, and vinegar. Stir to mix.

3. To make the dressing: In a screw-top jar, combine the oil, vinegar, mustard, and honey and shake to combine. Drizzle over the greens.

4. Place the salmon fillets on 4 plates, top with the bean salsa, and serve with the salad.

Per serving: 464 calories, 15 g carbohydrates, 45 g protein, 24 g fat, 6 g fiber

 **COOK'S TIP**

Mesclun is simply a mix of fresh, tender young salad leaves and may include a variety of lettuces such as iceberg, Romaine, mignonette, and oakleaf, plus baby spinach leaves, arugula, curly endive, broadleaf endive, nasturtium, snow pea shoots, radicchio, and sometimes edible flowers. You can buy it ready-made in most supermarkets, or mix your own to taste.

TUNA POACHED IN TOMATO AND FENNEL WITH CHILE CHICKPEA MASH

(photo on page 217)   *Serves 4*

Fresh fennel, with its mild anise flavor, has a natural affinity for fish and seafood. It's used extensively by cooks around the shores of the Mediterranean Sea. Mashed legumes make a great low-GI and nutrient-rich alternative to mashed potatoes. The mash also makes a delicious spread on its own, rather like hummus—and if you like it hot, add extra chile.

PREPARATION TIME: 20 MINUTES   COOKING TIME: 45 MINUTES

TUNA:

2   large fennel bulbs, or 4 baby fennel bulbs, thickly sliced (leafy tops reserved)
1   tablespoon extra-virgin olive oil
1   large red onion, sliced
2   cloves garlic, minced
1   can (15½ ounces) Italian tomatoes, chopped
1   cup dry white wine
2" long strip of lemon peel
1   bay leaf
1   pound tuna steaks, cut into large bite-sized chunks
    Freshly ground black pepper
2   tablespoons chopped flat-leaf parsley
    Lemon wedges

MASH:

1   can (15½ ounces) chickpeas, rinsed and drained
2   tablespoons chopped flat-leaf parsley
    Juice of ½ lemon
1   small red chile, seeded and thinly sliced
½   cup boiling water
    Freshly ground black pepper

1. To make the tuna: Chop 1 tablespoon of fennel leaves. Set aside. (Reserve the remainder for another recipe, if desired.) Heat the oil in a large saucepan over low heat and gently cook the sliced fennel, onion, and garlic for 10 minutes, or until the onion is golden and transparent. Add the tomatoes, wine, lemon peel, and bay leaf. Stir to combine. Bring to a simmer. Cook, covered, for 30 minutes, or until the vegetables are just cooked.

2. Place the tuna in the pan. Gently stir. Poach for 3 to 4 minutes, or until opaque.

3. Meanwhile, to make the mash: In the bowl of a food processor fitted with a metal blade, combine the chickpeas with the parsley, lemon juice, and chile. Purée, adding just enough of the boiling water to make a smooth, creamy mixture. Season to taste with pepper.

4. Remove the strip of lemon peel and bay leaf from the pan of tuna, and discard. Season to taste with pepper.

5. Place a scoop of mash on 4 plates and top with the tuna and vegetable mixture. Sprinkle with the chopped parsley and reserved fennel leaves. Serve with lemon wedges.

Per serving: 410 calories, 20 g carbohydrates, 39 g protein, 14 g fat, 9 g fiber

COOK'S TIP

Fennel is delicious thinly sliced and served raw in salads or cooked. Choose bulbs with green, sweet-smelling leaves. Remove the tough outer stalks as they are usually damaged or stringy; trim the base of the bulb; then halve, quarter, slice, or dice. Chop the feathery tops and use as a garnish, or add to sauces or dressings at the end of cooking time.

JUMBO SHRIMP WITH TOMATO-PESTO STUFFED RED PEPPERS

Serves 8

Late summer—when locally grown tomatoes and eggplant are at their peak—is the perfect time to partake of this special meal.

PREPARATION TIME: 20 MINUTES   COOKING TIME: 30 MINUTES

PESTO:

⅔   cup unblanched whole almonds
¼   cup extra-virgin olive oil
1½ bunches fresh basil
4   cloves garlic
    Salt and freshly ground black pepper

PEPPERS:

4   tablespoons olive oil, divided
4   cloves garlic, finely chopped
    Salt and freshly ground black pepper
12 small plum tomatoes halved lengthwise, seeded
½   bunch fresh basil, shredded
4   medium red bell peppers, halved lengthwise
1   cup uncooked penne pasta

SHRIMP:

    Olive oil spray
16 jumbo shrimp, shelled and deveined (tails optional)
8   Italian eggplants, halved lengthwise

1. To make the pesto: In a food processor fitted with a metal blade, grind the almonds coarsely. Add the oil, basil, and garlic. Process to a coarse paste. Season to taste with salt and black pepper, and set aside.

2. To prepare the peppers: Preheat the oven to 350°F.

3. Combine 2 tablespoons oil, garlic, and a pinch each of salt and black pepper. Use half the mixture to brush onto the tomatoes. (Set the remaining mixture aside to baste the shrimp and eggplant.) Top with the basil leaves. Place on a baking sheet with sides. Bake for 30 minutes, then set aside.

4. Place the bell pepper halves, cut side down, on a baking sheet and bake until they soften but do not lose shape. Remove and pat dry with paper towel. Take care to keep them from breaking.

5. Bring a large pot of salted water to a boil. Cook the penne for 9 to 11 minutes. Drain the pasta and return to the pot. Add the remaining 2 tablespoons oil and the reserved tomato-basil mixture. Toss to mix.

6. To make the shrimp: Preheat the grill. Coat a grill rack with oil spray. Brush the shrimp and eggplant with the reserved garlic and olive oil mixture (Step 3). Grill for 3 minutes, or until the shrimp is opaque and the eggplant is tender.

7. Place the pepper shells on plates. Spoon on the pasta mixture. Drape eggplant over the peppers. Place the shrimp to the side. Drizzle the reserved pesto over all.

Per serving: 243 calories, 18 g carbohydrates, 13 g protein, 14 g fat, 6 g fiber

TROUT WITH BARLEY RISOTTO

(photo on page 218)   *Serves 4*

Barley is one of the oldest cultivated cereals and has one of the lowest GI values of any food. It's also versatile: Add pearl barley to soups and stews, fuel your day with barley porridge, or make a barley risotto—all great ways to reduce the overall GI of a meal.

PREPARATION TIME: 15 MINUTES   COOKING TIME: 1 HOUR

1 tablespoon olive oil	2 tablespoons barbecue sauce
1 onion, finely chopped	Freshly ground black pepper
2 large cloves garlic, minced	4 trout fillets (about 5 ounces each)
2 cups (7 ounces) fresh shiitake mushrooms, sliced	Juice of ½ lemon
2 cups hot vegetable broth	1 tablespoon chopped dill leaves
1 cup pearl barley	Lemon wedges (optional)

1. Preheat the oven to 350°F. Heat the oil in a flameproof baking dish over medium heat and cook the onion and garlic for 3 minutes, or until soft. Add the mushrooms and cook for 1 to 2 minutes. Add the broth, barley, and barbecue sauce. Stir well. Season to taste with pepper.

2. Cover the dish. Bake for 40 to 45 minutes, or until the barley is partially cooked. Place the trout fillets on top of the barley mixture. Add the lemon juice and season to taste with pepper. Replace the lid and bake for 15 minutes.

3. Carefully remove the trout to plates. Spoon the barley slightly over the trout. Sprinkle with the dill and serve with lemon wedges, for garnish, if desired.

Per serving: 455 calories, 37 g carbohydrates, 43 g protein, 13 g fat, 8 g fiber

● ●

COOK'S TIP

To reduce the cooking time, cover the barley with water in the morning and leave to soak for the day.

GARLIC SHRIMP WITH CILANTRO PASTA

Serves 6

This dish is a triple winner—it is special enough for company, comes together in less than 20 minutes, and has a low GI.

PREPARATION TIME: 8 MINUTES   MARINATING TIME: 10 MINUTES
COOKING TIME: 11 MINUTES

Salt
Olive oil spray
1 pound jumbo shrimp, peeled and deveined
¼ cup + 1 teaspoon extra-virgin olive oil
4 cloves garlic, finely sliced

12 ounces spinach fettuccine
Salt and freshly ground black pepper
2 large red or yellow bell peppers, thinly sliced
½ bunch fresh cilantro, coarsely chopped

1. Bring a large pot of salted water to a boil.

2. Preheat the grill to medium-high. Coat a grill rack with oil spray.

3. In a large bowl, toss the shrimp with ¼ cup oil and the garlic. Set aside to marinate for 10 minutes.

4. When the water boils, add the pasta and cooked uncovered, stirring occasionally, for 11 minutes.

5. Grill the shrimp for 2 minutes, brushing occasionally with the marinade, until cooked. Season the shrimp to taste with salt and black pepper.

6. Drain the pasta and return to the pot. Toss in the remaining 1 teaspoon of olive oil.

7. On a large serving platter, combine the pasta, shrimp, bell pepper strips, and cilantro.

Per serving: 382 calories, 44 g carbohydrates, 25 g protein, 11 g fat, 1 g fiber

SHRIMP WITH QUINOA TABBOULEH

Serves 4

Quinoa is one of those versatile grains that you can make a meal of throughout the day—and it has a low GI of 53. This version of tabbouleh uses quinoa instead of bulgur wheat and is made with pistachios. The fresh, strong flavors of lime and basil complement the shrimp beautifully.

MARINATING TIME: 30 MINUTES   PREPARATION TIME: 15 MINUTES
COOKING TIME: 15 MINUTES

SHRIMP:

    Olive oil spray

24 large shrimp, peeled and deveined, with tails intact

    Grated peel and juice of 1 lemon

1 teaspoon ground cumin

2 jalapeño chile peppers, finely chopped

TABBOULEH:

1 cup quinoa, rinsed well

2 cups water

½ cup pistachio nuts, coarsely chopped

½ red onion, finely chopped

1 tomato, chopped

½ cup chopped basil

    Juice of 1 lime

1 tablespoon olive oil

1 teaspoon ground cumin

    Freshly ground black pepper

½ cup low-fat plain yogurt

1. To make the shrimp: Preheat the grill. Coat a grill rack with oil spray. In a mixing bowl, combine the shrimp, lemon peel and juice, cumin, and jalapeños. Mix well to coat the shrimp in the marinade. Refrigerate for 30 minutes to allow the flavors to develop. Soak 8 bamboo skewers in cold water for 30 minutes.

2. To make the tabbouleh: Put the quinoa in a saucepan and cover with the water. Bring to a boil, then reduce the heat and simmer for 10 minutes, or until the grains are tender and translucent. While still warm, transfer to a serving bowl. Add the nuts, onion, tomato, basil, lime juice, oil, and cumin. Season to taste with black pepper. Mix well and set aside.

3. Thread 3 shrimp onto each soaked skewer. Grill for 2 minutes on each side, or until the shrimp are opaque. Spoon the tabbouleh onto plates, top with 2 skewers per plate, and drizzle with the yogurt.

Per serving: 420 calories, 35 g carbohydrates, 34 g protein, 15 g fat, 5 g fiber

● ●
COOK'S TIPS

As a variation, use almonds or cashews instead of the pistachio nuts, or substitute mint leaves for the basil.

The shrimp can be broiled instead of grilled, if desired.

SHRIMP, BEAN, AND PEPPER PILAF

Serves 6

Turmeric, the root of a tropical cousin of ginger, lends its reddish-gold hue and pleasant pungency to this seafood concoction.

PREPARATION TIME: 10 MINUTES   COOKING TIME: 30 MINUTES

1	tablespoon canola oil
1	cup basmati rice
1	large onion, chopped
1	teaspoon ground turmeric or ginger
2	cups chicken or vegetable broth
1	can (14½ ounces) diced tomatoes
1	large green bell pepper, diced
2	cloves garlic, chopped
	Salt and freshly ground black pepper
2	pounds medium shrimp, peeled and deveined
1	can (15½ ounces) baby lima beans, rinsed and drained
1	red chile, seeded and finely sliced
½	bunch fresh cilantro, coarsely chopped

1. Heat the oil in a large, heavy frying pan. Add the rice, onion, and turmeric or ginger. Stir for 3 minutes before adding the broth, tomatoes with juice, bell pepper, and garlic. Season to taste with salt and black pepper.

2. Cover the pan and simmer for 20 minutes, or until the rice absorbs most of the liquid.

3. Gently stir the shrimp, beans, and chile into the pan. Cover and cook for 3 minutes, or until the shrimp are opaque.

4. Taste and adjust seasoning, if desired. Stir in the cilantro and serve immediately.

Per serving: 275 calories, 39 g carbohydrates, 24 g protein, 4 g fat, 6 g fiber

COOK'S TIP

This recipe can also be made with scallops.

SCALLOPS WITH ARUGULA SPAGHETTI

(photo on page 219)   *Serves 4*

If you have access to it, try wild arugula, which has a stronger flavor than ordinary arugula. It's perfect for salads with shaved Parmesan. Here the arugula's peppery bite complements the richness of the scallops.

PREPARATION TIME: 10 MINUTES   COOKING TIME: 15 MINUTES

	Salt
12	ounces dried spaghetti
2	tablespoons extra-virgin olive oil
2	cloves garlic, minced
1	red chile, seeded and finely chopped
14	ounces scallops, halved if large
3	plum tomatoes, peeled and chopped
	Juice of 1 lemon
1	cup packed arugula leaves
	Freshly ground black pepper

1. Bring a large pot of salted water to a boil. Cook the pasta until al dente.

2. Meanwhile, heat the oil in a large, deep frying pan or large saucepan over medium heat. Add the garlic and chile and cook, stirring, for 1 to 2 minutes, being careful that the garlic does not brown. Add the scallops and cook for 1 to 2 minutes on each side, or until just golden and opaque. Stir in the tomatoes and lemon juice and cook until heated through.

3. When the pasta is cooked, drain it thoroughly, then add to the sauce along with the arugula leaves. Season to taste with pepper, then lightly toss the ingredients together. Serve immediately.

Per serving: 440 calories, 62 g carbohydrates, 22 g protein, 11 g fat, 4 g fiber

• •

COOK'S TIP

To peel tomatoes, first remove the stems, then score a cross in the bottom of each tomato using a knife. Blanch the tomatoes in boiling water for 30 to 60 seconds. Transfer to a bowl of cold water, then peel the skin away from the cross.

FRESH MUSSELS WITH FETTUCCINE

(photo on page 220)   *Serves 6*

You can prepare the mussels and the sauce for this light, summery pasta dish in advance, and refrigerate if it's going to be longer than an hour before you cook the pasta. Or leave it at room temperature if you are planning to serve immediately.

PREPARATION TIME: 15 MINUTES   COOKING TIME: 15 MINUTES

	Salt
2¼	pounds fresh mussels in the shell
1	leek
⅓	cup extra-virgin olive oil, divided
¼	cup chopped kalamata olives
¼	cup torn basil leaves
4	large cloves garlic, crushed
	Juice of 1 lemon
	Freshly ground black pepper
12	ounces fettuccine
	Lemon wedges

1. Set a large pot of salted water over high heat.

2. Clean the mussels by thoroughly scrubbing the shells with a brush. Pull out the hairy beards and discard any broken mussels or any open mussels that don't close when tapped. Rinse well.

3. Place the mussels in a large pot, with only the water clinging to them, and place the pan over high heat. Cover the pan and shake over the heat until all the mussels have opened. Discard any mussels that do not open. Remove the mussels from their shells and place in a large serving dish (leave a few mussels in their shells for garnish, if desired).

4. Clean the leek in several changes of cold water. When no grit remains, cut into julienne strips. Heat 1 tablespoon oil in a frying pan over medium heat, add the leek, and cook for 3 minutes, or until tender and slightly brown around the edges. Add to the mussels in the serving dish, along with the olives, basil, garlic, lemon juice, and remaining oil. Season to taste with pepper.

5. When the water boils, add the pasta. Cook, stirring occasionally, until al dente. Remove the crushed garlic cloves from the mussel mixture and discard. Drain the pasta, add to the mussels, and toss well. Serve immediately with lemon wedges.

Per serving: 465 calories, 52 g carbohydrates, 27 g protein, 16 g fat, 3 g fiber

Recipe: Loukie Werle, Trattoria Pasta

COOK'S TIPS

Fish is quick and easy to cook. Cutlets of fish such as swordfish, salmon, cod, or mackerel take $2\frac{1}{2}$ to 3 minutes per side, or 5 to 6 minutes total. Try cooking them this way:

- In a nonstick pan over medium heat, with a film of oil or oil spray

- Under a preheated broiler or on a barbecue grill, brushed with flavored oil

- Steamed or poached with a little white wine or lemon juice

- Baked for 10 to 15 minutes in a preheated 375°F oven.

GARLIC AND PARSLEY SCALLOPS
WITH FETTUCCINE

Serves 6

Fresh herbs with their vibrant flavors and vividly colored leaves are true stalwarts of the healthy kitchen. Feel free to replace the parsley here with cilantro, basil, savory, tarragon, fennel, or other favorite fresh herb.

PREPARATION TIME: 5 MINUTES   COOKING TIME: 10 MINUTES

	Salt
2	packages (9 ounces each) fresh fettuccine
1	bunch flat-leaf parsley, coarsely chopped
4	cloves garlic, coarsely chopped
3	red chile peppers, coarsely chopped
1	tablespoon extra-virgin olive oil
24	sea scallops
	Freshly ground black pepper

1. Bring a pot of salted water to a boil. Cook the pasta for 3 minutes, then drain.

2. In a small bowl, combine the parsley, garlic, and chiles, and set aside.

3. Heat the olive oil in a heavy frying pan. Add the scallops. Cook for 2 minutes, turning once, until opaque. Remove from the pan.

4. Add the reserved parsley mixture to the pan and heat through. Add the pasta. Season to taste with salt and black pepper. Toss and serve immediately, topped with the scallops.

Per serving: 157 calories, 21 g carbohydrates, 10 g protein, 4 g fat, 2 g fiber

Chapter 9

CHICKEN, PORK, BEEF, AND LAMB

Feeling full immediately after eating and reducing hunger pangs between meals are just two of the weight-control benefits that protein provides. Protein also increases our metabolic rate for as long as three hours after eating. This means we burn more energy by the minute compared with the increase that occurs after eating carbohydrates or fats. Because meat and poultry contain no carbohydrates, they don't affect blood glucose as directly as carbohydrate foods, but they do contain primarily unhealthy saturated fat. Choose the leanest cuts whenever possible. Our recipes include the highest-quality, lowest-fat protein sources, presented in the delectable guises of Breaded Chicken on Roast Sweet Potato Salad, Sicilian Chicken, Pork with Honey-Glazed Apples, Grilled Steak with Chile Corn Salsa, and Roast Lamb and Vegetables with Thyme and Rosemary.

SWEET AND SOUR CHICKEN WITH CRACKED WHEAT SALAD

Serves 2

Bulgur wheat is a versatile low-GI cereal grain made from hard durum wheat that has been steamed, cracked, and dried. It is also known as cracked wheat. Use it in tabbouleh or add to pilafs, vegetable burgers, stuffings, stews, and even soups.

PREPARATION TIME: 20 MINUTES   COOKING TIME: 15 MINUTES

SALAD:

½   cup bulgur wheat
½   cup boiling water
2   tablespoons finely chopped mint
12   green beans
12   snow peas
8   thin spears asparagus
1¾ cups shredded or sliced cooked chicken
2   cups baby spinach or arugula leaves

DRESSING:

1   tablespoon white wine vinegar
1   tablespoon extra-virgin olive oil
2   teaspoons finely chopped lemon, with juice
2   teaspoons raw sugar
    Freshly ground black pepper

1. To make the salad: In a bowl, combine the bulgur wheat and water. Stir well. Cover and steam for 15 minutes, or until the water has been absorbed. Fluff up the grains with a fork, then mix in the mint.

2. Bring a saucepan of water to a boil. Put the beans, snow peas, and asparagus in the pan. Cook for 1 minute. Drain and rinse under cold running water to cool quickly. In a serving bowl, combine the vegetables with the chicken, spinach or arugula, and bulgur.

3. To make the dressing: In a screw-top jar, combine the vinegar, oil, lemon with juice, and sugar. Season to taste with pepper. Shake well to blend. Pour over the salad and toss to coat.

Per serving: 469 calories, 39 g carbohydrates, 35 g protein, 17 g fat, 9 g fiber

COOK'S TIPS

If you prefer, buy a cooked chicken to save time. Alternatively, gently poach a whole chicken breast in a covered saucepan in chicken broth (add a few leaves of fresh mint for extra flavor) for 10 minutes, or until the chicken is tender and cooked through. Remove from the saucepan and set aside until cool enough to slice or shred.

Raw sugar, such as demerara or turbinado, is sold in health food stores and some supermarkets. Good-quality brown sugar may be substituted.

BREADED CHICKEN ON ROAST SWEET POTATO SALAD

(photo on page 221)   *Serves 2*

Breaded pieces of tender chicken, layered on a tasty sweet potato salad and drizzled with a creamy honey mustard dressing, is the perfect dish for a lunch or light meal.

PREPARATION TIME: 20 MINUTES   COOKING TIME: 25 MINUTES

SALAD:

Olive oil spray

2 tablespoons balsamic vinegar

1 tablespoon olive oil

1 tablespoon brown sugar

1 sweet potato (about 10 ounces), cut into ¼" thick slices

CHICKEN:

2 tablespoons low-fat plain yogurt

2 tablespoons low-fat milk

1 cup dry whole grain bread crumbs

½ teaspoon paprika

Freshly ground black pepper

10½ ounces boneless, skinless chicken breasts or thighs, trimmed and cut in half

DRESSING:

1 tablespoon Dijon mustard

1 tablespoon ketchup

2 tablespoons low-fat plain yogurt

2 teaspoons lemon juice

1 teaspoon pure floral honey

Mixed green salad leaves

1 tablespoon chopped basil

1. To make salad: Preheat the oven to 425°F. Coat a shallow baking dish with oil spray. In a large bowl, combine the vinegar, oil, and brown sugar. Add the sweet potato and toss to coat. Transfer to the pan. Set aside.

2. To make the chicken: Line a baking sheet with parchment paper. Put the yogurt and milk in a shallow dish. Stir to blend. In another shallow bowl, combine the bread crumbs, paprika, and a pinch of pepper. Dip the chicken into the yogurt mixture, allow the excess to drain off, then coat in the bread crumbs. Put the chicken on the lined baking sheet.

3. Place the chicken and the reserved sweet potato in the oven. Bake the chicken for 20 minutes, or until golden brown and cooked through. Remove and slice into diagonal strips. Bake the sweet potato for 25 minutes, or until soft and starting to brown. Remove from the oven and leave for 10 minutes to cool a little.

4. Meanwhile, to make the dressing: Put the mustard, ketchup, yogurt, lemon juice, and honey in a small bowl. Stir to combine.

5. To serve, lay the salad leaves on a plate and top with sweet potato, a few more salad leaves, then more sweet potato. Lay the chicken on top of the salad and drizzle with the dressing. Scatter the basil on top.

Per serving: 595 calories, 58 g carbohydrates, 44 g protein, 19 g fat, 6 g fiber

COOK'S TIP

To make the dry whole grain bread crumbs, take 4 slices of a low-GI whole grain bread and break into small pieces. Spread out on a baking sheet and bake in a preheated 425°F oven for 5 minutes, or until golden brown. Cool slightly, then transfer to the bowl of a food processor fitted with a metal blade. Process into small crumbs.

THAI CHICKEN CURRY

Serves 8

Thanks to the wide availability of formerly exotic ingredients such as lemongrass, curry paste, and coconut milk, sophisticated dishes can be made at home with ease.

PREPARATION TIME: 5 MINUTES   COOKING TIME: 17 MINUTES

- 1   tablespoon canola oil
- 2   large onions, finely chopped
- 2   tablespoons Thai green curry paste
- 1½ cups chicken broth
- 1   cup low-fat coconut milk
- 1   cup water
- 1   stalk lemongrass, crushed
- 2   pounds boneless, skinless chicken breasts or thighs, trimmed of all visible fat, thinly sliced
- 2   green chiles, finely sliced
- 2   cups basmati rice
- 8   ounces green beans, sliced diagonally
- 1   bunch fresh cilantro, coarsely chopped, + extra for garnish

1. Heat the oil in a large, heavy frying pan and add the onions. Cook gently for 5 minutes. Add the curry paste and cook for 2 minutes, stirring.

2. Add the broth, coconut milk, water, and lemongrass to the pan. Simmer for 10 to 12 minutes to reduce the liquid. Add the chicken and chiles. Simmer gently until the chicken is tender.

3. Meanwhile, bring a large saucepan of water to a boil and slowly pour in the rice, stirring until the water returns to a boil. Boil for 11 minutes, then drain. Steam the green beans separately until just tender.

4. Remove and discard the lemongrass from the chicken mixture and add the beans and cilantro. Serve on a bed of hot rice with a garnish of cilantro.

Per serving: 401 calories, 43 g carbohydrates, 33 g protein, 11 g fat, 4 g fiber

COOK'S TIP

Jarred or canned Thai chili paste—a mixture of ground hot chiles, garlic, lemongrass, onion, lime, and other spices—is sold in the Asian section of most supermarkets.

CHICKEN BREASTS STUFFED WITH FETA AND SPINACH ON MASHED LENTILS

Serves 4

These chicken breasts are stuffed with a creamy mix of feta cheese, spinach, and sun-dried tomatoes and served on spicy lentil mash with a mixed green salad. Everyone will be coming back for more.

PREPARATION TIME: 20 MINUTES   COOKING TIME: 30 MINUTES

CHICKEN:

Olive oil spray
3   cups baby spinach leaves
⅓   cup crumbled reduced-fat feta cheese
¼   cup soft dry-pack sun-dried tomatoes
1   tablespoon low-fat cream cheese
Freshly ground black pepper
4   boneless, skinless chicken breasts (about 1¼ pounds), trimmed of all visible fat

LENTILS:

1   cup green lentils
¼   teaspoon ground turmeric
1   tablespoon olive oil
1   onion, finely chopped
2   cloves garlic, minced
Juice of ½ lemon
Freshly ground black pepper

1. To make the chicken: Preheat the oven to 400°F. Lightly coat a baking dish with oil spray. In the bowl of a food processor fitted with a metal blade, combine the spinach, feta, tomatoes, and cream cheese. Season to taste with pepper. Process until coarsely chopped.

2. Slice open each chicken breast lengthwise to create a pocket. Fill the pockets with the spinach stuffing. Place the chicken in the baking dish in a single layer. Cover with aluminum foil and bake for 30 minutes, or until cooked through and golden brown.

3. Meanwhile, to make the lentils: Put the lentils and turmeric in a saucepan over medium heat. Cover with water. Bring to a boil, then reduce the heat to a simmer and cook, partially covered, for 30 minutes, or until the lentils are soft. Drain the lentils and set aside.

4. Toward the end of cooking, heat the oil in a saucepan and cook the onion and garlic for 3 to 4 minutes, or until the onion is soft. Add the lemon juice and lentils. Season to taste with plenty of pepper. Smash some of the lentils with the back of a large spoon. Serve the chicken on a bed of lentils.

Per serving: 435 calories, 21 g carbohydrates, 49 g protein, 17 g fat, 8 g fiber

TANDOORI CHICKEN WITH HERBED RICE

Serves 4

This special dish takes its name from the tandoor, a traditional clay oven that's found from the Middle East to India. Fortunately for us, it tastes almost as good baked in our home oven.

PREPARATION TIME: 15 MINUTES   MARINATING TIME: 6 TO 8 HOURS
COOKING TIME: 20 MINUTES

- ½ cup tandoori paste
- 2 tablespoons + ½ cup low-fat plain yogurt
- 2 tablespoons lemon juice, divided
- 4 boneless, skinless chicken breasts (about 4½ ounces each)
- 1 cup basmati rice
- ⅓ cup fresh cilantro leaves, finely shredded
- ⅓ cup fresh mint leaves, finely shredded
- Grated peel of 1 small lime
- ½ cup finely chopped cucumber
- 2 ripe tomatoes, finely chopped
- ½ small red onion, finely chopped
- Pappadums
- ⅓ cup mango chutney

1. In a shallow glass or ceramic dish, combine the tandoori paste, 2 tablespoons yogurt, and 1 tablespoon lemon juice. Use a sharp knife to make 3 slits (about ½" deep) in each chicken breast. Add the chicken to the tandoori mixture. Spoon the paste all over the chicken, pushing it into the slits. Cover and place in the refrigerator for 6 to 8 hours to marinate.

2. Preheat the oven to 400°F. Place the chicken on a wire rack over a large baking dish and bake for 20 minutes, or until a thermometer inserted in the thickest portion registers 160°F and the juices run clear.

3. Meanwhile, cook the rice in a large saucepan of boiling water for 10 to 12 minutes, or until tender. Drain well and return to the pan. Set aside for 5 minutes, then add the cilantro, mint, and lime peel. Toss the rice with a fork to mix.

4. In a small serving bowl, combine the cucumber, tomatoes, onion, and the remaining ½ cup yogurt and 1 tablespoon lemon juice. Stir to mix.

5. Cook the pappadums in the microwave oven following the package instructions. Serve the chicken with the rice, cucumber-tomato salsa, pappadums, and chutney.

Per serving: 420 calories, 51 g carbohydrates, 42 g protein, 4.5 g fat, 3 g fiber

COOK'S TIP

Tandoori paste, a reddish blend of spices, garlic, and chiles, is sold in Indian food stores and some supermarkets. Pappadums are wafer-thin Indian flatbreads made from lentil flour. They are sold in Indian food stores. Crisp lavash may be used instead.

SICILIAN CHICKEN

Serves 4

The bright and lively flavors of this southern Italian chicken and pasta main dish really come through. Green olives may replace the kalamatas, and cauliflower can take the place of broccoli, if you like.

PREPARATION TIME: 10 MINUTES   COOKING TIME: 45 MINUTES

8	chicken drumsticks
1	tablespoon olive oil
1	yellow onion, cut into thin wedges
2	cloves garlic, crushed
1	can (28 ounces) diced tomatoes
⅔	cup kalamata olives
2	tablespoons tomato paste
8	ounces fusilli pasta, or other short pasta
10	ounces broccoli, cut into small florets
⅓	cup flat-leaf parsley, chopped
	Grated peel of ½ lemon
	Freshly ground black pepper

1. Wrap a piece of paper towel around the end of one drumstick. Hold the paper towel with one hand and pull off the skin with the other. Discard the skin and repeat with the remaining drumsticks.

2. Heat the olive oil in a large, heavy-based saucepan over medium heat. Add half the chicken. Cook for 3 to 4 minutes, turning occasionally, until well browned. Transfer to a plate and repeat with the remaining chicken. Set aside.

3. Add the onion and garlic to the pan and cook over medium heat, stirring occasionally, for 4 to 5 minutes, or until the onion softens. Return the chicken to the pan with the tomatoes, olives, and tomato paste. Increase the heat and bring to a boil. Reduce the heat and simmer, partially covered, for 20 minutes. Remove the lid and continue to cook for 5 to 10 minutes longer, or until the chicken is no longer pink in the center and the sauce thickens slightly.

4. Meanwhile, cook the pasta in a large saucepan of boiling water, following the package directions or until al dente, adding the broccoli for the last minute. Drain well and return to the pan.

5. Mix the parsley and lemon peel into the pasta. Toss well to combine and season to taste with pepper. Serve the chicken with the broccoli pasta.

Per serving: 582 calories, 60 g carbohydrates, 46 g protein, 16.5 g fat, 12 g fiber

CHICKEN, FENNEL, AND LEMON PAELLA

Serves 8

This splendid meal is lovely for serving to a group. The Green Bean, Tomato, and Olive Salad (page 160) goes well alongside.

PREPARATION TIME: 10 MINUTES   COOKING TIME: 30 MINUTES

- 1 tablespoon olive oil
- 1 medium fennel bulb, finely sliced
- 1 small onion, finely sliced
- 2 cloves garlic, coarsely chopped
- 1 pound chicken tenders
- 2 cups basmati rice
-   Salt and freshly ground black pepper
- 4 cups chicken broth, boiling
- ⅓ cup finely chopped fresh dill leaves + some sprigs for garnish
-   Grated peel and juice of ½ lemon
- 1 cup shaved Parmesan cheese

1. Preheat the oven to 400°F.

2. Heat the oil in a large, ovenproof, heavy frying pan. Add the fennel, onion, and garlic, and cook until they become opaque, approximately 2 minutes. Remove and set aside.

3. Add the chicken and cook for 3 to 4 minutes, or until no longer pink and the juices run clear. Remove and set aside.

4. Stir in the rice and cook for 2 minutes. Season to taste with salt and pepper.

5. Add the chicken broth and bring to a boil. Stir to mix. Add the chopped dill, lemon peel and juice, and the reserved fennel mixture.

6. Place the pan in the oven. Bake, uncovered, for 20 minutes.

7. Add the Parmesan and reserved chicken. Toss gently with a fork to mix with the rice. Serve immediately, garnished with sprigs of dill.

Per serving: 312 calories, 43 g carbohydrates, 18 g protein, 8 g fat, 3 g fiber

CHICKEN AND BOK CHOY STIR-FRY

Serves 4

A lovely, quick dish for a weeknight dinner. If baby corn is not available, add ½ cup frozen corn kernels.

PREPARATION TIME: 10 MINUTES   COOKING TIME: 10 MINUTES

10 ounces dried egg noodles
2 teaspoons canola oil
2 cloves garlic, minced
2 tablespoons grated fresh ginger
1 pound boneless, skinless chicken breasts, cut into thin strips
3 heads bok choy, leaves and stems coarsely chopped
8 ears baby corn on the cob, halved
3 tablespoons soy sauce
1 tablespoon oyster sauce
1 red chile, seeded and thinly sliced
½ cup cashew nuts, toasted (see Cook's Tip, page 187)
4 scallions, thinly sliced

1. Cook the noodles in plenty of boiling water for 4 to 5 minutes. Rinse in cold water, drain well, and set aside.

2. Heat the oil in a wok and add the garlic and ginger. Stir-fry for a few seconds, or until aromatic, then add the chicken and stir-fry for 5 minutes, or until the chicken is no longer pink. Add the bok choy and corn and stir until the bok choy is wilted. Add the soy sauce, oyster sauce, and chile. Stir to coat the chicken in the sauce.

3. Add the reserved noodles and toss to heat through. Serve in bowls and scatter the cashews and scallions over top.

Per serving: 605 calories, 63 g carbohydrates, 42 g protein, 20 g fat, 5 g fiber

ROAST CHICKEN WITH APRICOT AND ALMOND STUFFING

Serves 6

This roast fowl is as comforting as an old-fashioned Sunday lunch, but the enticing Middle Eastern flavorings make it new.

PREPARATION TIME: 10 MINUTES   COOKING TIME: 1 HOUR 40 MINUTES

Canola oil spray
½ cup quick-cooking barley
12 dried apricots, coarsely chopped
⅓ cup coarsely chopped unblanched almonds
½ bunch flat-leaf parsley, coarsely chopped
Grated peel and juice of ½ lemon
1 egg, lightly beaten
Salt and freshly ground black pepper
1 broiler-fryer chicken (3 to 3½ pounds), trimmed of skin and all visible fat
1 tablespoon olive oil
2 cups chicken or vegetable broth

1. Preheat the oven to 350°F. Lightly coat a baking dish with oil spray.

2. In a bowl, combine the barley, apricots, almonds, parsley, lemon peel and juice, and egg. Season to taste with salt and pepper.

3. Stuff the barley mixture into the cavity of the chicken. Place, breast side up, in the prepared baking dish. Tie the legs together with kitchen string and rub the chicken with the oil. Pour the broth into the dish.

4. Cover the dish with aluminum foil. Bake for 1 hour, then remove the aluminum foil and bake 30 minutes, basting the chicken with the broth, until a thermometer inserted in a breast registers 180°F and the juices run clear.

5. Remove the chicken from the dish and discard the string. Keep the chicken warm while making the sauce.

6. Make a reduction sauce by simmering the broth in the baking dish over a medium heat to reduce by half. Season to taste with salt and pepper. Strain through a fine sieve. Serve hot.

Per serving: 365 calories, 16 g carbohydrates, 40 g protein, 16 g fat, 4 g fiber

MOROCCAN CHICKEN WITH SWEET POTATO, CARROTS, AND PRUNES

Serves 4

The combination of ginger, cinnamon, prunes, and honey gives this stew the exotic flavors of the southern Mediterranean. Serve this one-pot meal with a crispy salad and bread.

PREPARATION TIME: 15 MINUTES   COOKING TIME: 45 TO 50 MINUTES

1   tablespoon olive oil
20 pearl onions
2   sweet potatoes, cut into bite-size chunks (about 5 cups)
2   carrots, cut into bite-size chunks
1   tablespoon grated fresh ginger
12 pitted prunes
1   teaspoon ground cinnamon

1   teaspoon pure floral honey
1½ cups vegetable or chicken broth
    Freshly ground black pepper
4   boneless, skinless chicken breasts (about 1¼ pounds), trimmed of all visible fat, cut into quarters
2   tablespoons chopped cilantro leaves
2   tablespoons chopped mint

1. Preheat the oven to 350°F. Heat the oil in a large ovenproof pot over low heat, add the onions, and cook for 5 minutes, or until the onions are soft and golden. Add the sweet potatoes, carrots, and ginger and cook for 5 minutes, or until the vegetables start to color a little.

2. Stir in the prunes, cinnamon, and honey. Allow to heat through, then pour in the broth. Season to taste with pepper.

3. Lay the chicken pieces in the liquid, then cover the pot. Bake for 35 to 40 minutes, or until the chicken is cooked through. Stir in the cilantro and mint and serve.

Per serving: 460 calories, 47 g carbohydrates, 38 g protein, 13 g fat, 8 g fiber

 ACTIVITY TIP

Dancing in some form has always been important for humans all around the globe. Find a class close to you, hit the local nightspot, or simply throw on your favorite CD at home and get moving!

PORK WITH CREAMY MUSTARD SAUCE
AND RED CABBAGE

Serves 4

The hearty flavors in this meal are warming on a chilly autumn evening.
Close with fresh Maple-Nut Stewed Apples (page 337).

PREPARATION TIME: 10 MINUTES   COOKING TIME: 20 MINUTES

1   tablespoon olive oil, divided
5   cups thinly sliced red cabbage (about ½ large head)
2   carrots, grated
1   yellow onion, cut into thin wedges
½   cup chicken broth
4   boneless pork loin cutlets (about 5¼ ounces each), trimmed of all visible fat
1   cup orange juice
½   cup low-fat evaporated milk
1   tablespoon whole grain mustard
¼   cup chopped fresh dill leaves
    Salt and freshly ground black pepper

1. Heat ½ tablespoon of the oil in a large, heavy-based saucepan over medium heat. Add the cabbage, carrots, and onion. Cook, stirring, for 3 minutes. Add the broth, cover, and reduce the heat to low. Cook for 15 minutes, or until the vegetables are tender.

2. Meanwhile, heat the remaining ½ tablespoon oil in a large, heavy-based frying pan over medium heat. Add the pork and cook for 4 to 6 minutes on each side, or until lightly browned and no longer pink in the center. Transfer to a plate, cover loosely with aluminum foil, and set aside.

3. Increase the pan heat to high and add the orange juice, milk, and mustard. Bring to a boil, stirring. Boil uncovered for 6 to 7 minutes, stirring often, until the sauce reduces and thickens slightly. Return the meat to the pan and turn to coat in the sauce.

4. Stir the dill into the cooked cabbage mixture and season with salt and pepper. To serve, spoon the sauce over the cutlets and accompany with the cabbage mixture.

Per serving: 380 calories, 24 g carbohydrates, 40 g protein, 13 g fat, 4 g fiber

PORK WITH HONEY-GLAZED APPLES

(photo on page 222) *Serves 2*

Autumn's harvest ingredients—honey, apples, and pork—are ideal for cool weather suppers. Lentils gently simmered in broth until they are tender make a satisfying low-GI accompaniment.

PREPARATION TIME: 15 MINUTES   COOKING TIME: 25 MINUTES

PORK AND APPLES:

Olive oil spray

2 pork tenderloin medallions (7 ounces each)

2 teaspoons reduced-fat margarine spread

2 teaspoons olive oil

2 Granny Smith apples, cored and cut into $\frac{1}{4}$" thick slices

1 tablespoon pure floral honey

1 tablespoon lemon juice

$1\frac{1}{2}$ cups steamed green beans

LENTILS:

1 cup vegetable broth

$\frac{2}{3}$ cup split red lentils

1 bay leaf

1. To make the pork and apples: Coat a nonstick frying pan with oil spray and heat over medium-high heat. Add the pork to the pan and cook for 4 to 5 minutes on each side, until lightly browned and a thermometer inserted sideways in the center reaches 155°F and the juices run clear. Transfer to a plate and cover to keep warm.

2. Add the margarine and olive oil to the pan and reduce the heat to medium-low. Add the apple slices and cook for 7 minutes, stirring and turning occasionally, until the apples begin to brown. Add the honey and lemon juice and stir to coat the apples. Cook for 2 minutes, or until heated through.

3. Meanwhile, to make the lentils: Put the broth, lentils, and bay leaf in a saucepan. Bring to a boil, then reduce to a simmer and cook for 20 to 25 minutes, stirring occasionally (add water if the mixture becomes too dry). Cook until the lentils are very tender. Remove and discard the bay leaf. Mash some of the lentils with the back of a large spoon.

4. Serve a scoop of the lentil mash on individual plates, top with the pork and apples, and drizzle with the pan juices.

Per serving: 600 calories, 57 g carbohydrates, 63 g protein, 14 g fat, 15 g fiber

PORK VINDALOO

(photo on page 223)   *Serves 4*

Vindaloo curries are renowned for their heat, but if you like your vindaloo really fiery, add an extra green chile or two. Serve with Mung Bean Dhal (page 184) and Cucumber Raita (page 157) for an authentic dining experience.

PREPARATION TIME: 30 MINUTES   MARINATING TIME: 1 HOUR

COOKING TIME: 1 HOUR 30 MINUTES

MARINADE:

2–2½ tablespoons Vindaloo Curry Powder (page 285 or prepared), or more to taste

4   tablespoons white wine vinegar

1   tablespoon malt vinegar

VINDALOO:

1   pound 10 ounces pork loin or shoulder, cut into 1½" cubes

2   tablespoons olive oil

2   onions, thinly sliced

3   tomatoes, chopped

4   cloves garlic, thinly sliced

1½" piece fresh ginger, cut into matchsticks

2   green chiles, seeds removed, chopped

1   teaspoon brown sugar

1   cup water

½   cup chopped cilantro leaves

2   cups steamed basmati rice

1. To make the marinade: In a large bowl, combine 2 tablespoons curry powder and the vinegars together. Whisk to blend. Add the remaining curry powder if a hotter paste is desired.

2. To make the vindaloo: Add the pork to the marinade bowl and toss the pieces to coat. Cover and allow to marinate in the refrigerator for 1 hour (or more, if you have the time).

3. Heat the oil in a large pot over low heat and gently cook the onions until soft and golden. Add the tomatoes, garlic, ginger, chiles, and sugar. Stir well to combine.

4. Remove the pork from the marinade and add to the pot, reserving the marinade. Increase the heat and cook for 1 to 2 minutes, or until the meat is starting to brown. Add the water and the reserved marinade. Cover and simmer for 1 to 1½ hours, stirring occasionally, or until the meat is very tender and well cooked. Stir in the cilantro just before serving with the rice.

Per serving: 455 calories, 34 g carbohydrates, 46 g protein, 14 g fat, 4 g fiber

Recipe: Carol Selva Rajah, Gourmet Asian Cuisine

 **COOK'S TIP**

To obtain 2 cups cooked rice, you will need ⅔ cup raw rice.

VINDALOO CURRY POWDER

Makes about ⅔ cup

6–7 teaspoons chili powder
4 teaspoons white poppy seeds
3 teaspoons ground cumin
2 teaspoons mild paprika
1 teaspoon ground cinnamon
1 teaspoon ground ginger

½ teaspoon amchur powder
½ teaspoon freshly ground black pepper
¼ teaspoon ground cloves
Pinch of ground star anise

1. In a bowl, combine 6 to 7 teaspoons chili powder (depending upon desired heat), the poppy seeds, cumin, paprika, cinnamon, ginger, amchur powder, pepper, cloves, and star anise. Mix thoroughly.

2. Store in an airtight container.

Recipe: Liz and Ian Hemphill, Herbies Spices

 **COOK'S TIP**

Amchur powder, the ground flesh of unripe sun-dried mangoes, is used as a souring agent. It's sold in Indian groceries and some specialty food stores. If unavailable, leave it out of the Vindaloo Curry Powder blend. When using the curry powder in a recipe, simply add 1 teaspoon of lemon juice or vinegar.

PORK FILLET WITH SPICED PEARS AND BASMATI RICE

Serves 6

Apples aren't the only fruit that enhances pork. Warmly spiced pears also are fabulous. Steamed baby carrots go well with the fruity pork.

PREPARATION TIME: 10 MINUTES   COOKING TIME: 45 MINUTES

3   teaspoons olive oil, divided
2   medium sweet potatoes, diced
1   large onion, diced
3   cloves garlic, finely chopped, divided
1   cup basmati rice
1½ cups chicken broth
    Salt and freshly ground black pepper
4   cups water

4   Bosc pears, peeled, cored, and quartered
¼   cup granulated sugar
4   whole cloves
2   strips lemon peel
1   stick cinnamon
1   pound pork tenderloin medallions
⅓   cup dry white wine
½   bunch chives (optional)

1. Heat 2 teaspoons of the oil in a large saucepan with a tight-fitting lid over a moderate heat. Add the sweet potatoes, onion, and 2 of the chopped garlic cloves. Cook for 3 minutes, stirring.

2. Add the rice. Cook for 3 minutes, stirring to coat the ingredients in oil and partially cook.

3. Pour in the chicken broth. Season to taste with salt and pepper. Cover and turn the heat down to low. Simmer very gently for 15 minutes, or until all the broth is absorbed and the rice is cooked.

4. Meanwhile, in a large saucepan, place the water, pears, sugar, cloves, lemon peel, and cinnamon. Bring to a boil, then turn the heat down to gently simmer the pears, uncovered, for 20 minutes.

5. Heat the remaining 1 teaspoon of oil in a heavy frying pan and add the pork, browning on all sides. Continue to cook the meat over a medium heat for 15 minutes, or until a thermometer inserted in the center reaches 155°F and the juices run clear. Remove the meat from the pan and keep warm.

6. Add the wine and the remaining 1 chopped garlic clove to the pan juices. Simmer, stirring the sauce, for 3 minutes. Season to taste with salt and pepper.

7. Cut the meat into diagonal slices. To serve, place mounds of rice on warmed plates, top with the meat slices, and pour the wine sauce over the top. Garnish with chives, if using. Fan the pears on the plate and pour a little poaching juice over the top.

Per serving: 353 calories, 59 g carbohydrates, 22 g protein, 2 g fat, 6 g fiber

COOK'S TIP

Choose pork tenderloin medallions that are about 1" thick. If thicker, simply place between two sheets of waxed paper and pound with the smooth side of a meat mallet or a small heavy skillet.

ACTIVITY TIP

Research has shown that just 30 minutes of moderately intense exercise each day can help to improve your health. If you prefer, you can break this down to two sessions of 15 minutes, or even three sessions of 10 minutes, and you will still see some benefits.

SLOW-COOKED PORK AND VEGETABLES

Serves 6

As this satisfying stove-top stew illustrates, it takes a variety of foods to comprise a low-GI diet. The nutritional benefits of different foods are many and varied, and it is advisable to base your food choices on overall nutritional content.

PREPARATION TIME: 15 MINUTES   COOKING TIME: 1 HOUR 45 MINUTES

2½ pounds boneless pork loin or shoulder roast, cut into 1½" cubes

2 tablespoons unbleached or all-purpose flour

2 tablespoons olive oil, divided

1 cup white wine

1½ cups chicken broth

1 can (14 ounces) diced tomatoes

8 sprigs fresh thyme

1 pound scallions, chopped

3 carrots, cut into large pieces

5 medium turnips, cut into large pieces

Salt and freshly ground black pepper

1. Coat the pork in the flour. Heat 1 tablespoon of the oil in a large, heavy-based saucepan over medium-high heat. Add one-quarter of the meat and cook for 3 to 4 minutes, or until well browned. Remove from the pan and repeat with the remaining meat, adding the remaining 1 tablespoon oil when necessary. Remove all the meat from the pan and set aside.

2. Increase the heat to high and add the wine to the pan. Cook, scraping any browned bits off the bottom of the pan, for 2 to 3 minutes, or until the wine is reduced by half. Add the broth, tomatoes, thyme, and the reserved meat to the pan. Bring to a boil. Reduce the heat to low and cook, partially covered, for 30 minutes.

3. Add the scallions, carrots, and turnips to the pan. Continue to cook, partially covered, for 40 to 50 minutes, or until the vegetables and meat are very tender. Season to taste with salt and pepper.

Per serving: 430 calories, 21 g carbohydrates, 43 g protein, 16 g fat, 7 g fiber

● ●
COOK'S TIP

Pork shoulder roast is often labeled Boston butt.

Veal Tagine with Sweet Potatoes (*page 306*)

Grilled Steak with Chile Corn Salsa *(page 308)*

Marinated Steaks with Mexican Bean Salad *(page 310)*

Beef Fajitas (*page 313*)

Pan-Fried Lamb and Greens Salad with Tzatziki *(page 316)*

● 293

Roast Lamb and Vegetables with Thyme and Rosemary (*page 326*)

Grilled Chile Mint Lamb, Tomato, and Wheat Salad (*page 328*)

Honey Banana Cups *(page 330)*

296 ●

Syrupy Oranges with Frozen Yogurt *(page 333)*

Pears Poached in Champagne *(page 334)*

Citrus Granita *(page 338)*

Chocolate Mousse with Berries *(page 339)*

Fruit Soufflé (*page 340*)

Fresh Plum and Ricotta Strudel (*page 349*)

Scottish Oat Crackers *(page 352)*

Apple and Strawberry Crumble (*page 356*)

BEEFBURGERS WITH SALSA

(photo on page 224)   *Serves 4*

Using ground rump steak with all the fat trimmed off (ask your butcher to grind it for you) makes this burger a healthier choice than typical fatty hamburger. The delicious tomato and bean salsa moistens it beautifully.

PREPARATION TIME: 15 MINUTES   COOKING TIME: 1 HOUR 10 MINUTES

SALSA:
1   tablespoon olive oil
1   small onion, finely chopped
1   small red chile, seeded and finely chopped
3   cloves garlic, minced
1   teaspoon ground cumin

½   teaspoon sweet paprika
2   cans (14 ounces each) plum tomatoes
1   can (14 ounces) red kidney beans, rinsed and drained
3   tablespoons chopped flat-leaf parsley

BURGER:
1   pound, 2 ounces lean ground beef
½   onion, finely chopped
½   cup flat-leaf parsley, finely chopped

Freshly ground black pepper
1   tablespoon olive oil

1. To make the salsa: Heat the oil in a saucepan over medium heat. Add the onion and chile and cook for 5 minutes, or until the onion is soft. Add the garlic, cumin, and paprika and cook for 2 minutes. Break the tomatoes into chunks in a bowl, then add them to the pan. Bring to a boil, then reduce the heat and simmer for 30 minutes.

2. Add the beans, return to a boil, then reduce the heat and simmer for 20 minutes. Stir in the parsley.

3. To make the burgers: Preheat a grill or frying pan. In a mixing bowl, combine the meat, onion, and parsley. Season to taste with pepper. Shape the mixture into 4 patties. Brush each with a little oil, then cook on the grill or in a frying pan for 3 to 6 minutes on each side, turning once, until golden brown and no longer pink in the center.

4. Serve the burgers with the salsa.

Per serving: 380 calories, 18 g carbohydrates, 32 g protein, 19 g fat, 8 g fiber

Recipe: Judy Davie, The Food Coach

VEAL TAGINE WITH SWEET POTATOES

(photo on page 289)   *Serves 4*

The word tagine refers both to the Moroccan cooking pot—traditionally a round clay pot with a conical lid—as well as the stew cooked in it. If you don't have a tagine, a Dutch oven will do just as well. Serve this savory stew with steamed basmati rice or bulgur wheat.

PREPARATION TIME: 20 MINUTES   COOKING TIME: 1 HOUR 15 MINUTES

SPICE MIX:

5   teaspoons mild paprika
2   teaspoons ground coriander
1   teaspoon ground cinnamon
1   teaspoon cayenne pepper
½   teaspoon allspice
¼   teaspoon ground cloves
¼   teaspoon ground green cardamom

STEW:

1   pound, 2 ounces veal roast, trimmed and cut into 1" cubes
2   tablespoons extra-virgin olive oil
2   red onions, sliced
2   cloves garlic, minced
4   tomatoes (about 10 ounces), quartered
2   sweet potatoes (about 1 pound), thickly sliced
1   red bell pepper, sliced
1   cup water
¼   cup chopped cilantro leaves (optional)

1. To make the spice mix: In a large bowl, combine the paprika, coriander, cinnamon, cayenne, allspice, cloves, and cardamom. Stir to mix.

2. To make the stew: Toss the meat in the spice mix to coat. Heat the oil in a large pot over high heat and quickly brown the meat on all sides. Remove with a slotted spoon and set aside. Reduce the heat to medium. Add the onions and garlic and cook gently for 5 minutes, or until the onions are golden and translucent.

3. Return the meat to the pot. Add the tomatoes, sweet potatoes, pepper, and water. Stir gently to combine, then cover with a piece of parchment paper (this helps reduce evaporation) and the lid. Simmer gently for 1 hour, or until the meat is tender. Garnish with cilantro, if using.

Per serving: 335 calories, 23 g carbohydrates, 31 g protein, 12 g fat, 4 g fiber

Spice Mix Recipe: Liz and Ian Hamphill, Herbies Spices

COOK'S TIPS

The pods of green cardamom are bright green and not to be confused with brown cardamom, as they are not interchangeable in recipes. Green cardamom has a sweet eucalyptus-like aroma that adds a light, fresh taste to spice mixes. Brown has a distinct "musty-smoky" flavor. You can buy green cardamom in larger supermarkets and spice stores.

Boneless, skinless turkey breast may replace the veal in this dish, if desired.

GRILLED STEAK WITH CHILE CORN SALSA

(photo on page 290)   *Serves 2*

This versatile corn salsa is delicious served with steaks cut from beef eye-of-round or rump roast. It complements other meats too, including thinly sliced rare roast beef and grilled chicken sausages.

PREPARATION TIME: 10 MINUTES   COOKING TIME: 10 TO 12 MINUTES

SALSA:

2 ears corn on the cob
1 tomato, seeded and finely chopped
½ red onion, finely chopped
2 small red chiles, seeded, finely chopped
½ bunch chives, finely chopped, divided
½ bunch cilantro, finely chopped, divided
2 tablespoons balsamic vinegar
2 tablespoons extra-virgin olive oil

STEAK:

   Olive oil spray
2 small lean beef steaks (about 3½ ounces each)
1 bunch arugula leaves

1. To make the salsa: Put the corn in a saucepan of boiling water and cook for 5 minutes. Drain and allow to cool slightly. Use a sharp knife to cut the kernels from the cobs, then place them in a large bowl.

2. Add the tomato, onion, chiles, half the chives, half the cilantro, the vinegar, and oil. Toss to mix completely. Set aside.

3. To make the steak: Preheat a grill or frying pan. Coat lightly with oil spray. Cook the steaks for 2 to 4 minutes each side, until browned and cooked to desired doneness. A thermometer inserted in the center registers 145°F for medium-rare, 160°F for medium, and 165°F for well-done.

4. To serve, put a steak on each plate, spoon a small mound of salsa on each steak, and serve with the arugula. Garnish with the remaining chives and cilantro.

Per serving: 495 calories, 30 g carbohydrates, 31 g protein, 26 g fat, 10 g fiber

Chile Corn Salsa Recipe: Luke Mangan

GRILLED BEEF WITH THAI NOODLE SALAD

Serves 4

The combination of sizzling grilled beef with cool refreshing noodles and herbs is irresistible.

PREPARATION TIME: 25 MINUTES   COOKING TIME: 10 MINUTES

2 ounces dried rice vermicelli	1½ tablespoons lime juice
2 cups bean sprouts	1 tablespoon fish sauce
1 carrot, cut into thin strips	1 tablespoon + 1 teaspoon canola oil
1 cucumber, cut into thin strips	1 teaspoon granulated sugar
1 red bell pepper, cut into thin strips	1 small fresh red chile, finely chopped
1 bunch mint, coarsely chopped	4 beef tenderloin steaks, trimmed of excess fat (about 4½ ounces each)
1 bunch cilantro, leaves only, coarsely chopped	Freshly ground black pepper

1. Place the vermicelli in a bowl and cover with cold water. Let stand for 5 minutes, or until the noodles are translucent. Drain and cut into short lengths.

2. Meanwhile, in a large serving bowl, combine the bean sprouts, carrot, cucumber, bell pepper, mint, cilantro, and the noodles. Toss well. In a small bowl, combine the lime juice, fish sauce, 1 tablespoon oil, sugar, and chile. Whisk to blend. Set aside.

3. Preheat a grill or frying pan on medium-high. Brush the steaks with the remaining 1 teaspoon oil. Season to taste with pepper. Cook, turning frequently, for 10 minutes, or until desired doneness. A thermometer inserted in the center of the steak registers 145°F for medium-rare, 160°F for medium, and 165°F for well-done. Set aside for 5 minutes.

4. Add the reserved dressing to the noodle mixture and toss to coat. Serve the noodle salad with the steaks.

Per serving: 289 calories, 24 g carbohydrates, 29 g protein, 10 g fat, 4 g fiber

COOK'S TIP

Southeast Asian fish sauce, or *nam pla*, is sold in many supermarkets and Asian food stores. Soy sauce may be substituted.

MARINATED STEAKS WITH MEXICAN BEAN SALAD

(*photo on page 291*)   *Serves 4*

Game meats, such as caribou or venison, are also a good alternative, being incredibly lean and packed with essential nutrients, including iron and zinc.

SOAKING TIME: OVERNIGHT   MARINATING TIME: 1 TO 2 HOURS

PREPARATION TIME: 10 MINUTES   COOKING TIME: 45 TO 50 MINUTES

MARINADE FOR STEAK:

½   cup red wine

1   tablespoon olive oil

1   tablespoon soy sauce

2   teaspoons liquid smoke

½   teaspoon paprika

    Freshly ground black pepper

4   lean beef fillets (about 5 ounces each)

SALAD:

1½ cups dry black beans

½   red bell pepper, finely chopped

3   scallions, thinly sliced

1   red chile, finely chopped

1   tablespoon extra-virgin olive oil

    Pinch of cayenne pepper

    Olive oil spray

8   spears asparagus

1   tablespoon Bourbon whiskey

1. To make the marinade for the steak: Combine the wine, oil, soy sauce, liquid smoke, paprika, and a pinch of pepper in a glass bowl. Put the steaks in a large resealable plastic bag and pour in the marinade. Squeeze out the excess air and seal the bag. Marinate in the refrigerator for 1 to 2 hours, turning the steaks occasionally.

2. Meanwhile, to make the salad: Soak the beans overnight in water. The next day, drain the beans and transfer to a saucepan. Cover with water and bring to

a boil. Cook for 30 to 40 minutes, or until al dente (cooking time will vary depending on the size of the beans and their soaking time). Transfer to a bowl and allow to cool. Add the bell pepper, scallions, chile, oil, and cayenne. Stir to mix. Cover and set aside.

3. Heat a grill or frying pan. Coat with oil spray. Cook the asparagus for 2 to 3 minutes, or until slightly browned. Remove and set aside.

4. Remove the steaks from the marinade, reserving the marinade, and pat dry with paper towels. Cook on the grill for 3 to 5 minutes on each side, or until desired doneness. A thermometer inserted in the center of the steak registers 145°F for medium-rare, 160°F for medium, and 165°F for well-done.

5. Put the reserved marinade in a small saucepan and add the Bourbon. Heat gently and simmer for 4 to 5 minutes to reduce and thicken the sauce.

6. To serve, spoon a little of the sauce over the steaks and serve with the salad and grilled asparagus.

Per serving: 460 calories, 31 g carbohydrates, 50 g protein, 12 g fat, 15 g fiber

Recipe: Steffan Rössner

MEDITERRANEAN BEEF STEW

Serves 6

Like all good stews, this one benefits in flavor if made in advance. After preparing it, cool completely, then refrigerate for several days or freeze for several weeks. Reheat gently before serving over noodles or rice.

PREPARATION TIME: 20 MINUTES   COOKING TIME: 1 HOUR 40 MINUTES

- 1 tablespoon olive oil
- 1 large onion, thinly sliced
- 2 pounds beef eye-of-round roast, cut into 1" cubes
- ½ cup red wine
  Salt and freshly ground pepper
- 1 cup crushed tomatoes
- 1 large bay leaf
- 1 cup dried porcini mushrooms, rehydrated in 1 cup warm water
- 1 pound baby carrots, halved
- 1 teaspoon finely chopped fresh thyme
- 1½ tablespoons finely chopped fresh parsley

1. Heat the oil in a large skillet. Add the onion and cook for 2 minutes. Add the meat and cook for 3 minutes, or until all sides are browned.

2. Add the wine. Season to taste with salt and pepper. Add the tomatoes and bay leaf. Bring to a boil, then simmer for 1 hour.

3. With a slotted spoon, remove the mushrooms from the soaking water. Strain the soaking water through a fine sieve. Add the mushrooms and water to the stew mixture.

4. Add the carrots, thyme, and parsley and mix well. Simmer for 30 minutes. Remove and discard the bay leaf.

Per serving: 414 calories, 13 g carbohydrates, 31 g protein, 25 g fat, 3 g fiber

BEEF FAJITAS

(*photo on page 292*)   *Serves 4*

This recipe makes enough for three rolls for each person. Serve the fajitas accompanied with your choice of grated cheese, shredded lettuce, guacamole, yogurt, tomato salsa, and refried beans.

PREPARATION TIME: 15 MINUTES   COOKING TIME: 15 MINUTES

2	tablespoons olive oil
1	pound, 2 ounces beef rump steak, thinly sliced
1	red onion, sliced
1	red bell pepper, sliced
1	yellow bell pepper, sliced
1–2	jalapeño chiles, seeded and finely chopped
2	tablespoons tomato paste
2	teaspoons sweet paprika
1	teaspoon ground cumin
1	teaspoon ground coriander
½	teaspoon chili powder
	Juice of 1 lime
2	tablespoons chopped cilantro leaves
12	flour tortillas

1. Heat the oil in a large frying pan over medium heat. Cook the meat, in batches, for 3 to 4 minutes each batch, or until brown. Remove from the pan.

2. Add the onion, bell peppers, and chiles to the pan. Cook for 3 minutes. Stir in the tomato paste, paprika, cumin, coriander, chili powder, and lime juice. Return all the meat to the pan and cook for 2 to 3 minutes, or until heated through. Stir in the cilantro leaves.

3. Heat the tortillas following the package instructions. Spoon a portion of the beef mixture onto a plate with a tortilla. Place some of the beef mixture on one side of a tortilla, add accompaniments of your choice, and roll up.

Per serving: 590 calories, 58 g carbohydrates, 38 g protein, 22 g fat, 5 g fiber

BEEF STROGANOFF

Serves 4

Beef stroganoff is usually loaded with sour cream, which pushes up the saturated fat content. This version uses low-fat yogurt instead of sour cream. The GI of this recipe is medium, which is due to the basmati rice—to lower the GI, you may prefer to use half rice and half barley.

PREPARATION TIME: 15 MINUTES   COOKING TIME: 20 MINUTES

1½ cups basmati rice	2 large cloves garlic, minced
2 cups water	8 ounces mushrooms, sliced
1 pound, 2 ounces lean beef, cut into strips	Grated peel and juice of 1 orange
1 tablespoon olive oil	½ teaspoon dried dill, or 1 tablespoon chopped fresh dill
1 red onion, thinly sliced	Freshly ground black pepper
1 onion, thinly sliced	1 cup low-fat plain yogurt

1. Wash the rice and put it in a large saucepan with the water. Cover with the lid and bring to a boil, then reduce the heat and simmer for 10 minutes. Turn off the heat and leave to stand, without removing the lid, until ready to serve.

2. Meanwhile, heat a large nonstick frying pan over medium heat. Dry-fry the meat, in small batches, for 2 minutes. Remove the meat.

3. Using the same pan, heat the oil over medium heat. Add the onion and garlic and cook for 5 minutes, or until the onion is soft. Add the mushrooms and cook for 3 minutes. Return the meat to the pan.

4. Add the orange peel and juice and the dill and season to taste with lots of pepper. Turn off the heat before mixing in the yogurt.

5. Spoon the steamed rice onto plates and top with the stroganoff.

Per serving: 540 calories, 70 g carbohydrates, 39 g protein, 10 g fat, 3 g fiber

Recipe: Isobel McMillan

RACK OF LAMB WITH LEMON
AND ROSEMARY ON POTATO-GARLIC MASH *Serves 6*

Because meats have virtually no carbohydrates, they rank Zero on the GI index.
So, with appropriate portions of well-trimmed lean meats, these protein- and
nutrient-rich foods can add variety and flavor to our diets.

PREPARATION TIME: 10 MINUTES   COOKING TIME: 40 MINUTES+ 5 MINUTES STANDING TIME

- 2 racks of lamb, 6 chops each, trimmed of all visible fat
- 3 cloves garlic, halved
  Peel of 1 lemon
- 6 sprigs fresh rosemary, coarsely chopped + 6 sprigs for garnish
  Freshly ground black pepper
- 2 tablespoons olive oil
  Potato-Garlic Mash (page 174)

1. Preheat the oven to 400°F.

2. Cut a tunnel between the bone and the meat of the lamb, and fill
   with garlic halves, lemon peel, and some of the chopped rosemary.

3. Pierce the meat and insert the remaining chopped rosemary over the surface
   of the meat.

4. Place the meat in a baking dish. Season with pepper, then drizzle with oil.

5. Bake for 35 to 40 minutes, or until a thermometer inserted in the center
   registers 145°F for medium-rare, 160°F for medium, or 165°F for well-done.

6. Let the meat stand for 5 minutes in a warm place before cutting into chops.
   Serve on a bed of hot Potato-Garlic Mash. Decorate each plate with a sprig
   of fresh rosemary.

Per serving (with mash): 467 calories, 28 g carbohydrates, 19 g protein, 31 g fat,
4 g fiber

Per serving (without mash): 330 calories, 1 g carbohydrates, 16 g protein, 28 g fat,
0 g fiber

PAN-FRIED LAMB AND GREENS SALAD WITH TZATZIKI

(photo on page 293)   *Serves 4*

Tzatziki is a traditional Greek cucumber and yogurt dip and makes a delicious dressing for this lamb salad. It is often served as a dip with grape leaves or vegetable platters. You can find prepared tzatziki in the refrigerated section of some supermarkets.

PREPARATION TIME: 20 MINUTES   COOKING TIME: 10 MINUTES

TZATZIKI:

½ cucumber
1   cup low-fat plain yogurt
    Juice of ½ lemon
1   tablespoon chopped mint
1   clove garlic, minced

SALAD:

    Olive oil spray
1   pound, 2 ounces lamb fillets
    Freshly ground black pepper
2   cups arugula leaves
2   cups baby spinach leaves
1   cup cherry tomatoes, halved
½   cucumber, sliced
½   cup peas, cooked al dente
½   red onion, thinly sliced
1   red bell pepper, thinly sliced
2   tablespoons extra-virgin olive oil
    Juice of ½ lemon

1. To make the tzatziki: Grate the cucumber into a bowl. Empty the bowl onto a clean kitchen towel and squeeze out the water in the cucumber. Return to the bowl. Add the yogurt, lemon juice, mint, and garlic. Stir to mix well. Set aside.

2. To make the salad: Heat a nonstick frying pan over medium heat. Coat lightly with oil spray. Season the lamb to taste with pepper and cook for 3 minutes on each side. The meat should still be pink in the middle. Remove from the pan and allow to rest for a few minutes before cutting into thin slices.

3. Meanwhile, in a serving bowl, combine the arugula, spinach, tomatoes, cucumber, peas, onion, bell pepper, oil, and lemon juice. Toss to mix.

4. Divide the salad among 4 plates. Lay the meat slices over the salad and top with a generous spoonful of the reserved tzatziki.

Per serving: 305 calories, 10 g carbohydrates, 33 g protein, 14 g fat, 4 g fiber

ACTIVITY TIP

Try out a new activity. For example, join a dance class—salsa, ballroom, line dancing, or jazz. Go rollerblading with friends, book golf or tennis lessons, or take your children to the park. You can't afford not to exercise, so find something you enjoy and get moving!

LAMB BURGERS WITH SWEET POTATO CHIPS AND SPINACH SALAD

Serves 6

This recipe is actually a whole meal in one. For variety, you can replace the lamb with extra-lean ground beef or pork tenderloin that you grind in the food processor.

PREPARATION TIME: 20 MINUTES   COOKING TIME: 50 MINUTES

CHIPS:

2¾ pounds sweet potatoes, peeled and cut into thick slices
1   tablespoon olive oil
    Salt and freshly ground black pepper

BURGERS:

1¼ pounds extra lean ground lamb
1   cup fresh bread crumbs, made from Pepperidge Farm Sprouted Wheat bread
⅓   cup fresh parsley, finely chopped
⅓   cup fresh mint, finely chopped
1   egg
1   clove garlic, crushed
½   tablespoon olive oil

SPINACH SALAD:

4   cups baby spinach leaves
12 cherry tomatoes
1   tablespoon lemon juice
    Freshly ground black pepper
1   jar (12 ounces) mild tomato salsa dip

1. To make the chips: Preheat the oven to 425°F. Line 2 large baking sheets with nonstick baking paper.

2. Place the sweet potatoes and olive oil in a large bowl. Season to taste with salt and pepper. Toss well to coat. Spread the potatoes in a single layer over the prepared baking sheets. Bake for 45 to 50 minutes, rotating the sheets once, until cooked through and crisp.

3. Meanwhile, to make the burgers: In a large bowl, combine the meat, bread crumbs, parsley, mint, egg, and garlic. Use clean hands to mix until well combined. Divide the mixture into 6 portions and shape each into a patty. Heat the oil in a large frying pan over medium heat. Add the patties and cook for 4 to 5 minutes on each side, or until the meat is no longer pink and a thermometer inserted in the center of a patty registers 160°F.

4. To make the salad: In a small serving bowl, combine the spinach, tomatoes, lemon juice, and pepper.

5. Serve the burgers with the sweet potato chips, salad, and salsa.

Per serving: 467 calories, 39 g carbohydrates, 27 g protein, 11 g fat, 8 g fiber

LAMB CUTLETS WITH PEA PILAF

Serves 4

Cardamom, which is related to ginger, grows in pulpy pods the size of chickpeas. Encased in the pods are many tiny aromatic seeds with a spicy sweet flavor. Before using, lightly crush the pods in a mortar and pestle or with the side of a chopping knife.

PREPARATION TIME: 15 MINUTES   MARINATING TIME: 1 HOUR
COOKING TIME: 30 MINUTES

MARINADE AND MEAT:

½   cup low-fat plain yogurt
1   teaspoon ground coriander
1   teaspoon ground cumin
2   teaspoons grated fresh ginger
8   lean lamb cutlets

PILAF:

2   teaspoons canola oil
1   small onion, halved and sliced
⅔   cup basmati rice
4   cardamom pods, lightly crushed
½   teaspoon ground turmeric
7   ounces cauliflower (½ small head), cut into small florets
1   cup vegetable broth
1   head broccoli (about 12 ounces), cut into small florets
1   cup fresh or frozen green peas
    Olive oil spray

1. To make the marinade and meat: Combine the yogurt with the coriander, cumin, and ginger. Place the meat in a nonmetallic dish and spread the yogurt mixture over the meat. Cover and refrigerate for 1 hour.

2. To make the pilaf: Heat the oil in a large saucepan and add the onion. Cook over medium heat for 3 to 5 minutes, stirring often, until the onion is soft and lightly golden. Add the rice, cardamom pods, and turmeric. Cook, stirring, for 30 seconds.

3. Add the cauliflower and broth. Stir once, then cover and bring to a boil. Reduce the heat to very low and cook for 10 minutes. Add the broccoli and peas and cook for 10 minutes. Remove from the heat and allow to stand, covered, for 5 minutes.

4. Meanwhile, heat a grill or nonstick frying pan. Coat the grill rack or pan with oil spray. Cook the meat over medium-high heat for 4 to 6 minutes on each side, or until lightly browned and no longer pink in the center. Serve the meat with the pilaf.

Per serving: 420 calories, 34 g carbohydrates, 43 g protein, 12.5 g fat, 6 g fiber

BALSAMIC LAMB
WITH SWEET POTATO MASH

Serves 4

This elegant main course is delicious proof that low-GI eating can be truly gourmet.

PREPARATION TIME: 10 MINUTES   MARINATING TIME: 6 HOURS OR OVERNIGHT
COOKING TIME: 20 MINUTES

¼   cup balsamic vinegar
4   teaspoons extra-virgin olive oil, divided
1   clove garlic, crushed
1   tablespoon chopped fresh rosemary leaves
4   lamb loin chops, well-trimmed (about 4 ounces each)
1¾ pounds sweet potatoes, cut into chunks
2   tablespoons low-fat milk, warmed
    Salt and freshly ground black pepper
½   cup beef broth
7   ounces green beans, steamed
14 ounces yellow squash, steamed

1. In a shallow glass dish, combine the vinegar, 2 teaspoons of oil, garlic, and rosemary. Add the meat and toss to coat. Cover and refrigerate for 6 hours or overnight to marinate.

2. Remove the meat from the marinade. Reserve the marinade.

3. In a large saucepan, combine the sweet potatoes with hot water to cover. Cook for 20 minutes, or until very tender. Drain well and mash until smooth. Add the milk and use a wooden spoon to beat until smooth. Season with salt and pepper to taste.

4. Meanwhile, heat the remaining 2 teaspoons oil in a large frying pan over medium-high heat. Add the meat. Cook for 4 to 6 minutes on each side, or until a thermometer inserted in the center registers 145°F for medium-rare, 160°F for medium, or 165°F for well-done. Remove the meat. Increase the heat to high and add the broth and the reserved marinade to the pan. Simmer for 2 minutes, or until the sauce reduces and thickens.

5. Divide the potatoes among 4 plates. Thickly slice the meat and place over the mash. Spoon the sauce over top and serve with the beans and squash.

Per serving: 370 calories, 33 g carbohydrates, 36 g protein, 10 g fat, 10 g fiber

SLOW-ROAST LAMB WITH CHICKPEAS

Serves 4

This recipe is perfect for a dinner party or family get-together, as everything can be prepared in advance and pulled from the oven when you are ready to eat. Potatoes are usually served with a roast but unnecessary here, as a chickpea and tomato sauce provides the starchy accompaniment.

PREPARATION TIME: 15 MINUTES   COOKING TIME: 3 HOURS

2	tablespoons olive oil
	Juice of 1 lemon
4	large cloves garlic, minced
1	teaspoon ground cumin
	Freshly ground black pepper
2¼	pounds leg-of-lamb, large pieces of visible fat removed
2	onions, chopped
1	can (14 ounces) chopped tomatoes
1	cup vegetable broth
¼	cup tomato paste
1	tablespoon pure floral honey
1	cinnamon stick
¼	teaspoon ground cloves
1	can (14 ounces) chickpeas, rinsed and drained

1. Preheat the oven to 325°F. In a bowl, combine the oil, lemon juice, garlic, cumin, and a pinch of pepper. Whisk to mix.

2. Put the meat in a large, nonstick flameproof baking pan. Rub the oil mixture over the meat. Cook over medium heat, turning as needed, to brown on all sides. Remove from the pan and set aside.

3. Add the onions to the hot pan. Cook for 4 to 5 minutes, or until soft and translucent. Add the tomatoes, broth, tomato paste, honey, cinnamon, and cloves. Mix well. Return the meat to the pan and spoon over the sauce. Cover with a tight lid or aluminum foil.

4. Roast for 2½ to 3 hours, or until a thermometer inserted in the center registers 165°F for well-done. Remove the meat, set aside, and keep warm. Place the pan over medium heat. Add the chickpeas and heat through. Remove and discard the cinnamon stick.

5. Slice the meat and serve with the chickpea tomato sauce spooned over the top.

Per serving: 360 calories, 25 g carbohydrates, 30 g protein, 15 g fat, 7 g fiber

 **ACTIVITY TIP**

A balanced exercise program—including aerobic, resistance, and stretching exercises—will give you the best results. Variety is also important because the body becomes efficient at anything it does repeatedly, so after a while you'll need to add something new to your exercise program.

ROAST LAMB AND VEGETABLES
WITH THYME AND ROSEMARY

(photo on page 294)   *Serves 6*

This is your traditional roast with a flavorsome, healthy Mediterranean twist.
Roasting vegetables brings out their natural sweetness and is an easy way
of serving a great assortment.

PREPARATION TIME: 20 MINUTES   MARINATING TIME: 6 HOURS OR OVERNIGHT
COOKING TIME: 50 MINUTES   STANDING TIME: 10 MINUTES

2   tablespoons coarsely chopped thyme
3   tablespoons olive oil, divided
2¼ pounds boneless leg of lamb
5   sprigs thyme, each sprig broken into 3 pieces
3   sweet potatoes (about 2¾ pounds), cut into 1" chunks
6   zucchini (about 1 pound), cut in half lengthwise
3   large red onions, each cut into 8 wedges
1   red bell pepper, cut into thick strips
3   sprigs rosemary
3   cloves garlic, each cut into 5 slices
2   tablespoons lemon juice

1. Combine the chopped thyme and 1 tablespoon of the oil in a small bowl. Put
the meat into a large glass dish and use your hands to coat the lamb in the
thyme mixture.

2. Roll up the meat and tie with kitchen string, to keep the shape and ensure it
will cook evenly. Using a sharp knife, cut 15 evenly spaced slits, about ¾" deep
and ½" long, into the top of the meat. Insert a sprig of thyme into each slit.
Cover with plastic wrap and refrigerate for at least 6 hours or overnight.

3. Preheat the oven to 350°F. Put the sweet potatoes, zucchini, onions, and pepper in a large roasting pan and scatter the leaves from the rosemary over top. Drizzle with 1 tablespoon of the oil and toss gently to coat. Place the meat on top of the vegetables. Insert a slice of garlic into each slit with the thyme.

4. In a screw-top jar, combine the lemon juice and the remaining 1 tablespoon of oil. Shake to blend. Drizzle over the meat.

5. Roast, basting with the pan juices occasionally, for 50 minutes, or until a thermometer inserted in the center registers 145°F for medium-rare, 160°F for medium, or 165°F for well-done. Turn off the oven. Transfer the meat to a platter. Cover with aluminum foil and set aside for 10 minutes to rest.

6. Return the vegetables to the oven to keep warm until the meat is sliced and served.

Per serving: 490 calories, 37 g carbohydrates, 40 g protein, 19 g fat, 7 g fiber

ACTIVITY TIP

A recent study found that those who walked regularly with a dog lost more weight than those who walked alone. If you don't have a dog, offer to walk a neighbor's—you will both end up reaping the rewards.

GRILLED CHILE MINT LAMB, TOMATO, AND WHEAT SALAD

(photo on page 295)   *Serves 2*

This tasty salad uses the classic flavor combination of lamb, mint, and tomatoes.
Pork or beef tenderloin or chicken or turkey breast can replace the lamb, if desired.

PREPARATION TIME: 15 MINUTES   COOKING TIME: 8 MINUTES   STANDING TIME: 10 MINUTES

½   cup bulgur wheat
½   cup boiling water
9   ounces lamb fillet, trimmed of all visible fat
2   teaspoons extra-virgin olive oil + extra for brushing meat
1   cup mint leaves, coarsely torn
4   small tomatoes, cut into eighths, or 8 cherry tomatoes, halved
½   red bell pepper, sliced into strips
1   small cucumber, sliced into rounds
1   red chile, seeds removed and thinly sliced (optional)
    Grated peel of 1 lemon
    Juice of 1½ lemons
    Freshly ground black pepper

1. Put the bulgur wheat in a serving bowl and pour the boiling water over top. Cover with aluminum foil (or plastic wrap or a plate). Allow to steam for 15 minutes, or until the water is absorbed.

2. Meanwhile, preheat a grill or frying pan. Lightly brush the meat with a little oil. Cook on a grill or pan for 3 to 4 minutes on each side, or until a thermometer inserted in the center registers 145°F for medium-rare, 160°F for medium, or 165°F for well-done. Remove the meat, wrap in aluminum foil and allow to stand for 10 minutes.

3. Fluff the bulgur with a fork. Add the mint, tomatoes, bell pepper, cucumber, chile (if using), lemon peel and juice, and the 2 teaspoons oil. Season to taste with pepper. Toss to mix well.

4. Slice the meat thinly across the grain. Toss with the salad ingredients or serve on top of the salad.

Per serving: 405 calories, 37 g carbohydrates, 34 g protein, 11 g fat, 10 g fiber

DESSERTS AND SWEET TREATS

Eating on the low-GI diet means enjoying desserts that are good for the spirits—and the body. Not feeling deprived is a big psychological boost for any dieter. Many of the ingredients used to prepare yummy desserts, such as fruit and dairy products, have a low GI. They make a valuable contribution to our daily intake of healthful foods and, being carbohydrate-rich, add to our feeling of fullness. So savor Apple and Strawberry Crumble, Chocolate Mousse with Berries, Baked Ricotta Cheesecake, Poached Pears with Rich Chocolate Sauce, or any of our other luscious recipes for desserts and sweet treats.

Chapter 10

HONEY BANANA CUPS

(photo on page 296)   *Serves 2*

Unlike most other fruit, bananas contain both sugars and starch. The less ripe the banana, the lower its GI. As the banana ripens, the starch turns to sugars and the GI increases.

PREPARATION TIME: 5 MINUTES

1	cup low-fat honey-flavored yogurt	2	passion fruit
1	large banana, just ripe, peeled and sliced	2	coconut macaroons

1. Spoon the yogurt into 2 small cups, dividing evenly between them.

2. Divide the banana between the 2 cups and spoon the passion fruit over the top.

3. Serve with a coconut macaroon.

Per serving: 190 calories, 31 g carbohydrates, 8 g protein, 3 g fat, 5 g fiber

ITALIAN STRAWBERRIES

                                                         Serves 4

Genuine balsamic vinegar, which is made from the naturally sweet unfermented juice of wine grapes, is more like a liqueur than an acidic condiment. In northern Italy, it often takes the place of lemon juice in dressing luscious ripe strawberries.

PREPARATION TIME: 5 MINUTES

4	cups strawberries, sliced		Mint leaves
2	tablespoons balsamic vinegar	1	cup low-fat ice cream or frozen yogurt
2	tablespoons sugar		

1. In a mixing bowl, combine the strawberries, vinegar, and sugar. Toss gently to mix.

2. Divide the strawberries among 4 bowls and garnish with the mint leaves.

3. Using a small ice cream scooper, divide the ice cream or frozen yogurt into 8 small scoops and place 2 in each bowl.

Per serving: 120 calories, 21 g carbohydrates, 4 g protein, 2 g fat, 3 g fiber

Recipe: Steffan Rössner

SOFTLY SIMMERED PEACHES

Serves 4

Prepare this easy dish in summer when locally grown fruit can be purchased at a farmers' market. If you have the patience to wait, refrigerate the poached peaches overnight for a guaranteed heat-busting treat.

PREPARATION TIME: 5 MINUTES   COOKING TIME: 12 MINUTES

- 4   ripe peaches
- 1   teaspoon sugar
-      Dash of ground cinnamon
-      Pinch of ground nutmeg (optional)

1. Drop the peaches in a pot of boiling water for 2 minutes. Remove with a slotted spoon and run under cold water. Peel. Cut the peaches in half and remove the pits.

2. Place peach halves, cut side down, in a high-sided skillet with 1" of boiling water. Sprinkle with the sugar, cinnamon, and nutmeg, if desired.

3. Cover and simmer for 10 minutes, or until tender. Serve warm or at room temperature.

Per serving: 49 calories, 10 g carbohydrates, 1 g protein, 0 g fat, 2 g fiber

POACHED PEACHES IN LEMON-GINGER SYRUP

Serves 6

Aromatics such as lemon and ginger add exciting flavors to just about any food, with no negative nutritional consequences. So use them with a free hand.

PREPARATION TIME: 2 MINUTES   COOKING TIME: 12 MINUTES

2	cups dry white wine
½	cup sugar
1½	teaspoons grated lemon peel
1½	tablespoons lemon juice
1"x½"	piece fresh ginger, thinly sliced
6	large peaches, halved
	Low-fat plain yogurt (optional)

1. In a large saucepan, combine the wine, sugar, lemon peel, lemon juice, ginger, and 2 cups water. Simmer over medium heat for 5 minutes.

2. Add the peaches. Simmer for 5 minutes. Remove the peach halves with a slotted spoon and peel away their skins. Simmer the syrup to reduce by half, then strain.

3. Serve the peaches with a dollop of yogurt, if desired, and a drizzle of syrup.

Per serving: 160 calories, 25 g carbohydrates, 2 g protein, 0 g fat, 2 g fiber

COOK'S TIP

The cooled poaching syrup can be passed through a fine strainer and refrigerated in a jar for up to 1 week. It can be used to poach more peaches, plums, nectarines, pears, or apples.

SYRUPY ORANGES WITH FROZEN YOGURT

(photo on page 297)   *Serves 2*

So the only fruit you have is oranges? You can still make a delicious dessert. Not only that, you'll also be boosting your fruit intake and enjoying all the health benefits of a single orange.

PREPARATION TIME: 10 MINUTES   COOKING TIME: 15 MINUTES

    Juice of 1 orange
2   tablespoons sugar
2   large oranges, cut into ½" thick slices
1   tablespoon brandy or Cointreau™ liqueur (optional)
1   cup peach or passion fruit frozen yogurt
4   slices nut quick bread, thinly sliced (optional)

1. In a frying pan, combine the orange juice, sugar, and ¼ cup water. Cook, stirring, over medium heat until the sugar dissolves. Reduce the heat to low. Simmer for 10 to 12 minutes to reduce the syrup.

2. Add the oranges and brandy or liqueur, if using, to the pan. Bring to a simmer for 3 minutes.

3. Spoon the oranges and syrup into 2 bowls. Top with a scoop of frozen yogurt. Serve with the nut bread, if desired.

Per serving: 300 calories, 55 g carbohydrates, 6 g protein, 4 g fat, 4 g fiber

COOK'S TIP

Navel oranges are the best choice for this recipe.

PEARS POACHED IN CHAMPAGNE

(photo on page 298)   *Serves 4*

This elegant dessert makes the perfect ending to a meal. Although vanilla beans are a little expensive, the wonderful fragrance and flavor that they impart to the poaching syrup is unsurpassed. If preferred, substitute the vanilla bean with 1 teaspoon pure, or natural, vanilla extract.

PREPARATION TIME: 10 MINUTES   COOKING TIME: 35 MINUTES

- 1½ cups champagne or sparkling white wine
- ½ cup orange juice
- ½ cup sugar
- 1 vanilla bean, split
- 4 ripe but firm pears, peeled, quartered, and cored
  Low-fat plain yogurt (optional)

1. In a large saucepan, combine the champagne or wine, orange juice, sugar, vanilla bean, and 1 cup water. Cook, stirring until the sugar dissolves, then bring to a boil and simmer for 5 minutes.

2. Add the pears to the pan. Simmer for 20 to 30 minutes, or until the pears are tender (the cooking time will vary according to how ripe the pears are). Remove from the heat. Allow the pears to cool in the syrup.

3. When cool, spoon into 4 small bowls. Serve with a spoonful of yogurt, if desired.

Per serving: 255 calories, 51 g carbohydrates, 1 g protein, trace fat, 3 g fiber

 COOK'S TIP

Vanilla beans are readily available from spice shops, gourmet food stores, and many supermarkets. A good bean is dark brown or black, slightly moist to touch, as pliable as a piece of licorice, and immediately fragrant. You should be able to wrap a vanilla bean tightly around your finger—if you can't, then it's too dry.

CRANBERRY POACHED PEARS WITH CUSTARD

Serves 6

These fruits look like garnet jewels after taking on the color of the cranberry juice. Bosc and Anjou pears both hold their shapes well and are particularly good for cooking.

PREPARATION TIME: 5 MINUTES   COOKING TIME: 45 TO 55 MINUTES

PEARS:
- 4 cups cranberry juice
- ¼ cup sugar
- 3 star anise
- 1 stick cinnamon, broken
- 6 ripe but firm pears, peeled

CUSTARD:
- 1 can (12¾ ounces) light evaporated milk
- ¼ cup sugar
- 2 egg yolks
- 1 teaspoon vanilla extract

1. To make the pears: In a saucepan large enough to hold the pears in a single layer, combine the cranberry juice, sugar, star anise, and cinnamon. Cook, stirring, over low heat until the sugar dissolves. Increase the heat and bring to a simmer.

2. Add the pears to the pan. Cook for 40 to 50 minutes, turning occasionally, or until the pears are tender.

3. Meanwhile, to make the custard: In a saucepan, heat the evaporated milk until warmed through. In a heatproof bowl, whisk the sugar, egg yolks, and vanilla until smooth. Whisk the warm milk into the egg yolk mixture until well combined. Pour the mixture back into the saucepan. Cook, stirring constantly, over low heat for 10 to 15 minutes, or until the custard thickens and coats the back of a wooden spoon.

4. Remove the pears from the poaching syrup. Serve with a little of the syrup and the custard.

Per serving: 317 calories, 65 g carbohydrates, 7 g protein, 4 g fat, 5 g fiber

POACHED PEARS WITH RICH CHOCOLATE SAUCE

Serves 6

Who would imagine that dark, decadent chocolate sauce could be part of a low-GI way of eating? The sauce can also be served over reduced-fat ice cream or frozen yogurt.

PREPARATION TIME: 10 MINUTES   COOKING TIME: 30 MINUTES

PEARS:
1   cup sugar
1   cinnamon stick
    Grated peel and juice of 1 lemon
6   ripe but firm pears, peeled, cored, and quartered

SAUCE:
4   ounces dark chocolate, finely chopped
1   tablespoon canola oil
    Low-fat whipped cream (optional)

1. To make the pears: In a large saucepan, heat the sugar, cinnamon, lemon peel and juice, and 6 cups water. Simmer for 5 minutes. Add the pears. Simmer for 20 minutes. Remove from the heat and allow the pears to cool.

2. To make the sauce: In a small saucepan, combine the chocolate, oil, and 5 teaspoons cold water. Cook over low heat, stirring occasionally, until melted.

3. With a slotted spoon, transfer the pears to a serving bowl. Pour the chocolate sauce over the pears. Serve immediately with a dollop of whipped cream, if desired.

Per serving: 291 calories, 54 g carbohydrates, 2 g protein, 10 g fat, 5 g fiber

COOK'S TIP

The cooled poaching syrup can be passed through a fine strainer and refrigerated in a jar for up to 1 week. It can be used to poach more pears, plums, nectarines, peaches, or apples.

MAPLE-NUT STEWED APPLES

Serves 4

*This warm fruit compote also makes a delicious side dish
with ham and eggs for brunch.*

PREPARATION TIME: 20 MINUTES   COOKING TIME: 20 MINUTES

4	medium baking apples
¼	cup toasted walnuts, coarsely chopped (see Cook's Tip, page 187)
¼	cup dried currants
1	teaspoon ground cinnamon
2	tablespoons pure maple syrup
¼	cup cooking sherry or white wine

1. Wash and core the apples and remove 1" of peel around the top. Set aside.

2. In a small bowl, combine the walnuts, currants, and cinnamon. Drizzle the maple syrup over the mixture and mix to coat well.

3. Arrange the apples in shallow saucepan large enough to hold them in a single layer. Fill each center with one-quarter of the nut mixture. Add the sherry or wine and just enough water to cover the bottom of the pan.

4. Cover the apples loosely with aluminum foil. Simmer over low heat for 20 minutes, or until tender.

5. Before serving, drizzle some stewing liquid over each apple. Serve warm.

Per serving: 173 calories, 37 g carbohydrates, 1 g protein, 3 g fat, 4 g fiber

CITRUS GRANITA

(photo on page 299)   *Serves 6*

This refreshing, citrus-flavored ice is the perfect end to a heavy or spicy meal. The granita should look like a fluffy pile of dry pink crystals. To allow adequate time for the granita to freeze, it is best to prepare this recipe a day ahead.

PREPARATION TIME: 5 MINUTES   COOKING TIME: 5 MINUTES
FREEZING TIME: 5 TO 6 HOURS

½   cup sugar
2   whole star anise
2½ cups fresh pink grapefruit juice

1. In a saucepan, combine the sugar, star anise, and ⅓ cup water. Bring to a boil over medium heat, stirring occasionally, until the sugar has dissolved. Remove from the heat. Discard the star anise and allow the sugar syrup to cool to room temperature.

2. Add the grapefruit juice to the cooled syrup. Stir to mix. Pour the mixture into a 13" x 9" freezerproof dish. Cover tightly with plastic wrap. Put the dish in the freezer for 45 minutes, or until the mixture is icy around the edge of the dish. Using a fork, scrape the edges to distribute the frozen portions evenly.

3. Cover and freeze again for 45 minutes, or until the mixture is icy around the edges and the overall texture is slushy. Use the fork to distribute the frozen portions evenly. Cover and return to the freezer for 3 hours, or until frozen solid.

4. Remove from the freezer. Using a fork, scrape the granita down the length of the pan, forming icy flakes. Return to the freezer for at least 1 hour, for the final freezing.

5. To serve, scoop the flaked granita into tall goblets or parfait glasses.

Per serving: 100 calories, 25 g carbohydrates, 1 g protein, 0 g fat, 0 g fiber

Recipe: Emma Pemberton

CHOCOLATE MOUSSE WITH BERRIES

(photo on page 300)   *Serves 6*

*This is a delectable version of a traditionally high-fat favorite. It can
be made up to 2 days ahead and is very easy to prepare. For best results,
use a good-quality cocoa powder.*

PREPARATION TIME: 10 MINUTES   COOKING TIME: 5 MINUTES
CHILLING TIME: 2 TO 3 HOURS

¼   cup cocoa powder, sifted
½   cup sugar
2   teaspoons unflavored gelatin
1½ cups evaporated fat-free milk
½   cup light cream
1   cup strawberries or raspberries
6   scoops low-fat ice cream (optional)

1. In a saucepan, combine the cocoa, sugar, and gelatin. Whisk to mix. Whisk in
about ¼ cup of the milk to form a smooth paste. Set over medium heat. Cook,
stirring, for 3 minutes to dissolve the sugar and gelatin, then gradually stir in
the remaining milk. Cook, stirring, until the liquid is hot but not boiling.

2. Remove from the heat. Stir in the cream. Divide the mixture among six
½-cup dessert dishes or ramekins. Refrigerate for several hours until set.

3. Serve with the fresh berries and a scoop of ice cream, if desired.

Per serving: 190 calories, 28 g carbohydrates, 8 g protein, 5 g fat, 2 g fiber

 ACTIVITY TIP

Working with a personal trainer can be a great way to improve
your health and fitness. A good trainer will design an exercise
program tailored to your needs and fitness level, as well as
provide motivation and support. Many trainers now offer
services for a reasonable rate, and you can choose to use a
health club or train at home or outdoors.

FRUIT SOUFFLÉ

(photo on page 301) *Serves 4*

This soufflé is made with semolina, which has a low-GI of 55. Semolina is a coarse grain made from the first millings of the creamy yellow endosperm from wheat grain (the finer grain, when milled from durum wheat, is used to make pasta). Here the semolina is cooked with low-GI fruit to make a delicious, hot soufflé.

PREPARATION TIME: 15 MINUTES   COOKING TIME: 30 TO 35 MINUTES

Canola oil spray
1   pound mixed fresh fruit, such as apples, rhubarb, and/or berries
2   tablespoons brown sugar, divided
2½ cups fat-free milk
5   tablespoons semolina
1   egg, separated
Grated nutmeg

1. Preheat the oven to 350°F. Lightly coat a 5-cup baking dish or four 1-cup soufflé dishes with oil spray. Set aside.

2. Chop the fruit (except if using berries). Place in a saucepan with 1 tablespoon sugar and ¼ cup water. Bring to a boil, then reduce the heat. Cover and simmer for 5 to 10 minutes, or until the fruit is soft. Spoon the fruit into the prepared baking dish or soufflé dishes.

3. Put the milk in a saucepan and heat until just coming to a boil. Sprinkle the semolina and the remaining 1 tablespoon sugar over the milk. Cook, stirring, until the mixture thickens, then continue to cook for 1 minute. Remove the pan from the heat. Stir in the egg yolk and allow to cool slightly.

4. In the bowl of an electric mixer, whip the egg white until stiff peaks form. Fold into the semolina mixture. Spoon the mixture over the fruit and sprinkle with the nutmeg. Bake for 20 minutes, or until the soufflé has risen and is golden. Serve hot.

Per serving: 180 calories, 32 g carbohydrates, 10 g protein, 2 g fat, 3 g fiber

BERRY AND VANILLA CRÈME DESSERT

Serves 4

This is a tasty, simple dessert that can be made with fresh berries in summer—strawberries, blueberries, and blackberries—or frozen berries when they are out of season. Berries not only have a low GI but are also incredibly rich in disease-fighting antioxidants.

PREPARATION TIME: 15 MINUTES   MARINATING TIME: 15 MINUTES
CHILLING TIME: 2 TO 3 HOURS

	Juice of 1 orange
1	tablespoon brown sugar
1	tablespoon sweet wine
1¼	cups mixed fresh or frozen berries
½	cup (4 ounces) low-fat cream cheese, at room temperature
¼	cup low-fat sour cream
4	teaspoons confectioners' sugar
1	teaspoon vanilla extract
8	ladyfingers

1. In a bowl, combine the orange juice, sugar, and wine. Add the berries and allow to marinate for 15 minutes.

2. In a mixing bowl, combine the cream cheese and sour cream. Stir with a wooden spoon until smooth. Sift in the confectioners' sugar, add the vanilla, and stir well to combine. Set aside.

3. Choose 4 small glasses with a wide base. Cut a ladyfinger to cover the base of each glass. Add a spoonful of berries and a drizzle of marinade over the ladyfinger, then top with a spoonful of vanilla crème. Top with another layer of ladyfinger, the berries, marinade, and vanilla crème. Chill for several hours.

Per serving: 230 calories, 27 g carbohydrates, 6 g protein, 10 g fat, 4 g fiber

LEMON SEMOLINA PUDDING WITH BERRY COULIS

Serves 6

Pale yellow semolina—coarsely ground from the durum wheat berries—is most associated with genuine Italian dried pasta, but it's also a wonderful low-GI cereal grain for a variety of desserts and other delectable dishes.

PREPARATION TIME: 10 MINUTES   COOLING TIME: 10 MINUTES

COOKING TIME: 20 MINUTES

	Canola oil spray
2	cups 1% milk
½	cup fine semolina
¼	cup granulated sugar
1	teaspoon vanilla extract
	Grated peel of 1 large lemon
1	egg, lightly beaten
10	ounces blackberries, strawberries, or raspberries + extra for garnish (optional)
2	tablespoons confectioners' sugar
¼–½	cup white wine or apple juice

1. Preheat the oven to 350°F. Lightly coat six ½-cup soufflé dishes with oil spray. Line the base of each dish with parchment paper.

2. In a saucepan, combine the milk, semolina, and granulated sugar. Stir to mix. Bring to a boil, stirring constantly. Reduce the heat and stir for 1 minute. Remove from the heat. Stir in the vanilla and lemon peel.

3. Cover the surface of the mixture with plastic wrap to prevent a skin from forming. Allow to cool for 10 minutes. When cooled, stir in the egg.

4. Spoon the mixture into the prepared dishes and place them into a baking pan with enough boiling water to reach halfway up the sides of the dishes. Cover loosely with a large sheet of aluminum foil. Carefully slide the pan into the oven and bake for 15 minutes, or until set. Remove from the pan of water. Holding the dishes with an oven mitt, run a knife around the edge of each pudding and turn out onto serving plates. Remove the piece of parchment paper.

5. Meanwhile, in the bowl of a food processor fitted with a metal blade, or through a food mill, purée most of the berries with the confectioners' sugar. (Reserve some whole berries for decoration, if desired). Thin the coulis with up to ½ cup white wine or apple juice.

6. Pour the coulis around the puddings, and decorate with whole berries, if desired.

Per serving: 195 calories, 35 g carbohydrates, 8 g protein, 3 g fat, 2 g fiber

RAISIN BREAD AND BUTTER PUDDING

Serves 4

A sweet and moist bread pudding may seem like the height of comfort food indulgence, but it fits well into a sensible eating plan.

PREPARATION TIME: 5 MINUTES   COOKING TIME: 1 HOUR

   Canola oil spray
2½ cups 1% milk
4   eggs
½   cup sugar
2   teaspoons vanilla extract
2–3   slices raisin bread, crusts removed
2   teaspoons reduced-fat margarine spread

1. Preheat the oven to 325°F. Lightly coat a 6-cup baking dish with oil spray.

2. Pour the milk, eggs, sugar, and vanilla into the dish. Whisk together until blended.

3. Lightly spread the raisin bread with margarine. Cut each slice diagonally. Arrange, margarine side up, on top of the milk mixture.

4. Bake for 1 hour, or until the bread puffs up and turns golden brown.

Per serving: 364 calories, 56 g carbohydrates, 18 g protein, 9 g fat, 2 g fiber

SUMMER PUDDING

Serves 4

This cool, fruity bread pudding is sure to become a summer favorite. Vary the berry combination according to what is ripe at the markets.

PREPARATION TIME: 10 MINUTES   COOKING TIME: 5 MINUTES

CHILLING TIME: OVERNIGHT

10 ounces fresh or frozen raspberries, blackberries, or mulberries

¼ cup raw sugar

¼ cup red wine

1 cinnamon stick

Canola oil spray

8 slices day-old bread, crusts removed, divided

Low-fat whipped cream (optional)

1. Reserve a few berries for decoration, if desired. Then in a medium saucepan, combine the remaining berries, the sugar, wine, cinnamon, and ¼ cup water. Gently simmer for 5 minutes, until the berries are plump and slightly softened. Discard the cinnamon and cool.

2. Coat a 6-cup bowl or mold with oil spray. Cut 6 slices of the bread into triangles and line them in the bowl, overlapping so they form a shell for the berries when the pudding is turned out.

3. Spoon a little of the berry juice over the slices to moisten them and, with a slotted spoon, fill the bowl with the berries. Pour ¼ cup of the berry juice over the berries and reserve any remaining juice.

4. Top with the remaining 2 slices of bread, which have been cut to make a lid. Cover with plastic wrap. Place a plate on top and refrigerate overnight.

5. Turn out onto a white plate, decorate with reserved berries and any reserved juice, and serve with a dollop of whipped cream, if desired.

Per serving: 243 calories, 49 g carbohydrates, 9 g protein, 2 g fat, 7 g fiber

 COOK'S TIP

Raw sugar, such as demerara or turbinado, is sold in natural food stores and some supermarkets. Good-quality brown sugar may be substituted.

FRAGRANT RICE PUDDING WITH PLUMS

Serves 4

Balancing foods is an important part of low-GI eating. As this dessert is pretty high in carbs, it would be best served after a simple low-carb meal such as grilled meat or fish with a salad.

PREPARATION TIME: 10 MINUTES   COOKING TIME: 25 MINUTES

- ½ cup basmati rice
- 2 cups low-fat milk
- 1½ tablespoons sugar
- 1 cardamom pod, lightly crushed
  Grated peel of 1 small orange
- ½ teaspoon vanilla extract
- ½ cinnamon stick
- 8 plums
- ¼ cup pistachios, chopped

1. Cook the rice in a saucepan of boiling water for 5 minutes. Drain and return to the pan with the milk, sugar, cardamom pod, orange peel, vanilla, and cinnamon.

2. Bring to a boil. Reduce the heat to low. Cook, stirring, for 15 to 20 minutes, or until the rice is tender and creamy and the liquid is almost all absorbed. Stir constantly toward the end of the cooking time, to prevent sticking.

3. Meanwhile, place the plums in a medium saucepan and cover with water. Slowly bring to a boil. Reduce the heat to low and simmer for 10 minutes. Remove the fruit with a slotted spoon. Cool slightly and slip off the skins.

4. Remove and discard the cinnamon and cardamom from the rice mixture. Serve immediately with the plums, sprinkled with pistachios.

Per serving: 296 calories, 52 g carbohydrates, 10 g protein, 4.5 g fat, 3 g fiber

BAKED RICOTTA CHEESECAKE

Serves 10

Cheesecake is possibly everyone's favorite dessert. This creamy dream can be garnished with a few fresh berries or sliced peaches in summer.

PREPARATION TIME: 20 MINUTES   COOKING TIME: 1 HOUR 10 MINUTES

STANDING AND COOLING TIME: 2 HOURS   CHILLING TIME: 3 TO 4 HOURS

CRUST:

Canola oil spray

12 Honey Oatmeal Cookies (page 353)

7 tablespoons reduced-fat margarine spread, melted

FILLING:

2½ cups reduced-fat ricotta cheese

10½ ounces silken tofu, well drained

Grated peel of 1 lemon

1 teaspoon vanilla extract

3 eggs

⅓ cup pure floral honey + extra for garnish

1. To make the crust: Preheat the oven to 325°F. Coat the base of an 8" springform pan with oil spray. Line with parchment paper and coat lightly with oil spray.

2. Place the cookies in the bowl of a food processor fitted with a metal blade. Process until fine crumbs appear. You should have 2 cups of crumbs. Transfer to a bowl and stir in the melted margarine. Spoon the mixture onto the base of the lined pan and use a spoon to spread evenly and press down firmly. Place the pan in the refrigerator while you make the filling.

3. To make the filling: Wipe out the food processor bowl with a paper towel. Place the ricotta, tofu, lemon peel, and vanilla in the bowl of the food processor fitted with a metal blade. Process until smooth. Add the eggs and ⅓ cup honey. Pulse until smooth and well blended.

4. Pour the ricotta mixture over the chilled cookie crumbs. Bake for 60 to 70 minutes, or until the cheesecake is just set in the middle.

5. Turn off the oven. Leave the cheesecake in the oven with the door slightly ajar for 1 hour to cool. Remove and keep at room temperature until cooled completely. Cover with plastic wrap and refrigerate for 3 to 4 hours.

6. To serve, drizzle each piece of cheesecake with 1 teaspoon honey.

Per serving: 298 calories, 29 g carbohydrates, 12 g protein, 15 g fat, 0 g fiber

CHERRY STRUDEL

Serves 8

Strudel looks like one of those fussy pastry shop desserts, but by using purchased filo pastry, it's actually super simple to prepare at home.

PREPARATION TIME: 20 MINUTES   COOKING TIME: 20 MINUTES

8	ounces reduced-fat ricotta cheese
1	egg, lightly beaten
1	tablespoon pure floral honey
1	teaspoon vanilla extract
5	sheets whole wheat filo pastry
	Canola oil spray
⅓	cup finely chopped walnuts
8	ounces cherries, pitted

1. Preheat the oven to 375°F. Line a baking sheet with parchment paper.

2. In a mixing bowl, combine the ricotta, egg, honey, and vanilla. Mix until well blended.

3. Lay 1 filo sheet on a work surface. Coat lightly with oil spray, and top with another sheet. Coat lightly with oil spray and sprinkle evenly with the nuts. Top with the remaining pastry sheets, coating each lightly with oil spray (except for the last sheet).

4. Pile the ricotta mixture at one end of the pastry and spread out to be about 4" wide, leaving 1" bare pastry at each side and the ends. Arrange the cherries over the ricotta.

5. Fold the end and sides over and roll up. Place on the prepared sheet, seam side down. Coat lightly with oil spray. Bake for 20 minutes, or until golden brown. Allow to cool slightly before slicing.

Per serving: 139 calories, 13 g carbohydrates, 6 g protein, 7 g fat, 1 g fiber

COOK'S TIPS

Look for 100% pure floral honey. The commercial blends have a higher GI value.

Whole wheat filo pastry is available in natural food stores.

FRESH PLUM AND RICOTTA STRUDEL

(photo on page 3o2)   *Serves 6*

*Plums and other blue-red fruit, such as cherries, blueberries, and cranberries,
are rich in a particular type of antioxidant known as anthocyanins.*

PREPARATION TIME: 20 MINUTES   COOKING TIME: 45 MINUTES

- 2   tablespoons reduced-fat margarine spread
- ½   cup fresh whole wheat bread crumbs
- ⅓   cup brown sugar, divided
- ½   teaspoon ground cinnamon
- 6   fresh plums, or 1 can (15 ounces) plums, drained well
     Canola oil spray
- 6   sheets filo pastry
- ½   cup reduced-fat ricotta cheese
     Low-fat vanilla ice cream (optional)

1. Melt the margarine in a saucepan over medium heat. Add the bread crumbs. Reserve 2 teaspoons sugar and add the remainder to the pan. Cook, stirring to break up any lumps, for 15 minutes. Remove from the heat and stir in the cinnamon. Allow to cool.

2. Cut the plums into halves, remove the pits, and thinly slice the flesh.

3. Preheat the oven to 375°F. Lightly coat a baking sheet with oil spray. Lay 2 sheets of filo pastry on top of each other. Lightly coat the top sheet with oil spray, then sprinkle over one-third of the crumb mixture. Top with 2 more filo sheets. Lightly coat the top sheet with oil spray. Sprinkle over another one-third of the crumbs. Top with the remaining 2 filo sheets. Coat with oil spray. Sprinkle over the remaining crumbs.

4. Spread the ricotta along the edge of the pastry. Arrange the plums on top and sprinkle with the reserved 2 teaspoons sugar. Roll up the pastry, jelly-roll style, tucking in the edges as you roll. Carefully transfer the roll to the prepared baking sheet. Lightly coat the top with oil spray and bake for 10 minutes. Reduce the heat to 350°F. Bake for 20 minutes, or until the pastry is crisp and brown. Serve warm with the ice cream, if desired.

Per serving: 205 calories, 30 g carbohydrates, 5 g protein, 6 g fat, 3 g fiber

Recipe: Catherine Saxelby

CHOCOLATE CHIP MUFFINS

Makes 12

Spicy tender muffins with pools of melted chocolate straight from the oven are irresistible!

PREPARATION TIME: 10 MINUTES   COOKING TIME: 25 MINUTES

Canola oil spray
1   cup sifted whole wheat flour
1   cup sifted all-purpose flour
1   tablespoon baking powder
1   cup lightly packed dark brown sugar
1   teaspoon apple pie spice mix or cinnamon
1   cup chocolate chips
1   cup buttermilk
2   eggs
1   tablespoon canola oil
1   teaspoon vanilla extract

1. Preheat the oven to 375°F. Lightly coat a 12-cup muffin pan with oil spray.

2. In a mixing bowl, combine the flours, baking powder, sugar, and spice mix or cinnamon. Fold in the chocolate chips.

3. In another large mixing bowl, combine the buttermilk, eggs, oil, and vanilla. Whisk until smooth.

4. Quickly stir the dry ingredients into the buttermilk mixture. Spoon the batter into the prepared pan.

5. Bake for 25 minutes, or until a wooden pick inserted in one muffin comes out clean.

Per muffin: 280 calories, 46 g carbohydrates, 7 g protein, 8 g fat, 2 g fiber

CHOCOLATE NUT BISCOTTI

Makes about 50

Biscotti keep for up to a month, so store them in an airtight tin to have on hand for dunking in coffee, tea, or milk.

PREPARATION TIME: 30 MINUTES   COOLING TIME: 30 MINUTES
COOKING TIME: 40 MINUTES

- ¾ cup sugar
- 2 eggs
- 1 cup stone-ground 100% whole wheat flour
- ½ cup cocoa powder
- ⅓ cup slivered almonds
- ⅓ cup pecans
- ⅓ cup hazelnuts

1. Preheat the oven to 350°F. Line a large baking sheet with parchment paper.

2. In the bowl of an electric mixer, whip the sugar and eggs together for 3 minutes, until they have increased in volume and are thick and pale.

3. Sift in the flour and cocoa powder and stir with a wooden spoon until almost combined. Add the nuts. With clean hands, mix until well combined.

4. Divide the mixture in half and shape into 2 logs about 6" long. Place the logs on the prepared sheet and flatten slightly to ¾" thick. Bake for 20 minutes, or until firm. Remove from the oven and allow to cool completely.

5. Heat the oven to 250°F. Cut the logs into slices about ⅓" thick. Spread out onto the lined baking sheets. Bake for 20 minutes, turning once. Allow to cool completely on wire racks.

Per biscotti: 48 calories, 5.5 g carbohydrates, 2 g protein, 2.5 g fat, 0 g fiber

· ·
COOK'S TIP

Feel free to vary the nuts mixture with walnuts or pistachios.
Add a variety or only one type, if desired.

SCOTTISH OAT CRACKERS

(photo on page 303)   *Makes 35*

Traditional crackers are made using lard or butter, both full of the saturated fats that we are recommending you cut down on. This recipe uses an unsaturated alternative instead of butter, and the result is equally delicious but altogether healthier.

PREPARATION TIME: 15 MINUTES   CHILLING TIME: 20 MINUTES
COOKING TIME: 15 TO 20 MINUTES

1⅓ cups coarse oats
½   cup whole wheat flour + extra for dusting
¾   teaspoon baking powder
¼   teaspoon salt
½   cup reduced-fat margarine spread
    Low-fat ricotta cheese
    Sliced strawberries and fresh figs

1. In the bowl of a food processor fitted with a metal blade, combine the oats, flour, baking powder, and salt. Add the margarine and process until the mixture resembles coarse bread crumbs. Slowly add 2 tablespoons very cold water until the mixture forms a stiff dough. Stop at this point, even if you haven't used all of the water.

2. Put the dough in a plastic bag. Place in the freezer for 20 minutes. Preheat the oven to 350°F.

3. Remove the dough and roll out on a floured work surface to ⅛" thick. Cut into rounds about 1½" in diameter. Place on a nonstick baking sheet. Bake for 15 to 20 minutes, or until golden. Transfer to a wire rack to cool.

4. To make the topping for the oat crackers, put a teaspoon of ricotta on each and top with a sliced strawberry or fig.

Per serving (2 crackers): 85 calories, 9 g carbohydrates, 2 g protein, 4 g fat, 1 g fiber

Per serving (2 crackers with toppings): 100 calories, 12 g carbohydrates, 3 g protein, 6 g fat, 2 g fiber

Recipe: Judy Davie, The Food Coach

COOK'S TIPS

Replace strawberries and figs with other fresh fruits in season: nectarines, peaches, plums, or pears.

Scottish oat crackers are also a delicious substitute for bread when served with soups and salads. In step 3, cut them into slightly larger rounds, about 2½" in diameter, if planning to serve them with soup.

HONEY OATMEAL COOKIES

Makes about 24

An ice-cold glass of fat-free milk for dunking is the only accompaniment these soft, chewy old-fashioned cookies require.

PREPARATION TIME: 10 MINUTES   COOKING TIME: 24 MINUTES

10	tablespoons reduced-fat margarine spread
½	cup pure floral honey
1	egg
¾	cup rolled oats
1	cup almond meal/flour (see Cook's Tip, page 354)
1	cup all-purpose flour
½	teaspoon ground cinnamon

1. Preheat the oven to 350°F. Line 2 baking sheets with parchment paper.

2. In the bowl of an electric mixer, beat the margarine and honey for 1 minute, or until well combined. Add the egg and beat until combined. Stir in the oats and almond meal/flour, then sift in the all-purpose flour and cinnamon. Stir until well combined.

3. Shape tablespoons of the mixture into balls and place about 1" apart on the prepared pans. Use a spoon to press down slightly. Bake for 10 to 12 minutes, or until light and golden, rotating the sheets around once in the oven during cooking. Transfer to a wire rack and repeat with any remaining mixture.

Per cookie: 115 calories, 12 g carbohydrates, 2 g protein, 6.5 g fat, 1 g fiber

APPLE AND RHUBARB CRUMBLE

Serves 8

Soluble fiber, such as that found in apple peel, does wonderful things such as lower cholesterol and regulate blood-glucose levels for long periods of time. For a more rustic—and healthier—dish, try leaving the peel on the apples.

PREPARATION TIME: 20 MINUTES   COOKING TIME: 30 TO 40 MINUTES

Canola oil spray

3   apples (such as Golden Delicious, Gala, or Fuji), peeled, cored, and cut into quarters

1   bunch rhubarb, cut into 1½" lengths (about 3 cups)

2   tablespoons superfine sugar

½   cup whole wheat pastry flour

1   cup almond meal/flour

7   tablespoons reduced-fat margarine spread

¾   cup untoasted muesli

½   cup firmly packed brown sugar

1. Preheat the oven to 400°F. Lightly coat an 8-cup baking dish with oil spray.

2. Layer the apples and rhubarb in the prepared dish, sprinkling sugar between layers.

3. In a mixing bowl, combine the flour and almond meal/flour. Use your hands to add the margarine until well combined and large crumbs start to form. Mix in the muesli and brown sugar.

4. Sprinkle the mixture evenly over the fruit. Cover with aluminum foil and bake for 20 minutes. Uncover and bake for 10 to 20 minutes, or until the fruit is tender and the topping golden brown. Allow to stand for 5 minutes before serving.

Per serving: 306 calories, 33 g carbohydrates, 7 g protein, 13 g fat, 4 g fiber

 **COOK'S TIP**

Almond meal/flour, very finely ground almonds, is available in natural food stores and some supermarkets. To prepare at home, place blanched or unblanched whole almonds in the bowl of a food processor fitted with a steel blade. Process until very finely ground.

INDIVIDUAL APPLE AND GINGER CRUMBLES *Serves 6*

Lightly sweetened fresh fruits combined with whole grains are among the easiest desserts to prepare—and so much better for your body than highly refined commercial pastries.

PREPARATION TIME: 10 MINUTES   COOKING TIME: 45 MINUTES

Canola oil spray	½ cup self-rising flour
6 Granny Smith apples, peeled, cored, and sliced	2 tablespoons reduced-fat margarine spread
2 tablespoons granulated sugar	¼ cup tightly packed dark brown sugar
1 cinnamon stick	½ cup rolled barley
3 whole cloves	½ teaspoon ground nutmeg
3 tablespoons coarsely chopped candied ginger, divided (optional)	Low-fat vanilla yogurt (optional)

1. Preheat the oven to 350°F. Coat six 1-cup soufflé dishes lightly with oil spray.

2. In a saucepan, combine the apples, granulated sugar, cinnamon, cloves, and 1 cup water. Simmer over medium-low heat for 15 minutes, or until the apples are just cooked. Remove and discard the cinnamon and cloves. Add 2 tablespoons ginger, if desired, to the pan.

3. Meanwhile, place the flour in a mixing bowl and cut in the margarine until crumbly. Mix in the brown sugar, barley, and nutmeg. Set aside.

4. Fill the prepared dishes with the apple mixture. Top with the crumble mixture.

5. Bake for 30 minutes, or until the topping is crisp and golden. Decorate the crumbles with the remaining 1 tablespoon ginger, if desired. Serve hot with a dollop of yogurt, if desired.

Per serving: 260 calories, 50 g carbohydrates, 3 g protein, 6 g fat, 4 g fiber

· ·
COOK'S TIP

Rolled barley is sold in natural food stores. Rolled oats or triticale may be substituted.

APPLE AND STRAWBERRY CRUMBLE

(photo on page 304)   *Serves 4*

Crumbles are real comfort food. Making the topping with rolled oats keeps the GI low and the fiber high, and the strawberries are rich in vitamin C and protective antioxidants.

PREPARATION TIME: 20 MINUTES   COOKING TIME: 20 TO 25 MINUTES

	Canola oil spray
3	cooking apples, such as Granny Smiths, peeled, cored, and sliced
2	tablespoons pure floral honey
1⅔	cups strawberries, hulled and halved
1	cup rolled oats
2	tablespoons brown sugar
2	tablespoons reduced-fat margarine spread, melted
½	teaspoon ground cinnamon
	Low-fat vanilla ice cream or custard (optional)

1. Preheat the oven to 400°F. Lightly coat a medium baking dish with oil spray.

2. In a saucepan, combine the apples, honey, and 2 tablespoons water. Bring to a boil. Reduce the heat to low. Cover and simmer for 3 to 4 minutes, or until the apples have softened a little. Remove from the heat and stir in the strawberries. Spoon the mixture into the prepared baking dish.

3. In the bowl of a food processor fitted with a metal blade, combine the oats, sugar, margarine, and cinnamon. Process until the mixture is coarsely ground. Pulse several times to mix. Spoon evenly over the fruit.

4. Bake for 15 to 20 minutes, or until the topping is crisp and golden. Serve with ice cream or custard, if desired.

Per serving: 280 calories, 48 g carbohydrates, 4 g protein, 8 g fat, 5 g fiber

ACTIVITY TIP

Develop an after-dinner walking habit
with your partner or a good friend.

part 3

LOW-GI
INFORMATION
RESOURCES

YOUR LOW-GI DIET FOODS

To make easy low-GI choices, you'll need to stock the right foods. Here are ideas for what to keep in your pantry, refrigerator, and freezer. These foods have optimum flavor and nutritional value and work well, in moderation, in a low-GI diet.

WHAT TO KEEP IN YOUR PANTRY

- **Asian sauces.** Hoisin, oyster, soy, and fish sauces are a good basic range. Also jarred or canned Thai curry pastes, Chinese garlic chili paste, and mirin (sweet rice wine) for genuine flavors.

- **Barley.** One of the oldest cultivated cereals, barley is very nutritious and high in soluble fiber. Look for products such as pearl barley to use in soups, stews, and pilafs.

- **Black pepper.** Buy freshly ground pepper or grind your own peppercorns.

- **Bread.** Low-GI options include whole grain, 100% stone-ground whole wheat, pumpernickel, sourdough, English muffins, flat bread, and pita.

- **Breakfast cereals.** These include traditional rolled oats, natural muesli, and low-GI packaged breakfast cereals.

- **Broth.** Make your own or buy prepared products, which are available in cans and aseptic containers or in cubes or granules. Look for low-salt options.

- **Bulgur wheat.** Use it to make tabbouleh, or add to vegetable burgers, stuffings, soups, and stews.

- **Canned evaporated fat-free milk.** This makes an excellent substitution for cream in pasta sauces.

- **Canned fish.** Keep a good stock of canned tuna packed in spring water, and canned sardines and salmon. Fish canned in oil contains about 10 times more fat than fish canned in water. If you prefer to buy tuna in oil, check the ingredient list closely for the type of oil used: Canola, olive, or soybean is best.

- **Canned fruit.** Have a variety of canned fruit on hand, including peaches, pears, apples, and nectarines. Choose the brands labeled with "no added sugar" and packed in juice.

- **Canned vegetables.** Sweet corn kernels and tomatoes can help to boost the vegetable content of a meal. Tomatoes, in particular, can be used freely because they are rich in anti-oxidants, as well as having a low-GI. Recipe-ready diced tomatoes are ultra-convenient for pasta sauces and other dishes.

- **Cornmeal.** One hundred percent stone-ground dried corn, either white or yellow, retains the most nutrients. It can be used for polenta, baking, and breading foods for oven frying.

- **Couscous.** Nutritious whole wheat couscous is now sold in many super-markets. It takes only minutes to soak it in hot water or broth as an ingre-dient in casseroles or an accompani-ment to braised dishes.

- **Curry pastes.** A tablespoon or so of jarred or canned Thai-style curry paste makes a delicious sauce base.

- **Dried fruit.** These include apricots, raisins, prunes, and apples.

- **Dried herbs.** Oregano, basil, ground coriander, thyme, and rosemary can be useful to have on standby in the pantry.

- **Honey.** Those with the lowest GI include the pure floral honeys, not the commercially blended types.

- **Jam.** A dollop of good-quality all-fruit spread (with no added sugar) on toast contains fewer calories than butter or margarine.

- **Legumes.** Stock a variety of legumes (dried or canned), including lentils, split peas, and beans. There are many bean varieties, including black, cannel-lini, chickpeas, lima, great Northern, white, kidney, and soybeans. Incor-porating them in a recipe, perhaps as a partial substitution for meat, will lower the fat content of the finished dish.

- **Mustard.** Whole grain mustard is useful as a sandwich spread, in salad dressings, and in sauces. Dijon-style mustard is a wonderful addition to sauces.

- **Noodles.** Many Asian noodles, such as udon and rice vermicelli, have low to intermediate GI values because of their dense texture, whether they are made from wheat or rice flour.

- **Nuts.** Try a handful of almonds, walnuts, pine nuts, or pecans (about 1 ounce) every other day. Try them sprinkled over your breakfast cereal, salad, or dessert, and enjoy unsalted nuts as a snack as well. Seeds such as sesame, sunflower, and flaxseed are delicious in both savory and sweet dishes.

- **Oils.** Try olive oil or canola oil for general use; some extra-virgin olive oil for salad dressings, marinades, and dishes that benefit from its flavor; and toasted sesame oil as a condiment for Asian-style stir-fries. Canola and olive oil cooking sprays are handy, too.

- **Pasta.** A great source of carbohydrates and B vitamins. Fresh or dried, the preparation is easy. Simply cook in boiling water until just tender, or al dente, drain, and top with your favorite sauce and a sprinkle of Parmesan cheese.

- **Quinoa.** This whole grain cooks in about 10 to 15 minutes and has a slightly chewy texture. It can be used as a substitute for rice, couscous, or bulgur wheat. It is very important to rinse the grains thoroughly before cooking.

- **Rice.** Basmati, brown, wild, short-grain white, and Uncle Ben's converted rice varieties have a much lower GI than, for example, jasmine rice.

- **Rolled oats.** Besides their use in oatmeal, oats can be added to cakes, muffins, breads, and desserts.

- **Salt.** Use in moderation.

- **Spices and seasoning blends.** Most spices and seasoning blends—including ground coriander, cumin, turmeric, cinnamon, paprika, nutmeg, and chili powder—should be bought in small quantities and stored in a cool, dark spot.

- **Tomato pasta sauce.** The classic meatless Italian tomato sauce is typically seasoned with onion, garlic, and oregano. Look for brands without high fructose corn syrup to avoid the unwanted calories. It can be used for pastas, pizzas, or braised meat and poultry.

- **Tomato paste.** Use in soups, sauces, and casseroles.

- **Vinegar.** White wine or red wine vinegar and balsamic vinegar are excellent as vinaigrette dressings in salads.

WHAT TO KEEP IN YOUR REFRIGERATOR

- **Bacon.** Bacon is a valuable ingredient in many dishes because of the flavor it offers. You can make a little bacon go a long way by trimming off all fat and chopping it finely. Ham is often a more economical and leaner way to go. In casseroles and soups, bacon or a ham bone imparts a fine flavor, with less fat.

- **Capers, olives, and anchovies.** These can be bought in jars and kept in the refrigerator. They are a tasty addition to pasta dishes, pizzas, and salads.

- **Cheese.** Reduced-fat Cheddar cheese, or other favorite reduced-fat types, are great to keep handy in the fridge. A block of Parmesan is indispensable and will keep for up to 1 month. Reduced-fat cottage and ricotta cheeses have a short life so are best bought as needed. They can be a good alternative to butter or margarine spread in a sandwich.

- **Condiments.** Keep jars of minced garlic, chile, or fresh ginger in the refrigerator to spice up your cooking in an instant. Ready-diced onions and bell peppers, sold in most supermarket produce sections, also speed healthy meal preparation.

- **Cream and sour cream.** Keep to very small amounts, as these are high in saturated fat. Substitute fat-free sour cream, which tastes very similar to the full-fat variety. A 16-ounce container of heavy cream can be poured into ice-cube trays and frozen, providing small servings of cream easily when you need it. Adding one ice-cube block (1 ounce) of cream to a dish adds only 5½ grams of fat.

- **Eggs.** To enhance your intake of omega-3 fats, we suggest using omega-3-enriched eggs. Although the yolk is high in cholesterol, the fat in eggs is predominantly monounsaturated, and therefore considered a "good fat."

- **Fish.** Try a variety of fresh fish.

- **Fresh fruit.** Almost all fruit makes an excellent low-GI snack. When in season, try apples, oranges, pears, grapes, grapefruit, peaches, apricots, strawberries, and mangoes.

- **Fresh herbs.** These are available in most supermarkets, and there really is no substitute for the flavor they impart. For variety, try parsley, basil, mint, chives, and cilantro.

- **Jarred vegetables.** Sun-dried tomatoes, artichoke hearts, and roasted eggplant and peppers are handy to keep as flavorsome additions to pastas and sandwiches.

- **Lemons.** A lemon is one of the most versatile ingredients in the low-GI kitchen. Try a squeeze along with ground black pepper on vegetables instead of a pat of butter. Lemon juice provides acidity that slows gastric emptying and lowers the GI value. Convenient frozen 100% pure lemon juice is now sold in most supermarkets.

- **Margarine.** Buy margarine spread in a tub. Look for the words "trans-fat free" and "light," "low-fat," "nonfat," or "fat-free" on the label. The first ingredient should say "liquid," as in "liquid canola oil."

- **Mayonnaise.** Select brands prepared with canola oil.

- **Meat and poultry.** Lean varieties are better—try lean beef, lamb fillets, pork fillets, chicken (breast or drumsticks), and turkey (breast).

- **Milk.** Fat-free or low-fat milk is best, or try low-fat calcium-enriched soy milk.

- **Tofu.** Add to stir-fries, casseroles, and smoothies.

- **Vegetables.** Keep a variety of seasonal vegetables on hand such as spinach, broccoli, cauliflower, Asian greens, asparagus, zucchini, and mushrooms. Bell peppers, scallions, and sprouts (mung bean and snowpea sprouts) are great to bulk up a salad. Sweet corn and sweet potato are essential to your low-GI food store.

- **Yogurt.** Low-fat natural yogurt provides the most calcium for the fewest calories. It also provides "friendly bacteria," protein, and riboflavin, and, unlike milk, is suitable for people who are lactose intolerant. Low-fat plain yogurt is a good substitute for sour cream. Have vanilla or fruit versions as a dessert, or use natural plain yogurt as a condiment in savory dishes. However, if using yogurt in a hot meal, make sure you add it at the last minute, and do not let it boil or it will curdle.

WHAT TO KEEP IN YOUR FREEZER

- **Filo pastry.** Unlike most other pastry, filo (also known as phyllo) is low in fat. To keep it that way, brush between the sheets with fat-free milk instead of melted butter when you prepare it. Look for it in the freezer section of the supermarket with other prepared pastry, and use it as a strudel wrap.

- **Frozen berries.** Blueberries, raspberries, and strawberries can make any dessert special, and with frozen ones, you don't have to wait until berry season to indulge. They're also a great addition to breakfasts and snacks.

- **Frozen meat, poultry, and seafood.** Boneless, skinless chicken breasts, pork tenderloins, and loose-pack shrimp are widely available. Take out just the amount you need to thaw for your recipe.

- **Frozen vegetables.** Keep a package of peas, beans, corn, spinach, or mixed vegetables in the freezer—these are handy to add to a quick meal.

- **Frozen yogurt.** This is a fantastic substitute for ice cream. Some products even have a similar creamy texture but much less fat.

- **Ice cream.** Ice cream is a source of carbohydrates, calcium, riboflavin, retinol, and protein. Reduced or low-fat ice cream is ideal for a quick dessert, served with fresh fruit.

What Is a Serving?

Bread/Cereal Group

1 slice bread

1 tortilla

$\frac{1}{2}$ cup cooked rice or pasta, or cooked cereal

1 ounce packaged cereal

2 medium cookies

3–4 small crackers

1 pancake (4")

Vegetable Group

$\frac{1}{2}$ cup chopped raw or cooked vegetables

1 cup raw leafy vegetables

$\frac{3}{4}$ cup (6 ounces) vegetable juice

$\frac{1}{2}$ cup cooked potatoes

10 french fries

Fruit Group

1 medium piece of fruit

$\frac{1}{2}$ cup chopped, cooked, or canned fruit in juice

1 melon wedge

$\frac{1}{4}$ cup dried fruit

Dairy Group

1 cup (8 ounces) milk or yogurt

$1\frac{1}{2}$ ounces natural cheese

2 ounces processed cheese

$1\frac{1}{2}$ cups ice cream (regular or reduced-fat)

1 cup frozen yogurt

GET MOVING!

Did you notice that we used the word *moving*, not *exercising*? There's a good reason. Most people think of exercise as a formal and structured activity that they must do each day. Not so! Though some people can and do make a serious commitment to 20 to 30 minutes of exercise three to four times a week, the majority of us say that we're too busy and don't have the time. The result? Many of us make no attempt at all to move our bodies. We're loathe to make *any* effort or commitment: We're too tired, too rushed, too stressed, too hot, too cold—the list of excuses goes on. But there's good news: We don't need to *exercise*, we just need to *move*.

Used to be, experts hinted that unless we exercised vigorously and sustained it for 20 to 30 minutes, we needn't bother doing it in the first place. Now we know better: Research tells us that any amount of movement is better than none at all. Can you accumulate 30 minutes of moving around each day? We bet you could! Could you weed for say, 5 minutes in the morning, then walk around the neighborhood for 10 minutes later on, then walk up and down the stairs for 2 minutes? That's all it takes to reap important health benefits. And it doesn't need to be vigorous to be beneficial. Nor does it have to involve gyms, special equipment, or expensive accessories.

For most people, walking fits the bill perfectly. All of us were meant to walk upright—it's the easiest, safest, and most natural form of physical activity around.

WALKING FOR PLEASURE AND HEALTH

Walking keeps us fit, it's cheap and convenient, and it becomes even more important as we grow older. You can walk alone or with friends. In fact, talking while you walk can have important emotional benefits: Not only do our bodies produce calming hormones while we walk, but the talk itself can be great therapy—and good for relationships in general. So instead of saying, "How about a cup of coffee?" try, "Would you like to take a walk?" But don't hesitate to walk alone if you prefer, or with your dog—your pet will love you all the more for it. And you'll be able to (finally!) take some time to think and relax.

Walking regularly has scientifically proven benefits. According to the American Heart Association, regular exercise can:

- Help lower blood pressure
- Cut heart attack and diabetes risk
- Reduce insulin requirements if you have diabetes
- Help you stop smoking
- Control weight
- Increase levels of good HDL cholesterol
- Keep bones and joints strong
- Reduce colon cancer risk
- Improve mood
- Ease depression

How Often?

Try to walk every day. Ideally, you should accumulate 30 minutes or more on most days of the week. The good news is, you can do it in two 15-minute stints or six 5-minute stints. It doesn't matter!

How Hard?

You should be able to talk comfortably while you walk. Find a level that suits *you.*

GETTING STARTED

Before beginning a walking program, see your doctor if you have:

- Been inactive for some time
- A history of heart disease or chest pains
- Diabetes
- High blood pressure

  Or if you:

- Weigh more than you should
- Smoke

The Importance of Good Shoes

The most important walking equipment is a pair of sturdy, comfortable, lightweight walking shoes. If your feet feel good, you'll want to walk longer distances and stick with your walking program. It's worth the investment!

It Doesn't Have to Be Intense

A new study has revealed that greater physical activity is associated with a lower risk of developing type 2 diabetes. Researchers found that the exercise didn't have to be intense: Exercise of moderate duration and intensity—including walking—was associated with reduced risk of disease. While brisk walking was best, even the slow walkers benefited!

10 Important Tips

Here are a few things to keep in mind as you head out for your next walk.

- Wear a broad-brimmed hat and sunglasses, and use sunscreen on exposed skin. (Don't forget the tops of your feet if they're exposed.)

- Avoid the hours between 10 a.m. and 3 p.m., when the sun's rays are strongest. Walk on the shady side of the street.

- Wear well-cushioned, flat-soled shoes and layers of clothing that you can remove if you need to.

- Tell someone that you're going for a walk and what time you expect to return.

- Walk steadily. Let your arms swing; get a rhythm going.

- On all your walks, but especially on long or strenuous ones, drink water before you start and carry some with you. A small backpack can hold your water, sunscreen, hat, and glasses. Keep it stocked and ready to go.

- If your breathing becomes uncomfortable, slow down. Don't come to a sudden stop, which can make you dizzy.

- During the winter, wear a hat to keep warm. One-third of our body heat is lost through our heads!

- Avoid walking immediately after meals (wait about 15 minutes) or if you have a fever or bad cold.

- If you're walking in the dark, wear light-colored clothing so that motorists can see you. Carry a flashlight for added visibility.

- If you feel sore at first, don't worry; your body will adapt, and the soreness will decrease. Stretching for 2 minutes before and after your walk will help minimize aches and pains.

STAYING MOTIVATED

When we start a new exercise program, we tend to be raring to go! We enjoy being active, and nothing can interfere with our routine. But gradually—and often without our even knowing it—we start putting exercise on the back burner. Here are some easy ways to keep physical activity a priority in your life.

- Walk with a regular partner or group.

- Plan your walk in advance: Will it be an early-morning or late-evening stroll?

- Vary your walking location.

- Visit national parks and landmarks.

- Walk your dog (if you have one) at a regular time each day. Soon he'll be reminding you.

- Don't let rain put you off—take your umbrella along and enjoy the sounds.

Chocolate Mousse with Berries
(recipe on page 339)

INDEX

Underscored page references indicate boxed text. **Boldfaced** page references indicate photographs.

Fruit Soufflé, **301,** 340
health benefits from, 30
high-GI, alternatives to, 27
in low-GI diet, 4–5
low-GI choices, 5, 9, 17–18, 27
Mixed Grain Cereal with Dried Fruit Compote and
    Yogurt, **50,** 66
Mustard-Roasted Fruit Chutney, 107, **129**
serving sizes, 364
Three-Grain Muesli, 45, **49**

G

Garbanzo beans. *See* Chickpeas
Garlic
    Garlic and Parsley Scallops with Fettuccine,
        266
    Garlic Shrimp with Cilantro Pasta, 259
    Grilled Garlic Potatoes, 172
    Potato-Garlic Mash, 174
    Spaghetti Aglio e Olio Deluxe, 190
Glycemic Index (GI). *See also* Low-GI diet
    description of, x, 4
    development of, ix–x, 4
    high-GI foods, substitutes for, 26–27
    key factors influencing, 9
    on food labels, 12
    values and rankings, x, 4
Glycemic Load (GL), 10–11
Grains. *See also* Barley; Bulgur; Oats; Rice; Rye;
        Wheat
    Buckwheat Pancakes with Berries, **53,** 72
    Cornmeal, Pepper, and Chive Muffins, 108
    Fruity Quinoa Porridge, **51,** 67
    high-GI, alternatives to, 27
    low-GI choices, 7, 8, 27
    processed, about, 7
    Shrimp with Quinoa Tabbouleh, 260–61
Granita
    Citrus Granita, **299,** 338
Grapefruit
    Citrus Granita, **299,** 338
Green beans
    Green Bean, Tomato, and Olive Salad, 160
    Spicy Beef and Noodles, **144,** 228
Greens. *See also* Spinach
    Escarole and White Bean Soup, 145
    mesclun, about, 248

Pan-Fried Lamb and Greens Salad with Tzatziki,
    293, 316–17
Pork with Creamy Mustard Sauce and Red
    Cabbage, 282
Salmon with Bean Salsa and Mixed Greens Salad,
    216, 252–53
Scallops with Arugula Spaghetti, **219,** 263
Stir-Fried Greens, 168

H

Halibut
    Grilled Halibut with White Bean Salsa, 246
Ham
    Baby Pea and Ham Soup, 123
    Goat Cheese Wrap, 110
    Tortellini and Ham Salad, 186
Heart disease, ix, 7
Honey, buying, 348
Hypertension, 7

I

Ice cream
    Italian Strawberries, 330
    serving sizes, 364
Insulin, xi, 7
Iron, 6
Italian-style dishes
    Angel Hair Pasta with Grilled Vegetables, 193
    Asparagus Tomato Frittata, 102
    Bowties with Creamed Mushrooms, 191
    Chocolate Nut Biscotti, 351
    Escarole and White Bean Soup, 145
    Fettuccine with Smoked Turkey and Pine Nuts, 206
    Fettuccine with Vegetables and Sausage, 205
    Fresh Mussels with Fettuccine, **220,** 264–65
    Garlic and Parsley Scallops with Fettuccine, 266
    Italian Strawberries, 330
    Just-Plain-Good Pasta, 189
    Lentil and Ricotta Cannelloni, 198
    Lentil Bruschetta, 109
    Linguine with Salmon and Peas, **143,** 203
    Luscious Lentil Lasagna, 201
    Marinated Grilled Chicken Noodle Salad, 208
    Minestrone, 124–25, **133**
    Pasta with Beans Soup, 148
    Potato and Corn Frittata with Sugar Snap Peas
        Salad, 100–101